NEW CUTTING

GW00739113

ELEMENTARY

photocopiable resources by Chris Redston

Longman

TEACHER'S RESOURCE BOOK

jane comyns carr

with sarah cunningham   peter moor

Pearson Education Limited
Edinburgh Gate
Harlow
Essex CM20 2JE
England
and Associated Companies throughout the world.

www.longman.com/cuttingedge

© Pearson Education Limited 2005

Produced by Cambridge Publishing Management Ltd

Set in 8.5pt Congress Sans by Cambridge Publishing Management Ltd

Printed in the UK by Ashford Colour Press Ltd

ISBN 0582 82502 4

Illustrated by Pavely Arts, Kathy Baxendale, Graham Humphreys/The Art Market, Ed McLachlan

Contents

Introduction

New Cutting Edge Elementary at a glance

New Cutting Edge Elementary is aimed at young adults studying general English at an elementary level and provides material for approximately 120 hours of teaching. It is suitable for students studying in either a monolingual or multilingual classroom situation.

STUDENTS' BOOK **CLASS CDS/CASSETTES**	The *New Cutting Edge Elementary Students' Book* is divided into fifteen modules, each consisting of approximately eight hours of classroom material. Each module contains some or all of the following: • **reading** and/or **listening** and/or **vocabulary** – an introduction to the topic of the module, and incorporates speaking • **grammar** – input/revision in two *Language focus* sections with practice activities and integrated pronunciation work • **vocabulary** – includes a *Wordspot* section which focuses on common words (*have, get, take,* etc.) • **task preparation** – a stimulus or model for the task (often listening or reading) and *Useful language* for the task • **task** – extended speaking, often with an optional writing component • **Real life** section – language needed in more complex real-life situations, usually including listening and speaking • **writing skills** • a **Study** ... **Practise** ... **Remember!** section – to develop study skills, with practice activities and a self-assessment section for students to monitor their progress. At the back of the *Students' Book* you will find: • a **Mini-dictionary** which contains definitions, pronunciations and examples of key words and phrases from the *Students' Book* • a detailed **Language summary** covering the grammar in each module • **Tapescripts** for material on the Class CDs/Cassettes.
WORKBOOK **STUDENTS' CD/CASSETTE**	The *New Cutting Edge Elementary Workbook* is divided into fifteen modules, which consist of: • **grammar** – consolidation of the main language points covered in the *Students' Book* • **vocabulary** – additional practice and input • **skills work** – *Improve your writing* and *Listen and read* sections • **pronunciation** – focus on problem sounds and word stress. The optional **Students' CD/Cassette** features exercises on grammar and pronunciation. There are two versions of the *Workbook*, one with and the other without an **Answer key**.

TEACHER'S RESOURCE BOOK	The *New Cutting Edge Elementary Teacher's Resource Book* consists of three sections:
	• an **Introduction** and some **Teacher's tips** on:
	  – helping students with pronunciation
	  – working with lexical phrases
	  – making the most of the *Mini-dictionary*
	  – making tasks work
	  – responding to learners' individual language needs
	  – using the *Study ... Practise ... Remember!* and *Mini-check* sections
	
	• **Step-by-step teacher's notes** for each module, including alternative suggestions for different teaching situations (particularly for tasks), detailed language notes and integrated answer keys
	• a photocopiable **Resource bank**, including learner-training worksheets, communicative grammar practice activities and vocabulary extension activities.
	
	The teacher's notes section is **cross-referenced** to the *Resource bank* and the *Workbook*.

The thinking behind New Cutting Edge Elementary

Overview

New Cutting Edge Elementary has a multilayered, topic-based syllabus which includes thorough and comprehensive work on grammar, vocabulary, pronunciation and the skills of listening, reading, speaking and writing. Structured speaking tasks form a central part of each module. The course gives special emphasis to:

- communication
- the use of phrases and collocation
- active learning and study skills
- revision and recycling.

Topics and content

We aim to motivate learners by basing modules around up-to-date topics of international interest. Students are encouraged to learn more about the world and other cultures through the medium of English, and personalisation is strongly emphasised. The differing needs of monocultural and multicultural classes have been kept in mind throughout.

Approach to grammar

Learners are encouraged to take an active, systematic approach to developing their knowledge of grammar, and the opportunity to use new language is provided in a natural, communicative way. There are two Language focus sections in each module, in which grammar is presented using reading or listening texts. Each Language focus has a Grammar box focusing on the main language points, in which learners are encouraged to work out rules for themselves. This is followed up thoroughly through:

- a wide range of communicative and written practice exercises in the Students' Book
- the opportunity to use new grammar naturally in the speaking tasks (see below)
- the Study ... Practise ... Remember! and Mini-check sections, in which learners are encouraged to assess their progress and work on any remaining problems
- a Language summary section at the back of the Students' Book
- further practice in the Workbook.

(See Teacher's tips: using the Study ... Practise ... Remember! and Mini-check sections on page 14.)

Approach to vocabulary

A wide vocabulary is vital to communicative success, so new lexis is introduced and practised at every stage in the course. Particular attention has been paid to the selection of high-frequency, internationally useful words and phrases, drawing on information from the British National Corpus.

Vocabulary input is closely related to the topics and tasks in the modules, allowing for plenty of natural recycling. Further practice is provided in the Study ... Practise ... Remember! section at the end of each module and in the Workbook.

In order to communicate, fluent speakers make extensive use of 'prefabricated chunks' of language. For this reason,

New Cutting Edge Elementary gives particular emphasis to collocations and fixed phrases. These are integrated through:

- Wordspot sections, which focus on high-frequency words such as get, have and think
- the Useful language boxes in the speaking tasks
- Real life sections, which focus on phrases used in common everyday situations such as telephoning or making arrangements
- topic-based vocabulary lessons.

(See Teacher's tips: working with lexical phrases on pages 9–10.) In addition, more straightforward single-item vocabulary is also extended through the Vocabulary booster sections of the Workbook.

'Useful' vocabulary is partly individual to the learner. With this in mind, the speaking tasks in New Cutting Edge Elementary provide the opportunity for students to ask the teacher for the words and phrases they need. (See Teacher's tips: responding to learners' individual language needs on pages 13–14.)

To encourage learner independence, New Cutting Edge Elementary has a Mini-dictionary which includes entries for words and phrases appropriate to the level of the learners. Learners are encouraged to refer to the Mini-dictionary throughout the course, and there are study tips to help them to do this more effectively. (See Teacher's tips: making the most of the Mini-dictionary on pages 10–11.)

The speaking tasks

New Cutting Edge Elementary aims to integrate elements of a task-based approach into its overall methodology. There are structured speaking tasks in each module which include interviews, mini-talks, problem-solving and storytelling. Here the primary focus is on achieving a particular outcome or product, rather than on practising specific language. Learners are encouraged to find the language they need in order to express their own ideas.

The frequent performance of such tasks is regarded in this course as a central element in learners' progress. The tasks provide the opportunity for realistic and extended communication, and because learners are striving to express what they want to say, they are more likely to absorb the language that they are learning. Much of the grammar and vocabulary input in each module is therefore integrated around these tasks, which in turn provide a valuable opportunity for the teacher to revisit and recycle what has been studied.

In order to make the tasks work effectively in the classroom:

- they are graded carefully in terms of difficulty
- a model/stimulus is provided for what the student is expected to do
- useful language is provided to help students to express themselves
- thinking and planning time is included.

(See Teacher's tips: making tasks work on pages 11–12 and Responding to learners' individual language needs on pages 13–14.)

In addition to the tasks, New Cutting Edge Elementary offers many other opportunities for speaking, for example, through the discussion of texts, communicative practice exercises and the wide range of games and activities in the photocopiable Resource bank in the Teacher's Resource Book.

Other important elements in *New Cutting Edge Elementary*

Listening

New Cutting Edge Elementary places strong emphasis on listening. Listening material consists of:
- short extracts and mini-dialogues to introduce and practise new language
- words and sentences for close listening and to model pronunciation
- longer texts (interviews, songs, stories and conversations), some of which are authentic, often in the *Preparation* section as a model or stimulus for the task
- regular *Listen and read* sections in the *Workbook* to further develop students' confidence in this area.

Speaking

There is also a strong emphasis on speaking, as follows.
- The tasks provide a regular opportunity for extended and prepared speaking based around realistic topics and situations (see page 5).
- Much of the practice of grammar and lexis is through oral exercises and activities.
- The topics and reading texts in each module provide opportunities for follow-up discussion.
- There is regular integrated work on pronunciation.
- Most of the photocopiable activities in the *Resource bank* are oral.

Reading

There is a wide range of reading material in the *Students' Book*, including factual/scientific texts, stories, quizzes, forms, notes and e-mails. These texts are integrated in a number of different ways:
- extended texts specifically to develop reading skills
- texts which lead into grammar work and language analysis
- texts which provide a model or stimulus for tasks and a model for writing activities.

Note: for classes who do not have a lot of time to do reading in class, there are suggestions in the teacher's notes section on how to avoid this where appropriate.

Writing

Systematic work on writing skills is developed in *New Cutting Edge Elementary* through:
- regular writing sections in the *Students' Book*, which focus on writing e-mails and letters, composing narratives and reviews, drafting and redrafting, using linkers, etc.
- *Improve your writing* sections in the *Workbook*, which expand on the areas covered in the *Students' Book*
- written follow-up sections to many of the speaking tasks.

Pronunciation

Pronunciation work in *New Cutting Edge Elementary* is integrated with grammar and lexis, and in the *Real life* sections in special *Pronunciation* boxes. The focus in the *Students' Book*

is mainly on stress, weak forms and intonation, while the *Workbook* focuses on problem sounds and word stress. A range of activity types are used in the *Students' Book*, including discrimination exercises and dictation, and an equal emphasis is placed on understanding and reproducing. In addition, there are *Pronunciation spots* in the *Study ... Practise ... Remember!* sections, which focus on problem sounds. These activities are intended as quick warmers and fillers, and can be omitted if not required.

Learning skills

New Cutting Edge Elementary develops learning skills in a number of ways as follows:
- The discovery approach to grammar encourages learners to experiment with language and to work out rules for themselves.
- The task-based approach encourages learners to take a proactive role in their learning.
- Looking up words and phrases in the *Mini-dictionary* gives students constant practice of a range of dictionary skills.
- The *Study ...* section of *Study ... Practise ... Remember!* focuses on useful learning strategies, such as keeping notes and revision techniques. Learners are encouraged to share ideas about the most effective ways to learn.
- The *Resource bank* includes four learner-training worksheets aimed at developing students' awareness of the importance of taking an active role in the learning process.

Revision and recycling

Recycling is a key feature of *New Cutting Edge Elementary*. New language is explicitly recycled through:
- extra practice exercises in the *Study ... Practise ... Remember!* sections. These are designed to cover all the main grammar and vocabulary areas in the module. After trying the exercises, learners are encouraged to return to any parts of the module that they still feel unsure about to assess what they have (and have not) remembered from the module. (See *Teacher's tips: using the* Study ... Practise ... Remember! *and* Mini-check *sections on page 14.*)
- *Consolidation* spreads after Modules 5, 10 and 15. These combine grammar and vocabulary exercises with listening and speaking activities, recycling material from the previous five modules.
- three photocopiable tests in the *Resource bank* for use after Modules 5, 10 and 15.

In addition, the speaking tasks offer constant opportunities for learners to use what they have studied in a natural way, and for teachers to assess their progress and remind them of important points.

Teacher's tips

Helping students with pronunciation

When people say that you speak good English, very often they are reacting to your pronunciation – this is very important in creating a confident first impression as a speaker of a foreign language. Although most students today are learning English for communication in an international context (so the perfect reproduction of British vowels, for example, is not essential), a high frequency of pronunciation errors can make students hard to understand, and listeners, whether native speakers or not, may just switch off. Setting high standards for pronunciation, even if you are not aiming for native-speaker-like production, will help to achieve the right kind of comprehensibility.

❶ Give priority to pronunciation ... but be realistic

Don't wait for a *Pronunciation* box to come along in the *Students' Book*. Integrate pronunciation work whenever students have a problem. 'Little and often' is a particularly good principle with pronunciation.

On the other hand, think about what you want to achieve: clarity and confidence are what most students need, rather than perfection in every detail. Individuals vary widely in what they can achieve, so don't push too much when a particular student is getting frustrated or embarrassed. Leave it and come back to it again another day. A humorous, light-hearted approach also helps to alleviate stress!

❷ Drill ...

Choral and/or individual repetition is the simplest pronunciation activity to set up and possibly the most effective. It can help to build confidence, and is often popular with low-level students as long as you don't overdo it (see above). There are models on the CDs/cassettes that students can copy for most key language in *New Cutting Edge Elementary*.

❸ ... but make sure students can hear the correct pronunciation

Even if students cannot yet produce the target pronunciation, it will improve their listening skills if they can at least hear it; and it goes without saying that you cannot reproduce something that you haven't heard clearly!

There are various ways of doing this. At low levels, it is often helpful to repeat the word or phrase two or three times yourself, before you ask students to say it. Sometimes you need to isolate and repeat individual syllables or sounds, and exaggeration of features like stress and intonation can be helpful. Or you can contrast the correct pronunciation with what the students are producing, either with the way that that word or syllable is pronounced in their own language, or with a similar sound in English.

❹ Pay particular attention to words with irregular spelling

One of the biggest problems for learners of English is the relationship between sounds and spelling. Highlight and drill problem words on a consistent basis. Think about teaching students the phonemic alphabet – this gives them a valuable tool for dealing with problematic pronunciation by themselves, and for recording it. You can use the list of sounds on the inside front cover of the *Mini-dictionary* to teach it – but only teach a few symbols at a time, and make constant use of them, otherwise students will soon forget them again.

❺ Focus on the sounds that most affect students' comprehensibility

Consonants (particularly at the beginning and end of words) are probably more important than vowels here. Use any tips you know for helping students to reproduce them. You might focus them on a similar sound in their own language and then help them to adapt it, or use a trick like starting with /uː/ to get students to produce the /w/ sound. Anything that works is valid here! Sometimes it is useful to contrast the problem sound with the one that students are mistakenly producing, via a 'minimal pair' such as *tree* and *three*. Say the pair of words several times, then ask students to say which they can hear, before asking them to produce the words themselves.

❻ Pay attention to schwa /ə/

This is one vowel sound that you shouldn't ignore. It is by far the most common vowel sound in English, occurring in a very high percentage of multi-syllable words. Using it correctly will help students to sound more fluent, and increase their comprehensibility. At the beginning of the course, make sure that students can produce this sound, and focus on it whenever it occurs in new words. Be careful not to stress it accidentally though – syllables with schwa in them are not normally stressed. To avoid this, drill new words starting with the stressed syllable, then add the schwa sounds either before or afterwards, for example:

/ə/ /ə/
ten ... atten ... attention

Consistently marking schwa sounds when you write words on the board will also help:

/ə/ /ə/
attention

❼ *Focus consistently on word stress ...*

This is an easy area in which to correct students effectively. Get into the habit of focusing on word stress whenever you teach a new word with potential problems. If students have problems, try one of the following ideas when you drill:
- Exaggerate the stress.
- Clap, click your fingers, etc. on the stressed syllable.
- Mumble the stress pattern, before saying the word: *mm-MM-mm attention*.
- Isolate the stressed syllable first, then add the other syllables.

Don't forget to mark stressed syllables when you write new words on the board, by underlining or writing a blob over them, and encourage students to do the same when they write in their notebooks. Make sure that students know how word stress is marked in the *Mini-dictionary*.

❽ *... and sentence stress*

Sentence stress is one of the most important elements in helping students to be easy to understand when they speak, just as punctuation makes their written work more comprehensible. Try to focus on it little and often, for example, when you teach a new structure or phrase. You can use the same methods as for word stress to help students to hear and reproduce the sentence stress.

❾ *Make students aware of weak forms and word linking*

As students become more advanced, these features will also contribute to comprehensibility and fluency, and at any level they are important for the purposes of listening. As you teach new phrases and structures, draw students' attention to weak forms and word linking as appropriate, and give students the opportunity to practise them. You can use the same method as for schwa sounds if they have problems. However, do not worry too much if students do not produce the weak forms and word linking spontaneously – this is more likely to come naturally when students are more fluent. All you can do at this stage is to sow the seeds for the future.

❿ *Make students aware of intonation*

Intonation is a source of worry to many teachers and, consequently, students. Teachers worry that their students (or they themselves) cannot hear it, and that whatever they do their students don't seem to 'learn' it. In reality, there are few situations in which wrong intonation leads to serious misunderstanding. Where problems do occasionally occur is in the area of politeness, and sounding sufficiently enthusiastic (although, even here, in real life many other factors – such as facial expression – can counteract 'wrong' intonation!).

In *New Cutting Edge Elementary*, we focus on these limited areas for intonation work. Again the key idea is 'awareness': you probably won't 'teach' students the right intonation overnight, but by focusing on this problem you can help them to see the importance of it. They are more likely to improve their overall intonation via plenty of exposure to natural-sounding English, and this is something that will take time. If students have problems hearing and reproducing the intonation patterns that you choose to focus on, try some of the following ideas:

- Exaggerate the intonation pattern, before returning to a more normal model.
- Hum the intonation pattern before repeating the words (incidentally, this is very useful for hearing intonation patterns yourself, if you have difficulty).
- Use gestures to show the intonation pattern (rather like a conductor).
- Mark the intonation on the board using arrows.

Remember, though, that if students are getting frustrated, or cannot 'get' the correct intonation, it is probably best to leave it and come back to it another time!

Working with lexical phrases

❶ Become more aware of phrases and collocations yourself

Until recently, relatively little attention was given to the thousands of phrases and collocations that make up the lexis in English, along with the traditional one-word items. If necessary, look at the list of phrase types, and start noticing how common these 'prefabricated chunks' are in all types of English. They go far beyond areas traditionally dealt with in English-language courses – phrasal verbs, functional exponents and the occasional idiom, although of course they incorporate all of these.

> a **collocations** (common word combinations), including:
> - verbs + nouns (*leave school, have a drink*)
> - adjectives + nouns (*best friend, bad news*)
> - verbs + adverbs (*work hard*)
> - verbs + prepositions/particles, including phrasal verbs (*listen to, wait for*)
> - adjectives + prepositions (*interested in*)
>
> b **fixed phrases**, such as: *Excuse me. / Here you are.*
>
> c **whole sentences which act as phrases**, such as: *I don't know. / I agree with you.*

Such phrases blur the boundaries between 'vocabulary' and 'grammar' – in teaching these phrases, you will find that you are helping students with many problematic areas that are traditionally considered to be grammar, such as articles and prepositions. Many common examples of these structures are in fact fixed or semi-fixed phrases. We are not suggesting that work on chunks should entirely replace the traditional grammatical approach to such verb forms, but rather that it is a useful supplement.

❷ Make your students aware of phrases and collocations

Students should also know about the importance of such phrases. *Learner-training worksheet C* on page 156 of the *Resource bank* aims to develop students' awareness of such collocations.

❸ Feed in phrases on a 'little but often' basis

To avoid overloading students and ensure that your lexical input is useful, teach a few phrases relating to particular activities as you go along. For example, in a grammar practice activity, instead of simple answers such as *Yes, I do* or *No, I haven't*, feed in phrases like *It depends* or *I don't really care*. The same is true of discussions about reading/listening texts and writing activities.

❹ Introduce phrases in context, but drill them as short chunks

Phrases can be difficult to understand and be specific to certain situations, so it is important that they are introduced in context. However, students may retain them better if you drill just the phrase (for example, *have lunch, go for a walk*) rather than a full sentence with problems which might distract from the phrase itself. The drilling of such phrases can be a valuable opportunity to focus on pronunciation features such as weak forms and word linking.

❺ Point out patterns in phrases

Pointing out patterns will help students to remember phrases. Many do not fit into patterns, but you can often show similar phrases with the same construction, like this:

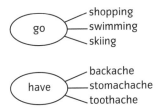

❻ Keep written records of phrases as phrases

One simple way to make your students more aware of collocation is to get into the habit of writing word combinations on the board wherever appropriate, rather than just individual words. The more students see these words together, the more likely they are to remember them as a unit. Rather than just writing up *housework* or *piano*, write up *do the housework* or *play the piano*. In sentences, collocations can be highlighted in colour or underlined – this is particularly important when the associated words are not actually next to each other in the sentence. Remind students to write down the collocations too, even if they 'know' the constituent words.

❼ Reinforce and recycle phrases as much as you can

This is particularly important with phrases which, for the reasons given above, can be hard to remember. Most revision games and activities that teachers do with single items of vocabulary can be adapted and used with phrases. You may find the following useful in addition:

> - **Making wall posters**: help students remember collocations by making a wall poster with a spidergram like those in the *Wordspot* sections of the *Students' Book*. Seeing the phrases on the wall like this every lesson can provide valuable reinforcement. There are many other areas for which wall posters would be effective, for example, common offers with *I'll* or common passive phrases. Always write the full phrase on the poster (*get married* not just *married*) and remove the old posters regularly, as they will lose impact if there are too many.
> - **Making a phrase bank**: copy the new words and phrases from the lesson onto slips of card or paper (large enough for students to read if you hold them up

at the front of the room) and keep them in a box or bag. This is a good record for you as well as the students of the phrases that you have studied – you can get them out whenever there are a few spare moments at the beginning or end of a lesson for some quick revision. Hold them up and, as appropriate, get students to give you:

- an explanation of the phrase
- a translation of the phrase
- synonyms
- opposites
- the pronunciation
- situations where they might say this
- a sentence including the phrase
- the missing word that you are holding your hand over (for example, *to* in the phrase *listen to the radio*)
- the phrase itself, based on a definition or translation that you have given them.

Making the most of the *Mini-dictionary*

The *New Cutting Edge Elementary Mini-dictionary* has been especially designed to be useful to, and usable by, Elementary students. It contains examples of most words, which are as self-explanatory as possible. We realise how difficult it may be for students at this level to understand definitions in English, although we have made a big effort to make these as simple as possible. We hope that students will develop the habit of using a monolingual dictionary, even if they cannot understand everything in it straight away. Obviously, however, students will still need support from the teacher to use the *Mini-dictionary* effectively.

❶ Show students the Mini-dictionary *at the beginning of the course*

Explain what the *Mini-dictionary* is, and reassure students that they don't need to understand all the definitions to use it. Obviously, students will not understand all the definitions immediately. Show them all the other information they can still find, such as opposites or word stress. Point out, too, that it is often easier to work out the meaning of a word from an example, rather than from a definition.

❷ Use the Mini-dictionary *together as a class, or in pairwork*

This will help to build up confidence in using a monolingual dictionary, as students work out together what they understand. Especially in the initial stages, it will help to make dictionary work less arduous and more sociable!

❸ Use it where appropriate in grammar lessons

Whenever you teach a grammatical area that is covered in the *Mini-dictionary*, for example, the Past simple or the comparative and superlative of adjectives, show students how the *Mini-dictionary* can help to answer their questions, even when you are not available to do so!

❹ Draw students' attention to information about collocation

The *Mini-dictionary* provides a lot of basic information about collocation, which will help students to use what they know effectively. Elementary students might not always be aware that collocations in English are often different from those in their first language, so whenever you look up a word together which has a problematic collocation, show how the *Mini-dictionary* examples can help with this.

❺ Vary your approach

If you always use the *Mini-dictionary* in the same way, students may get tired of it before long. Try using the *Mini-dictionary* in the following ways instead for a change:

a **Matching words to definitions on a handout:** make a worksheet with the new words in column A and their definitions from the *Mini-dictionary* mixed up in column B. Students match the words with the definitions.

b **Matching words to definitions on cards:** the same idea can be used by giving each group of students two small sets of cards with definitions and words to match.

c *I know it / I can guess it / I need to check it:* write the list of new words on the board, and tell students to copy it down marking the words ✔✔ if they already know it, ✔ if they can guess what it means (either from the context or because it is similar in their own language) and ✘ if they need to look it up. Students then compare answers in pairs to see if they can help each other, before looking up any words that neither of them know.

d **Looking up the five words you most need to know:** instead of pre-teaching the vocabulary in a reading text, set the first (gist-type) comprehension activity straight away, instructing students not to refer to the *Mini-dictionary* at this point. Check answers or establish that students cannot answer without some work on vocabulary. Tell them that they are only allowed to look up five words from the text – they have to choose the five that are most important to understanding the text. Demonstrate the difference between a 'key' unknown word in the text and one that can easily be ignored. Put students into pairs to select their five words, emphasising that they must not start using the *Mini-dictionary* until they have completed their list of five. After they have finished, compare the lists of words that different pairs chose and discuss how important they are to the text, before continuing with more detailed comprehension work.

e *True/False* **statements based on information in the** *Mini-dictionary:* write a list of statements about the target words on the board, then ask students to look them up to see if they are true or false, for example: *The phrase ... is very informal – true or false? The phrase means ... – true or false?*

Making tasks work

Treat tasks primarily as an opportunity for communication. Remember the main objective is for students to use the language that they know in order to achieve a particular communicative goal. Although it is virtually impossible to perform many of the tasks without using the language introduced earlier in the module, in others students may choose to use this language only once or twice, or not at all. Do not try to 'force-feed' it. Of course, if learners are seeking this language but have forgotten it, this is the ideal moment to remind them!

❶ *Make the task suit your class*

Students using this course will vary in age, background, interests and ability. All these students need to find the tasks motivating and 'doable', yet challenging at the same time. Do not be afraid to adapt the tasks to suit your class if this helps. The teacher's notes contain suggestions on how to adapt certain tasks for monolingual and multilingual groups, students of different ages and interests, large classes and weaker or stronger groups. We hope these suggestions will give you other ideas of your own on how to adapt the tasks.

❷ *Personalise it!*

Most tasks in *New Cutting Edge Elementary* have a model to introduce them. Sometimes these are recordings of people talking about something personal, for example, describing their family or finding something in common with other people. However, finding out about you, their teacher, may be more motivating, so you could try providing a personalised model instead. If you do this, remember to:
- plan what you are going to say, but do not write it out word for word, as this may sound unnatural
- bring in any photos or illustrations you can to help to bring your talk alive
- either pre-teach or explain as you go along any problematic vocabulary
- give students something to do as they are listening (the teacher's notes give suggestions on this where appropriate).

This approach may take a little courage at first, but students are likely to appreciate the variety it provides.

❸ *Set the final objective clearly before students start preparing*

Do not assume that students will work out where their preparations are leading if you do not tell them! Knowing that they will have to tell their story to the class, for example, may make a big difference to how carefully they prepare it.

❹ *Pay attention to seating arrangements*

Whether you have fixed desks or more portable furniture, when working in groups or pairs always make sure that students are sitting so that they can hear and speak to each other comfortably. Groups should be in a small circle or square rather than a line, for example. Empty desks between students may mean that they have to raise their voices to a level at which they feel self-conscious when speaking English – this can have an adverse effect on any pairwork or groupwork activity.

❺ *Give students time to think and plan*

Planning time is very important if low-level students are to produce the best language that they are capable of. It is particularly useful for building up the confidence of students who are normally reluctant to speak in class. The amount of time needed will vary from task to task, but normally about five minutes will suffice.

This planning time will sometimes mean a period of silence in class, something that teachers used to noisy, communicative classrooms can find unnerving. Remember that just because you cannot hear anything, this does not mean that nothing is happening! With storytelling and other activities, it may be useful to get students to go over what they are going to say, silently in their heads.

It may help to relieve any feelings of tension at this stage by playing some background music or, if practical in your school, by suggesting that students go somewhere else to prepare – another classroom if one is available.

Students may well find the idea of 'time to plan' strange at first, but, as with many other teaching and learning techniques, it is very much a question of training.

❻ *Make the most of the* Useful language *boxes*

The *Useful language* boxes are intended to help students with language they need to perform the tasks. It is important to get students to do something with the phrases in order to help students pronounce them and begin to learn them. Here are some suggestions.

- You can write the useful language on an overhead transparency. Give a definition/explanation to elicit each phrase, and then uncover it.
- Give some group and individual repetition if necessary, first with students looking at the phrase and then covering it up to encourage them to remember it.
- When you have looked at all the phrases, give students a minute to try and memorise them. Then remove the prompts, and students in pairs can try to say them to each other, or to write them down.
- If the *Useful language* box has a lot of questions, you could write the answers on the board and see if students can provide the questions. Don't write the questions. Give group and individual repetition practice of each question as needed, continually going back to earlier questions to see if students can remember them. At the end, students can look at the questions in the book.
- Elicit each phrase, as above, and write them up on the board until you have all the useful language up. Then ask students in pairs to read the phrases aloud to each other, and when they finish they should start again. Meanwhile you can start rubbing off individual words from the phrases and replace them with a dash. Start with smaller words, so that you leave the main

information words. Keep rubbing off more and more words until only dashes are left! See how much students can remember of this missing language.

- Write the phrases on cards and cut the phrases into two, for example, *I was ten / at the time*, so that students in groups can try to match the two halves. They can then check the *Useful language* box, and you can give group and individual practice.

❼ *Insist that students do the task in English!*

It may not be realistic to prevent students from using their own language completely, but they should understand that during the performance of the task (if not at the planning stage, when they may need their mother tongue to ask for new language) they must use English. At the beginning of the course, it may be useful to discuss the importance of this, and the best ways of implementing it. Students will be more tempted to use their own language if they find the task daunting, so do not be afraid to shorten or simplify tasks if necessary. However, planning and rehearsal time will make students less inclined to use their first language.

❽ *Let the students do the talking*

If students are hesitant, it is easy (with the best of intentions!) to intervene and speak for them. Some students will be only too happy to let you do this, and before long they won't even attempt to formulate full sentences, knowing that you will usually do it for them. Don't worry if they have to think for a little while before they can string their words together – they will get better at this eventually, but only if they have the opportunity to practise!

❾ *Give your feedback at the end ... and make it positive!*

Students at this level are bound to make a lot of errors in any kind of extended communication, and you may feel that you need to deal with these. It is usually best not to interrupt, however, but to make a note of any important points to deal with at the end. Keep these brief, though, and remember that at low levels any kind of extended speaking is a considerable challenge. Keep the emphasis on praise and positive feedback, and hopefully your students will be eager to do this kind of speaking task again!

❿ *Use written follow-up as consolidation*

Learners have more time to focus on correct language when writing, so encourage them to make use of any suggestions and corrections you made during the oral phase of the task. You could get them to read through and correct each other's written work if you have time.

Responding to learners' individual language needs

At appropriate points throughout the *Students' Book*, during the tasks and speaking activities, students are instructed to ask their teacher about any words or phrases they need. The ability to respond to students' individual language needs is central to a task-based approach, and you may find yourself doing this during pair/group/individual work and during preparation stages. The following suggestions are designed to help teachers who may feel daunted by the idea of unplanned, unpredictable input.

❶ Encourage students to ask about language

Students who take an active approach to their own learning are far more likely to succeed than those who sit back and expect the teacher to do it all for them. It is important to make students aware of this, and to convey to them your willingness to deal with their queries. Circulate during pair/group/individual work, making it clear that you are available to answer questions. Even if you cannot answer a query on the spot, let students know that you are happy to deal with it.

❷ Be responsive, but do not get sidetracked

One danger of this approach is that a teacher may get sidetracked by dominant students who want all their attention, leading to frustration and irritation among others. If you feel that this is happening, tell these students that you will answer their questions later, and move quickly on. Make sure that you keep moving round during pair/group/individual work. Keep a 'bird's-eye' view of the class, moving in to help students if they need it rather than spending too much time with one pair/group/individual.

❸ Encourage students to use what they already know

There is also a danger that students will become overdependent on you, perhaps asking you to translate large chunks for them, which they are very unlikely to retain. Always encourage students to use what they know first, only asking you if they really have no idea.

❹ Have strategies for dealing with questions you cannot answer

Have at least one bilingual dictionary in the classroom (especially for specialised/technical vocabulary) for students to refer to, although you may still need to check that they have found the right translation. If students ask for idioms and expressions, make sure you keep it simple – in most cases you will be able to come up with an adequate phrase, even if it is not precisely the phrase the student wanted. Finally, if all else fails, promise to find out for the next lesson!

❺ Note down important language points to be dealt with later

Note down any important language points that come up during tasks and discussions, and build in time slots to go over these later on. Write the errors on the board, and invite students to correct them, think of a better word, etc. Remember that it is also motivating (and can be just as instructive) to include examples of good language use as well as errors. Feedback slots can either be at the end of the lesson or, if time is a problem, at the beginning of the next.

❻ Select language points for correction slots carefully

Students are more likely to retain a few well-chosen points in these correction slots than a long list of miscellaneous language points. The following are helpful things to bear in mind.

> - **Usefulness:** many items may only be of interest to individual students – only bring up general language with the whole class.
> - **Quantity/Variety:** try to combine one or two more general points with a number of more specific/minor ones, including a mixture of grammar, vocabulary and pronunciation as far as possible.
> - **Level:** be careful not to present students with points above their level or which are too complex to deal with in a few minutes.
> - **Problems induced by students' mother tongue:** correction slots are an excellent opportunity to deal with L1-specific errors ('false friends', pronunciation, etc.) not usually mentioned in general English courses.
> - **Revision:** the correction slots are a very good opportunity to increase students' knowledge of complex language covered previously, as well as to remind them of smaller language points.

❼ Don't worry if you cannot think of 'creative' practice on the spot

If students encounter a genuine need for the language as they try to achieve a particular goal, it is more likely to be remembered than if it is introduced 'cold' by the teacher. In many cases, elaborate practice may be unnecessary – what is important is that you are dealing with the language at the moment it is most likely to be retained by the student. With lexis and small points of pronunciation, it may be enough to get students to repeat the word a few times and for you to write an example on the board, highlighting problems.

❽ Try some simple 'on the spot' practice activities

If you feel more work is needed, the following box includes some well-known activities which are relatively easy to adapt 'on the spot' (you can always provide a more substantial exercise later). A few examples should be enough for students to see how the structure is formed, and to increase awareness of it. These activities are also useful for practising phrases in the *Useful language* boxes in the tasks.

> a **Choral and individual drilling**
> b **Questions and answers:** ask questions prompting students to use the language item in the answer. For example, to practise the phrase *famous for*, ask

questions such as:

What's Monte Carlo famous for?	*It's famous for its casinos.*
What's Loch Ness famous for?	*It's famous for the Loch Ness Monster.*

Alternatively, give an example, then prompt students to ask each other questions, like this:

Monica, ask Henri about Venice.	*What's Venice famous for, Henri?*

c **Forming sentences/phrases from prompts:** for example, to practise the construction *is worth* + verb *-ing*, provide the example *The National Gallery is worth visiting*, then give prompts like this:

ROYAL PALACE / SEE	*The Royal Palace is worth seeing.*
THIS DICTIONARY / BUY	*This dictionary is worth buying.*

d **Substitutions:** give an example phrase/sentence, then provide prompts which can easily be substituted into the original. For example, to practise the non-use of the article, start with *I hate cats*, then prompt as follows:

LOVE	*I love cats.*
BABIES	*I love babies.*
DON'T LIKE	*I don't like babies.*

e **Transformations:** these are useful if there is another construction with almost the same meaning. Give one construction and ask students to say the same thing using another. For example, to practise *although*:

He's rich, but he's very mean.	*Although he's rich, he's very mean.*
She's over eighty, but she's very active.	*Although she's over eighty, she's very active.*

f **Combining shorter sentences/phrases:** give two short sentences and ask students to combine them with a more complex construction. For example, to practise *too ... to*:

She's very young. She can't do this job.	*She's too young to do this job.*
He's too old. He can't drive.	*He's too old to drive.*

g **Dictating sentences for students to complete:** dictate a few incomplete sentences including the phrase/structure, which students complete themselves, then compare with other students. For example, to practise *It takes ... to,* dictate:

It takes about three hours to get to ...,	*It only takes a few minutes to ...,*
It took me ages to ...	

Using the *Study ... Practise ... Remember!* and *Mini-check* sections

These sections are a fresh component in *New Cutting Edge Elementary*, replacing and extending the old *Do you remember?* sections. They occur at the end of each module except Modules 5, 10 and 15, where there is a more extensive *Consolidation* section.

The *Study ... Practise ... Remember!* and *Mini-check* sections have the following main aims:

- to ensure systematic consolidation of new language before learners move on to the next module
- to encourage learners to take responsibility for and assess their own progress
- to cover problem sounds which are not covered elsewhere.

❶ Use the different activities as warmers and fillers

The activities in the *Study ... Practise ... Remember!* sections are not intended to be used all together. They can be broken down into 'bite-sized' chunks and used as warmers or fillers when you have ten or fifteen minutes to spare. For example, you could do the *Study ...* section at the end of one lesson, use the *Pronunciation spot* as a warmer in another lesson and set the exercises in the *Practise ...* section (either together or separately) as warmers or fillers in other lessons. The *Mini-check* could be done as a short slot in the final lesson before you move on to the next module.

❷ Set homework based on these sections

If you are short of time in class, the *Practise ...* section could easily be set as homework. If you do this, draw learners' attention to the *Need to check?* rubric at the end of each exercise. It might be useful to explain in class where students should look (for example, in the *Language summary*) if they need to do further revision.

❸ Set aside time to answer students' questions

If you set the *Practise ...* section for homework, in the next lesson set aside some time for students to ask any questions they have, and to complete the *Remember!* self-assessment section, before getting students to do the *Mini-check*.

❹ Encourage students to take responsibility for their own progress

The approach throughout the *Study ... Practise ... Remember!* section is intended to encourage learner independence and personal responsibility for progress, and the *Mini-check* should also be presented to students in this light. Of course, it would be possible for learners to cheat and prepare beforehand (which in itself might be perfectly valid revision!), but explain to learners that these checks are for their own benefit and that if they cheat, they are cheating themselves. Of course, it is also a good opportunity for you to check informally how well they are progressing.

❺ Select the Pronunciation spots *that are most useful for your learners*

More than any other part of these sections, the *Pronunciation spots* are intended to stand alone. They can be used at any time as a warmer or filler. Some areas covered may not be a problem for your learners, in which case they can easily be omitted.

What English do you know?

(PAGES 6–7)

These two pages are not intended to be studied exercise by exercise before students begin Module 1. They are there for you to dip into if your students need revision of basic areas. Decide which exercises you want your class to do, or if individual students in your class need extra help, they could do some or all of the exercises for homework. In the Teacher's notes for the first few Modules, there are suggestions for using some of the exercises in combination with the work of the Module. Section 9 on basic classroom instructions is useful for all classes before beginning Module 1.

1 [TO.1] After students have matched the words, they listen to check their answers and repeat the pronunciation.

ANSWERS
2e   3b   4a   5f   6d

ADDITIONAL PRACTICE:

Workbook: Common words, page 4

2 [TO.2] Students write the numbers and then listen and copy the pronunciation. Check particularly that they put the stress on the second syllable in *thirteen*, *fourteen*, etc.

●   ●
thirteen   fourteen

ANSWERS
eight – 8   nine – 9   four – 4   sixteen – 16
fifteen – 15   five – 5   ten – 10   three – 3   zero – 0
seven – 7   two – 2   one – 1   seventeen – 17
twelve – 12   thirteen – 13   six – 6   twenty-one – 21
nineteen – 19   eleven – 11   eighteen – 18
fourteen – 14

Exercise 2: additional suggestions

- Students, in groups of about five or six, stand in a circle with a ball. They throw the ball to each other and count: the first student catching the ball has to say *zero*. He/She then throws it to another student who says *one*, and so on. Students count first from zero to twenty-one and then back down again.
- Mutual dictation: students write down ten of the numbers in any order. They then work in pairs and take it in turns to dictate the numbers to their partner.

ADDITIONAL PRACTICE:

Workbook: Numbers 0–21, page 4

3 [TO.3] After students have written the words, they listen to check their answers and repeat the pronunciation. Check particularly the difference between those which end in /s/ (books, desks, students) and those ending in /z/ (teachers, pens, chairs, girls, boys) and the pronunciation of *women* /wɪmɪn/.

ANSWERS
1 books   2 teachers   3 desks   4 chairs   5 students
6 girls   7 boys   8 men   9 women

Exercise 3: additional suggestion

Check the plural form with *-es*. Draw or bring in: a box, a match and a watch. Elicit the words and ask students how to make the plurals. Show them that after *x* and *ch* we add *-es*. Check pronunciation and drill the words: *boxes* /bɒksɪz/, *matches* /mætʃɪz/, *watches* /wɒtʃɪz/.

4 a [TO.4] Students listen and repeat the letters. You may need to pay particular attention to a, e, i, g, j, k, q, u, w and y.

Exercise 4a: additional suggestion

If students need extra practice before they do b, put them in pairs. Student A says a letter and Student B has to point to the letter he/she heard.

b Demonstrate with the class, by spelling your own name. Then students work in pairs and take turns to spell out their details to their partner, who writes them down.

5 If you are in a mono-nationality class, you could elicit the pronouns in the students' language. In a multi-national class, the students can tell their partner the pronouns in their different languages before matching.

ANSWERS
a I my   b you your   c he his   d she her   e it its
f we our   g they their

6 a [TO.5] After writing, students listen and check, then repeat. Point out that *one hundred* is also possible.

ANSWERS
twenty-two, twenty-three, twenty-four
thirty-six, thirty-seven, thirty-eight
forty-four, forty-five, forty-six
fifty-seven, fifty-eight, fifty-nine
sixty-seven, sixty-eight, sixty-nine
seventy-five, seventy-six, seventy-seven
eighty-two, eighty-three, eighty-four
ninety-eight, ninety-nine, a hundred

b [TO.6] Students listen and write the dictated numbers.

ANSWERS
a twenty-five   b eighty-eight   c fifty   d nineteen
e ninety   f a hundred   g thirteen   h seventy-five
i thirty   j twenty-three   k seventeen   l ninety-nine

c Students can work in pairs on this exercise and listen and check their partner's answers whilst the teacher circulates and checks.

ANSWERS

seventeen sixteen	sixty-five sixty-four
eighty-six eighty-five	fifty-four fifty-three
eleven ten	forty-five forty-four
thirteen twelve	a hundred ninety-nine
twenty-five twenty-four	ninety eighty-nine
seven six	thirty-three thirty-two
eighteen seventeen	

Exercise 6: additional suggestions

a Work on the difference between e.g. *thirteen* /θɜːˈtiːn/ and *thirty* /θɜːti/ showing students where the stress is and the different length of the final vowels. Give choral and individual repetition. Ask students to raise their right hand if they hear *thirteen* and their left if *thirty* and give listening practice for similar numbers (*fourteen, forty*, etc.). They can do the same in pairs with one saying a number and the other raising the relevant hand.

b Get students to play *Bingo!* They choose twelve numbers between 1 and 100, and write them in their notebooks. Call out numbers in any order, but make sure you have a note of which numbers you say. When students hear one of their numbers, they cross it out. The winner is the first student to cross out all their numbers. When they have done this, they shout out *Bingo!*

ADDITIONAL PRACTICE

Workbook: 4 Numbers 1–100, page 4

7 [TO.7] Get students to put the days in order and then listen, check and work on pronunciation.

ADDITIONAL PRACTICE

Workbook: 3, page 4

8 [TO.8] Establish that the people know each other. After matching and listening, students can practise in different pairs or stand up and mingle, speaking to as many people as possible.

ANSWERS
1 Fine, thanks, and you?
2 Bye, Kate. See you later.

9 **a** Students match the pictures.

ANSWERS
2 b   3 c   4 a   5 d   6 e

b Students follow the instructions on the tape.

module 1

People and places

Language focus 1 (PAGES 8–9)

be: names and countries

1 Students act out the conversation with all the students sitting near them or they can circulate introducing themselves to everyone.

2 **a** 🔲 [T1.1] As an introduction, ask students about the picture. Who are they, where are they? Elicit ideas on what they are saying. The characters are, from left to right: Ben, Emily, Carla and Ariel. Students can read the dialogue and check their predictions; they should then add the phrases from the box and listen to check their answers. Check students understand *fantastic*.

ANSWERS
2 Nice to meet you, Carla.
3 No, no! I'm from Buenos Aires.
4 Nice to meet you, too.
5 Really? Manchester's a fantastic city.

b Students decide if the sentences are true or false.

ANSWERS
1 True   2 False   3 True   4 False

Grammar

Write on the board *I'____ from Milan. _____ you from Milan too?* Ask students to complete the gaps and then complete the rest of the gaps in the *Grammar* box, using the conversation to help them. Drill the sentences as necessary. Referring to the full *Language summary A* on page 150, highlight:
* the change in word order: *He's > 's he?*
* the use of apostrophes for contracted forms
* pronunciation of the *s* so students are not saying *Where he from?*
* pronunciation of *Where are* /weərɑː/.

Refer students to *Language summary A* on page 150.

PRACTICE

1 **a** Students mingle, asking each other the questions. If they already know each other and/or are from the same country, use Activity 1A in the Resource bank.

b Circulate, giving help where needed. Check that in the feedback, they use *this is* and not *he is* or *she is* to introduce each other.

Pronunciation

See *Teacher's tips: helping students with pronunciation* on pages 7–8.

🔲 [T1.2] Play the recording for students to listen to the words. Help them hear the word stress by tapping or clapping at the same time. Then play the recording again, stopping after each word for choral and individual repetition.

2 Demonstrate, using the examples and drilling the questions if necessary. Encourage students to use *I think* when they are not sure. Students work in pairs asking and answering the questions.

ANSWERS
1 They're from Argentina.   2 He's from the USA.
3 They're from Germany.   4 They're from Thailand.
5 He's from Kuwait/the Gulf/Emirates
6 He's/She's from Poland.   7 They're from China.
8 He's/She's from Russia.

3 **a** Demonstrate the activity, which can be done in pairs or small groups.

b 🔲 [T1.3] Students listen and check.

ANSWERS

Hamburg	Germany	
Bangkok	Thailand	capital
San Diego	The USA	
Liverpool	Britain	
Warsaw	Poland	capital
St Petersburg	Russia	
Beijing	China	capital
Buenos Aires	Argentina	capital
Cairo	Egypt	capital
Barcelona	Spain	
Rome	Italy	capital
Monterrey	Mexico	

ADDITIONAL PRACTICE

RB **Resource bank:** 1A *Nice to meet you*, page 114

Workbook: Names and countries, page 5; Personal information: *be*, page 5

Vocabulary (PAGE 10)

1 **a** Students match the nationalities to the countries.

b 🔲 [T1.4] Students listen and check.

ANSWERS

1	Spain	Spanish	4 Turkey	Turkish
2	China	Chinese	5 Italy	Italian
3	the USA	American	6 Britain	British

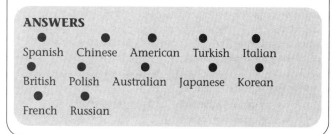

7	Poland	Polish	10	Korea	Korean
8	Australia	Australian	11	France	French
9	Japan	Japanese	12	Russia	Russian

Pronunciation

See *Teacher's tips: helping students with pronunciation* on pages 7–8.

[T1.5] Demonstrate the stress by clapping or tapping. Do a couple of examples with students, based on listening to the recording. Students continue on their own. Check the answers, drill as necessary.

> **ANSWERS**
>
> ● ● ● ● ●
> Spanish Chinese American Turkish Italian
> ● ● ● ● ●
> British Polish Australian Japanese Korean
> ● ●
> French Russian

Reading and listening (PAGE 10)

a Set up the quiz in a lively manner, showing the points system and putting students into pairs or small groups to answer the questions. Show them how to use their *Mini-dictionary* to find *currency/ies*. Set a time limit of about ten minutes, and circulate to see the groups are on-task.

b [T1.6] When the time is up, stop the quiz and elicit students' answers to each question before you play the correct answer on the recording. As you go along, check the types of company in C below (*car*, *electrical*, *fashion*). Students keep their scores and see who is the winner on points.

> **ANSWERS**
> A euro – France   lira – Italy   dollar – Australia
>   yen – Japan
> B 1 Thailand 2 Poland 3 Britain 4 Egypt
> C 1 Mercedes Benz – German 2 Hyundai – Korean
>   3 Sony – Japanese 4 Gucci – Italian
> D 1 Spanish 2 Arabic 3 Russian 4 Chinese
>   5 Italian
> E Nicole Kidman – Australian
>   Penelope Cruz – Spanish
>   Jennifer Lopez – American

ADDITIONAL PRACTICE

Workbook: Nationalities, page 6; Vocabulary booster: More countries and nationalities, page 6

Language focus 2 (PAGE 11)

be: personal information

1 The focus here is on short (contracted) forms of *be* in the positive and negative. Focus students on the photos and get them in pairs to match the sentences with the pictures. Either check new vocabulary before the activity, or check a few

words and encourage students to use the *Mini-dictionary* to find unknown words. *See Teacher's tips: making the most of the* Mini-dictionary *on pages 10–11.* Words and phrases to check: *airport, on holiday, on business, tourist, married, single, friends.* Drill the pronunciation of words as necessary, particularly *married* /'mærid/ and *on business* /ɒn 'bɪznɪs/.

2 [1.7] Play the recording for students to check their answers.
Andrei a, e, h, i, n
Marisol b, f, j, k, m
Toshi and Mariko c, d, g, l, o

ADDITIONAL ACTIVITY

If you have a low elementary class: get students to revise pronouns and possessive adjectives by using exercise 5 on page 7 of the *Students' Book.*

Grammar

[T1.8] Ask students to complete the table individually and then compare in pairs. Circulate and monitor. Then play the recording for students to listen and check their answers.

Check that students are writing the apostrophe in the correct place and that they understand that short forms are normal in spoken English. Encourage them to use short forms when speaking.

> **ANSWERS**
> I'm, he's, she's, they're, you aren't, he isn't, she isn't, it isn't, they aren't

Point out that:
• we also use short forms with nouns, for example *Maria's a student*.
• we use *'s* with *what's* and *where's* (but we use *what are* and *where are*).

Refer students to *Language summary A, B and E* on page 150 of the *Students' Book.*

> **Language note:**
> It is also possible to use alternative negative forms: *you're not, he's not,* etc. but we have decided to cover only one possibility at this point. You may wish to show your students both.

Pronunciation

See *Teacher's tips: helping students with pronunciation* on pages 7–8.

[T1.8] Using the recording script, students listen and repeat the short forms in sentences. Help them particularly with linking *you aren't* /juː ɑːnt/ *He isn't* /hiː ɪznt / *we aren't* /wiː ɑːnt/.

PRACTICE

1 a Demonstrate by writing some true and false sentences on the board: *His name's Mark. He's from Russia. He's a teacher.* Read each sentence aloud and ask students to say if it is true or false and to correct you if it is false. Students work individually to write their sentences.

b Ask a student to read out a couple of sentences and the class corrects him/her. Students continue in pairs. Circulate, and help as necessary.

2 This activity helps students to personalise the language. Write the two examples on the board and do them with one of the students in front of the class. Before students do the exercise, check the following or ask students to find them in their *Mini-dictionaries*: *school, classroom, small, politician, the evening, at work.* Circulate and help as necessary. At the end, have a quick class feedback on each question.

ADDITIONAL PRACTICE

Workbook: *is or are*, page 6; Negative sentences, page 6

Language focus 3 (PAGE 12)

Articles (1): *a/an* + jobs

1 [T1.9] Students match the jobs with the pictures, then listen to check.

> **Language note:**
>
> We have included *actress* as the female form of *actor* because *actress* is still very common, although women in the job often prefer to be called *actors.* However, nowadays *police officer* is used more commonly than *policeman/woman.* Also a *PA (personal assistant)* is more common than a *secretary.*

> **ANSWERS**
> a a police officer   b an engineer
> c a businessman and a businesswoman   d a footballer
> e a doctor and a nurse   f a musician   g a lawyer
> h an actor and an actress   i a PA, a personal assistant
> j a shop assistant   k a waiter and a waitress
> l a singer   m an electrician

Pronunciation

[T1.10] Get students to listen to the stresses and drill the pronunciation chorally and individually.

Drill other words, paying attention to the stress and also the *schwa* /ə/ ending of *actor* /ˈæktə/, *doctor* /ˈdɒktə/, *teacher* /ˈtiːtʃə/, *waiter* /ˈweɪtə/, *officer* /ˈɒfɪsə/, *singer* /ˈsɪŋə/, *lawyer* /ˈlɔːjə/ and to the stress in

●　　　●　　●　●　　　●　●
personal assistant,　shop assistant,　police officer,

●　　●　●
businessman/woman.

2 Students practise by pointing at the pictures and asking and answering questions in pairs.

Grammar

Write *He's _____ engineer* and *she's _____ actress* on the board and ask students to complete the gaps.

Go through the rule. Teach the words *vowel* and *consonant.* Emphasise that in English we use *a* or *an* when talking about jobs.

Refer students to *Language summary F* on page 150.

Note to teachers: In Module 5 we will be looking at some different uses of articles. However, you should point out individual uses as they appear in earlier modules, particularly if your students have no articles in their own language. Articles are included with new sets of vocabulary in *Cutting Edge Elementary.* Encourage your students to copy these into their notebooks.

> **Exercise 1 and 2: alternative suggestions**
>
> - Bring in your own pictures of jobs. Give one to a student and ask him/her to mime it while the other students guess the job. The student writes the word (with the stress marked) on the back of the picture and then 'teaches' the class the name of the job.
> - Use your own pictures and write the name of the jobs on the back, with the stress marked. Each student has a picture. They mingle asking each other *What's your job?* and teach each other the new words. Circulate and help with the pronunciation of the jobs.
> - *If you have a small class:* put pictures of jobs on a table/the floor. Say a job and ask students to point to it. If no-one knows the job, then teach it. After they've listened to you saying the jobs a few times, let them take it in turns to say a job and the others point to the correct picture. If you want to increase motivation, say a job and students try to pick up the picture before the others. The winner is the one with the most pictures at the end!
> - Students do exercise 1, have one minute to memorise the words and then close their books and try to write all the jobs. The winning student is the one who remembers the most.

PRACTICE

1 Demonstrate, using yourself as an example and then a stronger student. Students work in pairs. Circulate, helping where necessary.

2 Write the beginnings of the sentences on the board and show the students how to finish them. Circulate, helping where necessary.

3 a Demonstrate by making an example about a famous person on a large piece of card with the information written in the same way as on pages 138 and 140 of the

Students' Book. Hold it so that the students can't see. Check the meaning of *famous*. Tell students you have information about a famous person on the card and they have to ask questions to find out who it is, e.g. *Is it a man or a woman? How old is he? What's his job? Is he from Britain?* When students have guessed the person, show them the information on the card. Get students to look at the famous people on the two pages.

b Students work in pairs; as they do the activity, circulate and note any examples of good use and errors for analysis and feedback later.

c Once students have guessed the people on the cards, they can continue, using other famous people they know.

ADDITIONAL PRACTICE

Workbook: Indefinite article: *a(n)*, page 7; Vocabulary: Jobs, page 7

Language focus 4 (PAGE 13)

be: personal questions

1 a Focus students on the photograph by asking *Where is it? Who are they?* Elicit some ideas about what the people are saying. Demonstrate example 1 with the class and students work individually to choose the correct answers.

b [T1.11] Play the recording for students to check their answers

> **ANSWERS**
> 1 b 2 a 3 b 4 b 5 a 6 b 7 a 8 a

Grammar

Divide the board into two columns headed *Questions* and *Answers*. Write *I'm twenty-six; My phone number's 017153355; Yes, I am; Yes, he is.* in the *Answers* column and guide students to give you the matching questions from the *Grammar* box.

Highlight:
- the word order in the questions, using arrows to show the inversion of the subject and verb *you are > are you*
- the negative short answers *No, I'm not* and *No, he isn't.* The students should be able to give you these
- that we use short forms rather than repeating the full information in the question, for example *Yes, I am married*
- that we don't contract the positive short forms, for example not *Yes, she's*

Refer students to the *Language summary* on page 150.

2 Students ask and answer the questions from exercise 1, working in pairs. To enliven the activity, have them pretend to be market researchers interviewing someone visiting their town/country.

Pronunciation

See *Teacher's tips: helping students with pronunciation* on pages 7–8.

1 [T1.12] Use the recording or yourself to show the upward intonation of these 'yes/no' questions. You can use your hands to show how the voice rises after the stressed syllable. Drill, giving choral and individual repetition.

2 Students practise the questions and answers.

PRACTICE

1 Demonstrate an example and then students work individually to put the questions into the correct order. Circulate, helping where needed.

> **ANSWERS**
> b Are you twenty-one? c Is your teacher from Britain?
> d What's your e-mail address?
> e How old is your mother?
> f Where's Jennifer Lopez from? g Where's Manchester?
> h Are you single? i Are you from a big city?
> j Is your father a businessman?

2 Students work with a different partner and ask each other five or more of the questions. Circulate, listening particularly for students' use of the short forms. Make a note of problems and write some up on the board after the activity. Ask students to correct them.

ADDITIONAL PRACTICE

RB **Resource bank:** 1B, *The English class*, page 115; 1C *Short answer snap*, page 117

Workbook: *be:* personal questions: page 7; Listen and read, page 8

Task: Find information from documents (PAGES 14 and 15)

See *Teacher's tips: making tasks work* on pages 11–12.

Preparation: reading

1 Focus students on the photo of Hana and her Employee Personal Data card. Do the first example with the whole class, showing where to find the answer. Check *emergency* if necessary, but otherwise discourage students from trying to understand every word on the card. The aim here is to practise reading to extract specific information.

In the feedback, encourage students to give you the correct answers.

> **ANSWERS**
> a ✗ It's Hana b ✔ c ✗ It's 0795 323561
> d ✗ Depends on the current year
> e ✗ She's from the Czech Republic f ✔
> g ✔ It's 01904 776 544 h ✗ It's Dr Jo Boxer

2 Focus students on the *Useful language* box to revise personal questions. Students ask these questions about Hana and will have to change all the questions to the *she* forms.

Task: speaking

1 Divide the class into two groups, A and B. As look at Jamie's documents on page 15 and Bs look at Chrissie's documents on page 139. Each group completes the relevant part of the table on page 14. Before they start, check comprehension of *Mr*, *Mrs*, *Miss* and *Ms*. Students can work individually and then compare answers with another student in their group. Circulate and help as necessary.

> **Language note:**
> *Mr, Mrs, Miss* and *Ms* are only used with full names or surnames, for example *Mrs Betty Schwarz, Mr Gray*. Many women prefer to be addressed as *Ms* /mɪz/, as this does not draw attention to whether or not the woman is married.

> **ANSWERS**
> | Jamie | Chrissie |
> |---|---|
> | James Stuart Burden | Christina Elizabeth Nagano |
> | *DOB: 24.08.86 | *DOB: 10.10.82 |
> | 33b Park Street | 4685 Sterling Drive |
> | Glasgow | Boulder, Colorado 80301 |
> | G12 8AG | The United States |
> | Student | Marketing Manager |
> | Britain | The United States |
> | j.burden@glas.ac.uk | chrissie@creations.com |
> | 0141 228 4275 | 324 809 6439 |
> | ? | married |
>
> *The date of birth is given here rather than the age, as this will vary according to the current date.

Help students with the pronunciation of *Glasgow* /ˈglæzgəʊ/, *Boulder* /ˈbəʊldə/ and the e-mail addresses: *J. Burden at glaz dot ac dot UK; chrissie at creations dot com* (com = a company, ac = an academic institution such as a university).

2 Re-group students into A/B pairs. Check that they understand the task and re-focus them on the *Useful language box*. Ask two strong students to start asking and answering questions about Jamie in front of the class. Tell the students to keep their written information 'secret' from their partner and to write down the new answers in the table. Circulate, helping as necessary and collecting examples of any problems for error correction work later.

Follow-up writing: Done in class or as homework to provide a review of the Module.

Real life (PAGE 16)

Answering questions

1 This is a good opportunity to review numbers. See the Teacher's notes for *What English do you know?* for some additional ideas for practising these.

2 [T1.13] Focus students on the pictures. Play the recording and the students match the conversations to the pictures.

> **ANSWERS**
> Conversation 1 b   in a hotel
> Conversation 2 a   in a bank

3 **a** Work with the whole class to elicit possible questions for the missing information.

b Play the first conversation again and students complete the information. Then go onto the second conversation. If necessary, pause the recording, play parts of it at a time and give the students opportunities to listen to particularly problematic parts.

> **Language note:**
> Hotel room numbers are pronounced as separate numbers, e.g. *Room five three four (534)*, not *Room five hundred and thirty-four*. *0* is pronounced in hotel room numbers and telephone numbers as the letter *O* or as *zero (more commonly in the US).*

> **ANSWERS**
> a Rahman   b 14   c 7CK   d 01206 879879
> e 01206 765456   f British   g No
> h medical student   i 23   j Ream   k 201 758491
> l 615

4 **a** [T1.14] Play the recording, pausing after each question to allow students to write an answer.

b Students practise the questions in pairs.

Pronunciation

Students look at recording 14 on page 165. Play the recording again, or read the questions yourself. Students listen and repeat, paying particular attention to stress and intonation.

5 Students act out the conversations in pairs. Choose one or two pairs to act their's out in front of the class.

Study ... (PAGE 17)

Capital letters

It is an important basic writing skill to be able to use capital letters accurately, particularly if capital letters are used differently in your students' own language. *If you are in a mono-national situation:* you could start by eliciting when students use capital letters in their language and ask if they have noticed anything the same or different about English. *In a multi-national situation:* students can show their partners where they use capital letters (e.g. maybe for days of the week or for personal pronouns).

1 Encourage students to use their observation skills by looking back through the Module to decide which letters need to be capitalised.

> **ANSWERS**
> a What's your name?   b I'm here on business.
> c This is Emily.   d Are you Mrs Ream?

2 This is an introduction to how the *Mini-dictionary* can be a very helpful study tool for students. Do one example with them and they find the other examples themselves.

> **ANSWERS**
> English, Arabic, Poland, teacher, Saturday, notebook, December.

You could then draw together some categories on the board for using capital or lower case letters, particularly focusing on any differences between English and students' own languages. Refer students to *Language summary D* on page 150 and add other categories such as days of the week, languages, months, etc.

ADDITIONAL PRACTICE

Workbook: Punctuation: capital letters, page 8; Improve your writing: Addresses in English, page 9

Practise ... (PAGE 17)

This section can be done independently by students, which will encourage them to monitor their own learning and achievement. However, you can also use this section for further practice of the language areas covered in Module 1 or as a test. If you are testing students, make sure they do not look at the *Language summaries* until the end of each exercise or after they have finished all five exercises. Students can do this section for homework, or in class time if they need teacher guidance or if you want them to work in pairs/groups.

1–5 For each exercise, make sure students read the instructions carefully. Provide the answers either by checking as a whole class or by giving them a copy from the *Teacher's Book*.

> **ANSWERS**
> 1 Short forms of *be*
>   b He's a student. c I'm Marta.
>   d You're on holiday. e I'm not married.
>   f We aren't from Madrid. g We're from Malaga.
>   h She isn't at school. i They aren't American.
> 2 *be*
>   b This is Pablo. c What's your name?
>   d Where are you from? e They're Italian.
>   f I'm not a student. g She's twenty-three years old.
>   h We're on holiday. i How old is he?
> 3 b London Britain/the UK/England British/English
>   c Moscow Russia Russian
>   d Rome Italy Italian
>   e Madrid Spain Spanish
>   f Beijing China Chinese
>   g Warsaw Poland Polish
>   h Tokyo Japan Japanese
> 4 a/an + jobs
>   b a businessman c a nurse d an engineer
>   e a waiter f an electrician g a police officer
>   h a lawyer
> 5 b How c What d Where e How f What

Pronunciation spot (PAGE 17)

[T1.15] Get the students to listen to *American* on the recording or model it yourself and ask them where the stress is. Then show how some of the other, unstressed sounds reduce down to a *schwa*. As students listen and repeat each word, focus them on the stressed syllable as a first issue. Otherwise students can overemphasise the *schwa*. They need to become aware of it as a feature of weakened sounds because of stress.

[T1.16] Students listen and mark the stress and then listen and mark the /ə/ sounds.

> **ANSWERS**
>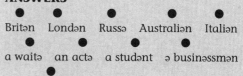
> Britən Londən Russə Australiən Italiən
> a waitə an actə a studənt ə businəssman
> ən electricən

From now on, you could decide to use the phonetic script when getting students to copy any new words with /ə/ in them.

Remember! (PAGE 17)

Read the REMEMBER! box with the students and get them to tick the ones they understand and are getting correct. If students have problems with a particular area, they can go over the relevant part of the Module/Language summary independently.

The *Mini-check* can be used as a test or as an independent self-check, or it could be used as revision after Module Two.

> **ANSWERS**
> 1 Britain 2 Spanish 3 Italy 4 Japan 5 'm
> 6 're 7 is 8 Are 9 Emily isn't a student.
> 10 My parents aren't from Barcelona.
> 11 You aren't in my class. 12 Are you married?
> 13 How old are you? 14 What's your job?
> 15 What's your telephone number? 16 musician
> 17 waiter 18 engineer 19 address
> 20 I'm from Turkey and Ahmed's from Dubai.

module 2

You and yours

Language focus 1 (PAGE 18)

this, that, these, those

1 [T2.1] Focus students on the pictures and ask them to circle the correct word. They work individually and then compare answers in pairs. This will help you to see how much they already know. Then play the recording for students to check their answers.

> **ANSWERS**
> 1 this   2 that, that's   3 those   4 These, This, this

Grammar

Write *here* and *there* in two columns on the board and ask students where to put *this (book)* and *that (book)*. Then elicit the plural forms in the correct columns:

	here	there
singular	*this*	*that*
plural	*these*	*those*

Refer students to *Language summary A* on page 150 of the *Students' Book*.

Pronunciation

See *Teacher's tips: helping students with pronunciation* on pages 7–8 of the *Teacher's Book*.

1 [T2.2] Play the recording and drill the four words chorally and individually. Pay particular attention to /ð/ and /θ/ sounds and to the difference between the singular /ðɪs/ and the plural /ðiːz/. Give some initial discrimination practice by saying *this, this, these, this, these, these* etc. slowly and then more quickly. Then do the same in phrases (*this pen, these books*). Students have to decide which they hear by holding up either their right or left hand.

The sounds /ð/ and /θ/ are further practised in the pronunciation spot at the end of the Module.

2 [T2.3] Play the recording and students write the eight sentences.

> **ANSWERS**
> a   What's this in English?
> b   Is this your pen?
> c   Is that your brother?
> d   This is my friend Ben.
> e   These are my parents.
> f   That's my teacher over there.
> g   Who are those children?
> h   Are these your books?

Students repeat the sentences. Help them to pronounce the

/s/ in *What's this? What's that?* by backchaining: *this > sthis > What's this?*

Students can also practise the original conversations on page 16, in pairs. Encourage stronger students to cover the words and try to remember the conversations.

PRACTICE

Students underline the correct alternative. They can do this individually and then check in pairs.

> **ANSWERS**
> 1 This   2 this is, this is   3 that   4 those
> 5 this   6 these   7 that   8 these

ADDITIONAL PRACTICE

Workbook: Identifying objects: *this, that, these, those,* page 10

Vocabulary (PAGE 19)

Everyday objects

1 Students work individually to find the objects in the photo.

> **ANSWERS**
> **From left to right**
> 1 a wallet   2 a credit card   3 a watch   4 photos
> 5 a diary   6 postcards   7 keys   8 a phone card
> 9 a brush   10 an identity card   11 a cheque book
> 12 a bottle of water   13 a camera   14 stamps
> 15 a packet of tissues   16 a dictionary   17 sweets
> 18 a mobile phone   19 coins
> 20 a packet of chewing gum   21 glasses

Demonstrate the speaking activity with a student using real objects, e.g. a mobile phone and some keys. Get a student to hold them and to ask the class questions. Students can then ask and answer in pairs using the pictures. Circulate and help as necessary, particularly with the pronunciation of the objects and questions.

> **Language note:**
> If your students speak a language which does not use articles, remind them to use *a/an* in front of a singular noun.

Pronunciation

[T2.4] Either use the recording or say the words in the box yourself. Ask students where the stress is. See *Teacher's tips: helping students with pronunciation* on pages 7–8 of the *Teacher's Book*.

Get students to listen to the full recording and mark the stress.

ANSWERS

photos a camera a bottle of water a credit card

keys stamps a mobile phone a brush a diary

coins a packet of chewing gum a watch

a cheque book a phone card postcards

a dictionary an identity card a packet of tissues

a wallet sweets glasses

Drill any words that your students find particularly problematic. Pay attention to the sounds in mobile / ˈməʊbaɪl/ identity /aɪˈdentɪti/ diary / ˈdaɪri/ tissues /tɪʃuːz/

2 Demonstrate the activity by pointing to an object across the room and asking *What's that in English?* and seeing if students know. Then get them to ask you, to see if they can accurately reproduce the question. Check the plural form in the same way. Students work in pairs. Likely objects could include *a cassette player, a video, an overhead projector, a white/blackboard, pens, chalks, a computer, a light, coats, scarves, chairs, a noticeboard, a picture, a register, a door, a ceiling, a wall, windows* and anything that can be seen outside the windows. Circulate and provide the word if the students don't know it. Collect a list of the words, which you or the students could write on the board.

ADDITIONAL PRACTICE

Resource bank: 2A *What's this?* page 116
Workbook: a/an or no article with objects and plurals, page 10

Language focus 2 (PAGE 20)

have got

1 [T2.5] Focus students on the pictures and check they understand the situation (*What's her problem? No phone card. Who is he?*). Play the recording and students complete the gaps.

ANSWERS
a I haven't got b Have you got? c I've got.

2 [T2.6] Introduce the form briefly by writing phrases based on the recording: *I've got my mobile* and *Have you got one/a phone card?* showing how the subject and object are inverted. Briefly drill this and go straight on to communicative listening practice of the question form: play the first two questions to demonstrate the activity.

Language note:
You may wish to explain the use of *one* to prevent the repetition of *have you got a phone card?*

3 a Demonstrate the activity and elicit/introduce the short answers, *Yes, I have.* and *No, I haven't.* Encourage additional information as in the example (*Here it is. It's at home*). Students work in pairs. Circulate, checking their use of language and helping where needed.

b Invite a stronger student to tell the class about their partner and see if *he/she* can produce the third person form correctly. Highlight and drill *He/She's got a(n) ...* . Students can tell the whole class or could turn to a new partner and tell them what they have found out about their original partner.

Language note:
We realise it is more natural to use *any* with some questions, for example *Have you got any coins?* but this language is introduced in Module 6. If you have a strong class, or if you think it's important, you may wish to teach *any* briefly at this point.
Students may know *I have* and *Do you have ...?* These mean the same as *I've got* and *Have you got ...? Do you have ...?* is slightly preferred in US English. In British English both are common.

Grammar

Write the examples on the board or use an overhead projector and ask students to complete the gaps. Encourage them to look back at exercises 1–3, to find or guess the answers.
1 Highlight:
  • the use of *'s* or *has* for the *he/she/it* forms
  • the contracted forms of *have* and *have not*
  • the word order of the questions
2 Write on the board *He's French* and *He's got a French car*, and ask students what *'s* means.
You may also want to check short answer forms at this point. Elicit the short answer to the question *Have you got your passport?* Write up the short answer *Yes, I have* and check the other short answer forms.
Refer students to *Language summary C* on page 151 of the *Students' Book*.

PRACTICE

1 Check *rich* and *brothers*. Students work individually and then check with a partner. Circulate and help as necessary. Check answers with the whole class.

ANSWERS
a 've got b haven't got c 've got d 's got
e Have .... got; 've got f Has .... got

2 a This gives more communicative practice. Begin by asking students to match the questions and answers and complete the gaps.

ANSWERS
1c Have 2d is 3b is 4a is

b Then get the students to choose something from the box and ask you similar questions. You may wish to drill the questions. Do the same with a strong pair in front of the whole class and then get students to work in pairs and have brief conversations. Stronger students may well develop the talking further. Circulate and note down any problems with the target form for error correction later.

ADDITIONAL PRACTICE

RB **Resource bank:** 2B *Who's got a Ferrari?* page 119

Workbook: have/has got 3, page 10; Questions and short answers, page 11; 5 *'s = is* or *has*, page 11

Reading and listening (PAGE 21)

My favourite thing

1 [2.7] Teach favourite /feɪvərɪt/ by saying *My favourite actor is ... My favourite colour is ... What about you?* If you wish to personalise the activity, start by bringing in one of your favourite objects (or a photo of it) and either talk simply about it or get students to ask you questions about it. Then focus students on the photos or put these on an overhead transparency, and ask them not to read the texts yet. The students predict the people's favourite things.

Teacher's note: We believe that sometimes it can be very useful for learners to listen and read at the same time, to help them to make sense of their reading and to see the relationship between sounds and spelling. However, this activity could first be used to give reading or listening practice, depending on which you think your class needs most.

Play the recording for students to listen and read and to check their predictions. The following words may be new to your students: *fast, comfortable, fantastic, pet, friendly, beautiful, professional, important, laptop, new, eyes.* You may wish to pre-teach some of these and/or ask students to look up others in the *mini-dictionary* after you have checked answers to the activity. You could write the words on the board, say them and ask students to listen and mark the word stress. Drill the words as necessary.

ANSWERS

Kemal	car
Lisa	pet cat
Tim	trumpet
Mo	computer

2 Students work in pairs and find the answers in the reading texts. Check answers with the whole class.

ANSWERS

a the car
   the computer/laptop
   the trumpet
   the car

b Billy, the cat
   Tim
   Billy

c Billy
   Tim
   Lisa

d the car
   the computer/laptop

Language notes:
- Point out that British people tend to use *he* and *she* for their pets.
- In the answers we use *the* because we know which one we are talking about.

3 Students close their books and tell each other about the people's favourite things. Student A can talk about Kemal and Tim and student B about Lisa and Mo. Circulate and help as needed.

Pronunciation

1 Students look at the tapescript on page 165. Demonstrate the activity on the board and let students work individually or in pairs.

2 [T2.8] Students listen and check their answers; they then practise saying the short form versions.

4 **a** Demonstrate on the board, writing about something important to you. Students work individually and write in their notebooks. Circulate and help if needed.

b Put students in small groups to talk about their favourite thing.

Language focus 3 (PAGE 22)

Family vocabulary; Possessive *'s*

For the following sections, you may wish to bring in some of your own family photos and encourage students to do the same.

1 Students at elementary level will know a fair number of words for family members. Check the meaning of *male, female* and *both* by doing the example on the board with the class.

Students can work individually or in pairs to complete the table. Circulate and help where needed. Encourage students to look up words in their *Mini-dictionary*.

Use this opportunity to discover if students are unsure about meanings. In the feedback check meaning as you go along and drill pronunciation e.g. daughter /dɔːtə/ girlfriend /gɜːlfrend/.

ANSWERS

male	female	both
husband	wife	
boyfriend	sisters	
grandson	girlfriend	
son	grandmother	
father	mother	
	daughter	

2 **a** Focus students on the photographs of famous people. Use one example as a whole class demonstration. Introduce the phrases *Maybe...* and *I'm sure...* It is not important whether students know the famous people. The point is for them to guess and thus have practice with the vocabulary. Students discuss the pictures in pairs.

b [T.9] Students listen and check.

ANSWERS
1 Steve Tyler and Liv Tyler: father and daughter
2 Lynne and David Beckham: sister and brother
3 Goldie Hawn and Kate Hudson: mother and daughter
4 Prince William and Queen Elizabeth: grandson and grandmother

Grammar

Write on the board:
William is the grandson of Queen Elizabeth.
Ask the students if they know another way to say this. Write the possessive *'s* form:
William is Queen Elizabeth's grandson.
Highlight that we usually use possessive *'s* with people.
Refer students to *Language summary F* on page 151 of the *Students' Book*.

PRACTICE

1 Demonstrate an example on the board and get students to write five further sentences in their notebooks. Circulate and help if needed.

2 Get students to add the words to the table. Go through each word checking the meaning or use pictures/photos/diagrams to elicit the words. Drill difficult ones, giving choral and individual repetition. The spelling of *nephew*, *niece* and *daughter* are particularly difficult.

ANSWERS

male	female	both
grandfather	granddaughter	children
uncle	aunt	parents
nephew	niece	grandparents

3 **a** Allow students a couple of minutes to study the vocabulary and spelling before they do the puzzle on page 144. They can do this individually as a competition.

ANSWERS
1 parents   2 niece   3 uncle   4 aunt
5 grandfather   6 cousin   7 grandmother
8 children   9 grandparents

b Give a few examples yourself: *Who's your mother's father? Who's your father's brother? Who's your grandfather's son?* Get two stronger students to demonstrate before students continue in pairs. Circulate and help as needed.

4 Encourage students to think of other famous related people from their own countries or internationally known e.g. the Clinton family, Jennifer Aniston and Brad Pitt, the Simpson family, the Beckhams and Julio and Junior Iglesias.

ADDITIONAL PRACTICE

RB **Resource bank:** 2C *The family*, page 121

Workbook: Vocabulary: Family vocabulary, page 12; Listen and read: A famous family, page 13; Possessive *'s*, page 14.

Task: Talk about your family tree
(PAGE 23)

Preparation: listening

See *Teacher's tips: making tasks work* on pages 11–12.

1 **a** Focus students on Alex and the photos of his family; ask them in pairs to guess the relationship between the people.

b Ask students to look at the family tree on page 146. It is very important that they understand how family trees are organised. Ask them to find Alex on the tree and then check their ideas.

2 [T2.10] Play the recording again and students number the people in the order they hear them.

ANSWERS
1 Alex   2 Elena   3 Enrique   4 Beatriz
5 Lucas   6 Lourdes   7 Roberto   8 Isabella
9 Bella   10 Mateo

3 Students check the words in bold. Words to check: *funny*, *lawyer*, *clever*. They can use their *Mini-dictionary* or ask you.

ANSWERS
a Alex   b Elena   c Enrique   d Beatriz
e Lucas   f Lourdes   g Lourdes
h Lourdes   i Roberto   j Isabella

Task: speaking

1 Demonstrate the activity by drawing your own family tree on the board and write in the names of six people. Or bring in photos of your family. Ask students to do whichever alternative you/they have chosen.

2 Allow students time to think about what to say and perhaps make some notes. Show them how to do this using your model on the board (*e.g. mother – very friendly, housewife, 42*). Circulate and encourage students to ask you for any particular vocabulary (e.g. they might want to say that their mother is *hard-working* or their father is retired, or their grandfather is *dead*).

Focus students on the *Useful language* box for completing the task. Write the phrases on the board, drill them and then rub out words to check if students can still remember the phrases.

Demonstrate the activity using your family tree or photos. Allow them time to react and ask you questions.

3 The students work in small groups and they ask and answer about their families. Circulate but don't interrupt unless there is a breakdown in communication. You can collect examples of good use of language and errors for feedback afterwards.

ADDITIONAL PRACTICE

Workbook: Improve your writing: Combining sentences, page 15; Writing about your family, page 15

Real life (PAGE 24)

Classroom language

1 Focus the students on the picture and establish the situation of students asking a teacher questions. Students work in pairs to decide on the best reply in each conversation.

2 [2.11] Play the recording for students to check their answers. They should also cross out the wrong answers.

ANSWERS
a 2 b 1 c 2 d 1 e 2 f 2 g 2 h 1

Pronunciation

See *Teacher's tips: helping students with pronunciation* on pages 7–8.

1 [2.12] Get students to look at the tapescript on page 165. Check the meaning of *polite* and ask them to listen. See if they can notice what makes it sound polite.

2 Students listen to each sentence and practise saying it in a polite way. They can just copy the way it is said. Or encourage them to start at a relatively high pitch in order to make the intonation sound more polite. Give choral and individual practice and help with showing where the main sentence stresses are.

3 a Students work in pairs to act out similar conversations.

b Students swap roles and do more. Circulate and help as needed.

Study ... (PAGE 25)

1 It is important for students to know the English names for grammar terms. This will help you if you are keeping English the medium of instruction in a monocultural class. Some students may not know all the terms in their own language, so, once you have demonstrated the activity, circulate and offer help and further examples, where needed.

Pay particular attention to any term which you know is different from the students' own languages. For example, syllables may be broken down differently or punctuation marks play a less important role.

Ask students to match the grammar words and examples. Alternatively, you could put these on cards and ask students in pairs to match them.

ANSWERS
b say, write
c beautiful, rich, important
d I, you, we
e from, on
f dic-tion-a-ry
g I've, he's, they're
h What? Where?
   ●
i comfortable
j . , ?

2 Look through one page from Module 0–2 and find some further examples as a whole class. Then, ask students to find further examples themselves or in pairs. Circulate, helping where needed.

As the grammar words are high frequency in an English class, you can work on the pronunciation of the difficult ones. Drill and give choral and individual repetition.

Practise ... (PAGE 25)

This section can be done independently by students, which will encourage them to monitor their own learning and achievement. Or you can use this section for further practice of the language covered in Module Two or as a test. Make sure they do not look at the *Language summaries* until the end of each exercise or after they have finished all five exercises. Students can do this section for homework.

1–5 Make sure students read the instructions carefully. Provide the answers either by checking as a whole class or by giving them a copy from the *Teacher's Book*.

ANSWERS
1 **Word groups**
a a computer, a DVD player, a mobile phone
b beautiful, friendly, clever
c a daughter, a niece, an aunt
d a son, a grandfather, a nephew
e cousins, friends, grandparents

2 **this, that, these, those**
b that
c this
d those
e these
f this

3a **have got**
2 Are you
3 Have you got
4 are you?
5 Are you
6 Have you got
7 Have you got
8 Have you got

4 's
b That's Anna's bag.
c She's got three sisters.

d   What's the matter?
e   He's Laura's cousin.

5
b   Can you say that again?
c   What does this word mean?
d   How do you say this word?
Encourage students to tick those they understand and
got correct. Encourage them to do extra study of
problematic areas.

Pronunciation spot

a   📼 [T2.13] The sounds /ð/ and /θ/ are problematic for
speakers of different languages and are worth spending
some time on at an early stage. Play the recording and
get students to listen to the two sounds in different
words. Show students the diagram of how to make the
sounds and get them practising. To help with the
position of the tongue you can ask students to place a
finger in front of their lips and make sure their tongue
touches it each time they make one of the sounds. To
differentiate between the two sounds, get students to
place a hand on their throat. With the voiced sound /ð/
they will feel a vibration and with the voiceless sound /θ/
there should be no vibration.

b   Students listen and repeat each word.

c   📼 [T2.14] Students listen and repeat the phrases.

ANSWERS
1   That thing over there.
2   Those three things.
3   Thank you for those things.
4   It's this Thursday.
5   This Thursday's fine.
6   That's the teacher over there.
7   It's three thirty-three.
8   There are thirteen of those things.

From now on, you could decide to use the phonetic script
when getting students to copy any new words with /ð/ or
/θ/ in them.

Remember! (PAGE 25)

Students do the *Mini-check* on page 160. Check answers as a
whole class, and ask students to tell you their scores out of 20.

ANSWERS
1 sister brother   2 aunt uncle   3 niece nephew
4 daughter son   5 c f   6 g b   7 h i   8 j e
9 a d   10 has got   11 Have you got
12 haven't got   13 've got   14 Has your brother got
15 hasn't got   16 These tissues are Jenny's.
17 How   18 What   19 How   20 What

module 3

Everyday life

Vocabulary (PAGE 26)

Common verbs

See *Teacher's tips: working with lexical phrases* on pages 9–10 and *making the most of the* Mini-dictionary on pages 10–11.

1 Ask students to put the verbs in the box in the correct place in the circles. They can start individually and then compare their answers with a partner. Let them check the meaning of any unknown words in their *Mini-dictionaries*.

> **ANSWERS**
> b work   c speak   d go   e study   f eat   g drink

2 [3.1] Play the recording for students to check their answers. Play again for repetition of the phrases and give extra choral and individual repetition where needed.

3 Ask students to add the words and phrases to the spidergrams.

> **ANSWERS**
> | | |
> |---|---|
> | live | with my parents, in a small town |
> | work | in an office |
> | speak | Chinese |
> | go | to the cinema a lot |
> | study | law |
> | eat | meat |
> | drink | beer, lemonade |

> **Language note:**
>
> In the UK people prefer the term flat, in most other countries they live in an apartment. Notice the use of *a lot* in some of these phrases. This is one of the most common chunks of language in spoken English.

ADDITIONAL PRACTICE

Workbook: Vocabulary: common verbs, page 16

Language focus 1 (PAGE 27)

Present simple questions

[T3.2] Play the first question and demonstrate what the students need to do. Then play the other questions.

Grammar

1 See if students can remember the first question on the recording (*Do you live in a big city?*). Write *I live in (the name of your city)* on the board. Under it write *... long hours*, and

ask students to provide the subject and the verb. Build up the table from the grammar box on the board. Remember the focus is on the question form and short answer. Highlight the meaning of the Present simple, i.e. that it is something which is always true (and not only at the present time). This is particularly important if your students speak a language which only has one present tense, where English has two.

2 See if students can remember the question about languages and elicit *Do you speak English?* onto the board. You may wish to use boxes/arrows/colours to show how we add the auxiliary verb do to make a question. Ask students to give you the answer to this question and write the short answers *Yes I do*, *No I don't* on the board. Highlight that:
we use *do* in these answers and not the main verb, i.e. not ~~Yes, I speak~~, but *Yes I do*.
an apostrophe = a missing letter. Ask them what it is in *don't*.
Refer students to *Language summary A* on page 151.

Pronunciation

See *Teacher's tips: helping students with pronunciation* on pages 7–8.

1 [3.2] Either play the examples again or model them yourself. Ask students to listen and tell you which words are stressed. These will be the main verb and the associated nouns. Tell students these are the important or information words. Point out the weakened form /d=jə/. Give choral and individual repetition.

2 Ask the students to look at the recording script on page 166 and drill the questions, stressing the main verbs and nouns. Give choral and individual repetition.

PRACTICE

1 Students work in pairs. Make sure students are using short answers, *Yes, I do* or *No, I don't*.

2 a Demonstrate the example on the board and get students writing five questions based on the collocations learnt earlier.

b Ask two students to demonstrate the activity in front of the class. They ask their questions to as many people as possible. They do not need to write the answers.

3 [T3.3] Students do the written practice individually. They can check their answers with a partner.

> **ANSWERS**
> a A: Do you eat meat?
>   B: No, I don't. I only eat fish.
> b A: Do you and your family live in a house?
>   B: No, we don't. We live in a flat.
> c A: Do your parents speak English?
>   B: Yes, they do.
> d A: Do you work for a big company?
>   B: No I don't, I work for a small company.
> e A: Do you and your friends go to the cinema a lot?
>   B: Yes, we do. We love the cinema.

4 a Demonstrate the activity with some true sentences about yourself. Students write eight sentences.

b Students read their sentences to a partner.

ADDITIONAL PRACTICE

RB **Resource bank:** 3A *Pick four cards*, page 123

Workbook: Present simple, Questions, page 16

Reading and vocabulary (PAGE 28)

1 a Ask students which words from the box they can see. In pairs, they can use the photos to discover or teach each other any new words with the help of the *Mini-dictionary*.

b [T3.4] Either model and drill the words yourself or use the recording as a model.

2 To arouse interest in the reading and listening texts, get the students to look at the photos and say whether things look different or the same.

3 Pre-teach this vocabulary by asking students to match the words.

> **ANSWERS**
> b open   close
> c a big meal   a snack
> d in the evening   in the morning
> e go to work   go home

4 Check comprehension of: *most + plural noun*. You could use percentages to help convey the meaning. You can check *usually/normally*. Students read the text and complete the gaps individually, and then compare with a partner.

> **ANSWERS**
> b in the evening   c a snack   d finish / go home
> e start   f open   g close

Listening (PAGE 29)

Life in Australia

1 [T3.5] Allow students time to read the questions. Demonstrate by playing the opening of the recording and asking which questions they hear. Play the rest of the recording and ask students to number the questions.

> **ANSWERS**
> 2 f   3 c   4 d   5 b   6 g   7 a

2 Do the example with the class and then play the full recording. Students tick the true statements. Be prepared to replay any sections

> **ANSWERS**
> Sentences b, e, g, i are true.

Language focus 2 (PAGE 29)

Present simple (positive and negative)

Elicit three positive sentences and three negative sentences from the students. Encourage them to look back at the reading text to find these.

> ## Grammar
>
> Project the table onto the board using an overhead projector. Alternatively, you could build up the table with the students, leaving gaps (*I _____ in a house*) to keep students involved. Elicit the negative form from the students.
> Refer students to *Language summary A* on page 152 of the *Students' Book*.

PRACTICE

1 Do the example with the class on the board, and then ask students to complete the exercise individually.

2 a Write on the board:

In Britain children start school at about nine o'clock.
In Poland children start school at eight o'clock.

    Elicit what is necessary to join the sentences (change to *they*, addition of *but* and check the meaning of *but*) and then ask students to write three more sentences.

b Students write three sentences to link Britain and Australia.

3 You can use this to practise the negative sentences in particular. Get students to make six sentences about themselves beginning and then explaining using the positive, as in the example. Students write six sentences individually and then talk to their partner.

ADDITIONAL PRACTICE

RB **Resource bank:** 3B *Pronoun stars*, page 124

Workbook: Present simple page 16; Positive and negative pages 16 and 17; Vocabulary: opposites, page 18

Real life (PAGE 30)

Days and times

If you have a low elementary class you can start by revising numbers, using exercise 2 on page 6 of the *Students' Book*.

1 a [T3.6] Check *in the morning, in the afternoon, in the evening*. Focus students on the pictures of the clocks/places and play the first example to demonstrate the activity. Students mark the time on the clocks.

> **ANSWERS**
> 2 Sao Paolo   one o'clock
> 3 London   four o'clock
> 4 Moscow   eight o'clock
> 5 Tokyo   one o'clock
> 6 Auckland   four o'clock

b Drill the question form and give choral and individual practice. See if the students can remember that e.g. In Los Angeles *it's nine o'clock in the morning* and encourage them to add the part of the day each time.

2 Focus students on the pictures of the watches and get them to match them with the times.

ANSWERS
1 f   2 a   3 d   4 e   5 b   6 c

At this point it is useful to have a clock with moveable hands available and check *past* and *to* with *5,10, 20, 25 and half past, quarter past and quarter to*. Demonstrate meaning very carefully for the students whose way of telling time may be different in their language.

3 [T3.7] Do the first one as an example. Students work individually and then listen and check.

ANSWERS
b   quarter past seven
c   half past nine
d   twenty to nine
e   quarter to seven
f   five past twelve
g   quarter to three
h   ten past three
i   twenty-five past nine
j   ten to eight
k   five to three
l   twenty-five to ten

Pronunciation

See *Teacher's tips: helping students with pronunciation* on pages 7–8.

1 Either play the recording again, or say these times yourself highlighting the stresses. Drill, giving choral and individual repetition. Highlight the use of the *schwa* in *to* /tə/.

2 Students listen and repeat each of the times above.

4 Divide each pair into Student A and Student B and direct them to the relevant page. Check what kind of text it is, e.g. *a TV guide*, and ask some brief orientation questions to help them skim it: *Films? Football? Famous people?* Make it very clear it is not important to understand everything, just the times.

Ask students to ask their partner questions to complete their gaps. Check by asking: *Is your information the same or different?* so that Student Bs realise they have different information from Student As.

Elicit and drill the question in the example. Focus on the use of *on* (as in *on TV*). Elicit the answer from one of the Student Bs and show Student As where they need to write it. Elicit Student B's first question: *What time is Holiday on?* Drill this and then get an answer from Student A. Show Student Bs where to write it.

5 Students work in pairs to discuss the questions. At this point allow freer speaking, so don't correct.
Refer students to *Language summary C* on page 152.

> **Language note:**
> Point out that when we have for example 11.02, 11.03, 11.04 etc. we use *minutes: one minute past eleven*, etc.

ADDITIONAL PRACTICE

RB **Resource bank:** 3C *Time pelmanism*, page 125
Workbook: Telling the time, page 19; Prepositions of time: *in, at or to*, page 19

Vocabulary and speaking (PAGE 31)

Daily routines

1 Focus students on the pictures and choose two examples to elicit a positive and negative response. Make sure that the students can identify the verbs with the activities. Then students tick or cross out the activities for themselves.

2 Students complete their individual clocks. Circulate, helping as needed.

3 Choose a stronger student and ask them some questions about their 'clock' and routines. Then ask the student to ask you and elicit the question form: *What time do you get up?* Drill, working on stress, and give choral and individual repetition. Practise with other questions. Put students into pairs to ask and answer questions based on the 'clocks'.

4 Put students into new pairs to ask and answer the questions.

5 Focus students on the example given. Students write their answers in their notebooks.

ADDITIONAL PRACTICE

Workbook: 11 Vocabulary, daily routines, page 19

Task: Find things in common
(PAGE 32)

See *Teacher's tips: making tasks work* on pages 11–12.

Preparation: listening

1 [3.8] Play the first conversation and elicit the correct topic. Check the following words: *love, never, hungry, horrible, sometimes*. Play the listening for students to listen and number the rest of the topics. Replay any conversations necessary and give them time to compare answers.

ANSWERS
1 breakfast
2 age
3 married or single
4 meat
5 where you live
6 nationality
7 brothers and sisters

2 Let students listen to extract 1 again and establish that the speakers are different. Get students to write an X beside breakfast in exercise 1. Then play extract 2 and establish that here the speakers have something in common so they can tick the topic. Students continue individually and then compare with a partner. Replay the conversations as many times as necessary. Check answers.

ANSWERS
Conversation 1   ✗
Conversation 2   ✔
Conversation 3   ✔
Conversation 4   ✗
Conversation 5   ✗
Conversation 6   ✗
Conversation 7   ✔

3 The students look at the four conversations and decide which are the same and which are different.

ANSWERS
a the same   b different   c the same   d different

ADDITIONAL PRACTICE

Workbook: *too, both* and *neither*, page 21

Task: speaking

1 Put students in pairs. Write the possible topics on the board and elicit a few possible questions. Then focus them on the questions in the *Useful language* box. Students then work together. Make sure both students write down all the questions.

2 Students work with a new partner. Ask them to find five things they have in common, positive or negative.

3 Demonstrate with a student and write the results on the board:

Do you go out to the cinema a lot? Me (✔) Maria (✔) We both go out to the cinema a lot. Check the meaning of *both*.

Students then report back in small groups or with the whole class.

Language note:

If you have an odd number of students in your class, with a group of three, you will need to introduce *all of us* and *none of us* for the feedback stage.

Study ... (PAGE 33)
Remembering spelling

Noticing spelling tendencies and rules is an important study skill and one which we return to on several occasions in the Study sections of Cutting Edge. This is a simple introduction to English spelling and concerns doubled letters.

1 Write up on the board *office* and *wallet* and ask students what is the same about their spelling. (They both have doubled consonants.) Underline the doubled letters and then get students to find more examples in the list.

2 Give two minutes study/memorising time.

3 [T3.9] Play the recording and conduct this as a spelling 'test'.

Practise ... (PAGE 33)

This section can be done independently by students to monitor their own learning and achievement. However, you can also use this section for further practice of the language areas covered in Module Three or as a test. If you are testing students, make sure they do not look at the *Language summaries* until the end of each exercise or after they have finished all five exercises. Students can do this section for homework, or in class time if they need teacher guidance or if you want them to work in pairs/groups.

1–5 For each exercise, make sure students read the instructions carefully. Provide the answers either by checking as a whole class or by giving them a copy from the *Teacher's Book*.

ANSWERS
1 **Common verbs**
c   go home
d   study
e   finish
f   go to bed
g   have breakfast
h   read a book

2 **Verb forms**
a   , don't
b   Haven't, have,
c   do
d   are
e   aren't

3 **Vocabulary**
b   an office
c   a garden
d   a newspaper
e   a shop
f   a beach

4 **Times**
b   half past three

c   quarter past six
d   ten past five
e   eleven o'clock
f   quarter to six
g   twenty-five to ten
h   five to four

5   Prepositions
b   at, in
c   at
d   on
e   at

Pronunciation spot

This links well with a focus on spelling in this section and builds on work on word stress.

a 🔊 [T3.10] Say the words *chocolate* and *breakfast* and ask students how many syllables they can hear. Play the recording and students write in the boxes the number of syllables.

ANSWERS

chocolate	2
breakfast	2
camera	2
different	2
restaurant	2
favourite	2
Saturday	3
business	2
comfortable	3
dictionary	3

Language note: It is possible to pronounce some of these so there are more syllables (e.g. favourite 3) but the reduced pronunciation is more common.

b Write *chocolate* on the board and ask students which syllable is not pronounced (o). Get the students to cross out the silent syllables.

ANSWERS

rest~~au~~rant   breakfast   fav~~ou~~rite   Saturday   cam~~e~~ra
business   diff~~e~~rent   comf~~or~~table   diction~~a~~ry

c Students listen and practise. Give plenty of drilling of particularly key ones such as *comfortable* and *business*.

Remember! (PAGE 33)

Encourage the students to tick the items they understand and got correct and to do extra study at home where there were problems.

ANSWERS
1 go   2 have   3 speak   4 get   5 drink
6 open   7 Do, don't, -   8 do, -   9 -, have
10 Do, do   11 office   12 beach   13 cinema
14 city centre   15 half past eight
16 quarter to seven   17 twenty past three
18 at   19 on   20 at

module 4

Loves and hates

Listening (PAGE 34)

Celebrity loves and hates

1 Focus the students on the pictures and get them to match these to the words in the box. In the feedback, check the meaning and drill the pronunciation of any difficult ones. Demonstrate the personalisation stage, using yourself as an example and especially checking the meaning and pronunciation of *I'm frightened of* /aɪm fraɪtənd of/.

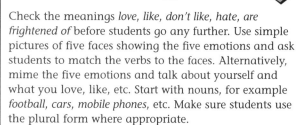

Exercise 1: additional suggestion

Check the meanings *love, like, don't like, hate, are frightened of* before students go any further. Use simple pictures of five faces showing the five emotions and ask students to match the verbs to the faces. Alternatively, mime the five emotions and talk about yourself and what you love, like, etc. Start with nouns, for example *football, cars, mobile phones*, etc. Make sure students use the plural form where appropriate.

2 [T4.1] Focus students on the celebrities (you may wish to teach this word). Do students know any of them? Play the first example on the tape to demonstrate what students have to do. Then play the whole recording and students match the people to the items in the box. It doesn't matter that students won't understand the full content of the extracts.

ANSWERS

Cameron Diaz	TV
Britney Spears	dolls
Harrison Ford	housework
Dean Cain	flying
Johnny Depp	clowns
Woody Allen	spiders, dogs, crowds.

Before listening again, introduce *face* and *plane*.

3 Play the first extract again and elicit that Cameron Diaz hates TV. They should put a cross next to TV in the box. Play the remainder of the tape. Students can work individually and then check their answers. Circulate and help where necessary. Play any problematic parts of the tape again.

ANSWERS

Britney Spears loves dolls
Harrison Ford loves housework
Dean Cain hates flying
Johnny Depp hates clowns
Woody Allen hates spiders, dogs, children

4 Ask students to complete the sentences using verbs in the box. Demonstrate on the board, using the first example. Check the meaning of *never*.

ANSWERS

b doesn't have   c hates   d loves   e goes   f has

Language focus 1 (PAGE 35)

Present simple: *he* and *she*; *like ...ing*; Activities

Grammar

Ask students to tell you what they remember about Woody Allen and spiders and elicit onto the board: *He hates spiders*.

Then elicit about Britney Spears: *She loves dolls*; and Johnny Depp: *He doesn't like clowns*; and Cameron Diaz: *She doesn't watch TV*.

Highlight:
• the third person -*s*.
• the use of *doesn't*.
• that we don't say ~~*She doesn't likes*~~.
• The use of the plural noun form after *likes* and *hates*.

Elicit the *he/she* forms of *have*, *go* and *do* and add these to the board, focusing on the spelling.

Language note:

At this point we are not making a big issue of the use of the -*ing* form, preferring to treat the activities as lexical items. But you may wish to highlight the form briefly as you go along.

PRACTICE

1 a Ask students to close their books and elicit onto the board the names of the celebrities. Name 'Cameron Diaz' and see if students can remember something about her. Put students into pairs to test each other.

b [T4.2] Focus the students on the tapescript and drill the positive and negative verbs. Pay particular attention to the final 's' and to the pronunciation of *doesn't* /dʌzənt/. There is a specific pronunciation slot on the final 's' on page 41.

2 a Focus students on the pictures and get them to match these with the words in the box. Encourage them to use their *Mini-dictionary* if necessary.

ANSWERS

1 cats   2 cooking   3 driving   4 cycling   5 salad
6 reading   7 running   8 swimming
9 computer games

b Get students to ask you about the pictures. Model possible replies: *Yes, I love it/them. / Yes, I do. / It's/They're okay. / No, I don't. / No, I hate it/them*. Remind students that we don't say *Yes I like* or *Yes I like cooking*. Students work in pairs. Circulate and help, particularly with natural replies. You may wish to allow time for reporting back. Students could tell you one thing that they had in common and one thing that was different.

3 a Demonstrate the activity by using the prompts to talk about yourself. Write the information on the board. Ask students to write about themselves. Circulate and help with any vocabulary.

b Collect all the pieces of writing and distribute them to different students. Focus them on the example in the speech bubble. Get a strong student to start, and make sure he/she does not say the name. The other students listen and guess who it is. Keep checking that students are using the final -s. Encourage them to correct themselves and each other.

Pronunciation

1 🔲 [T4.3] Focus students on the tapescript and play the first example. Write 1, 2, 3 on the board and elicit the number of syllables in *likes*. Write *likes* under 1. Do the same for the *watches*, putting it under 2. Continue with the other examples.

ANSWERS

1	2	3
likes	watches	finishes
loves	opens	understands
hates	closes	
starts	studies	
goes		
does		

2 Drill the individual verbs as needed. Students usually have difficulty with adding a final syllable in examples such as *watches* and *finishes*, so you may need to spend more time on these. Then get students to read the tapescripts aloud in pairs. Circulate and help individuals as needed.

ADDITIONAL PRACTICE

RB **Resource bank:** 4A *Things you love and hate*, page 126

Workbook: Present simple: Spelling, page 22; Present simple with *he/she/it*, page 22; *like, love, hate + -ing*, page 24

Reading (PAGE 36)

1 Focus students on the photos and ask who they are. You can check their jobs: Madonna – pop singer; Catherine Zeta Jones – actress/film star.

2 Write the two questions on the board and give students half a minute to read quickly and find the answers. This is to help students understand some key points of the text and they should not worry about words they don't understand.

ANSWERS
Madonna is American and lives in London.
Catherine Zeta Jones is British and lives in Hollywood. (You may wish to show students on a map where Wales is.)

3 a Students use their *Mini-dictionaries* to find the meanings of the words in bold. Alternatively, you can elicit these. Check the meaning carefully. You may wish to drill

ordinary /ˈɔːdənəri/ and *theatre* /ˈθɪətə/ or any others if necessary. Also check the meaning of *more* by telling students two things you enjoy and which one you enjoy more.

b Do the first example with the class. Students work individually first. They then check their answers in pairs. Encourage them to read in order to identify main information from a text and not to try and understand each word.

ANSWERS
1 Madonna   2 Catherine Zeta Jones   3 Madonna
4 Catherine Zeta Jones   5 Madonna   6 Madonna
7 Catherine Zeta Jones   8 Madonna

Language focus 2 (PAGE 37)

Present simple questions: *he* and *she*

Grammar

1 Write *She likes London* and *She misses the USA* about Madonna on the board and elicit/introduce the questions. Write the questions up above the answers and use colours/arrows/boxes to show students how to make the question form. Highlight that the -s from *likes* has moved to the auxiliary verb *do* to make *does*. So we don't say ~~Does she likes?~~

2 Elicit/introduce the short answers *Yes, she does* and *No, she doesn't*.

Highlight:
• the use of the auxiliary *does* in the short answers.
• that we don't say ~~Yes, she likes.~~

Drill the question forms and short answers. Say the first question and ask students which words are stressed:

● ●

Does she like London?

Show them how we weaken does to /dʒ/ and build up the sentence with them: *London, like London, she like London, does she like London.* Contrast the weak form of does /dʒ/ in the questions with the strong form /dʌz/ and /dʌznt/ in the short answers and drill both.

Refer students to *Language summary B* on page 152 of the *Students' Book*.

Grammar: alternative suggestion

If you have a small class: you can use Cuisenaire rods (small coloured rods traditionally used for mathematics) to show the transformation from the statement to the question form.

Use four rods to show: *She likes England,* with one rod representing '*s*' on the end of *likes*. Show: *Does she like England?* using the same four colours plus a new colour to represent do. Move the '*s*' rod to the end of *do*. This shows visually how the third person marker '*s*' or '*es*' moves from the main verb *likes* to the auxiliary *does*.

PRACTICE

1 **a** Do the first example on the board. Students complete it individually. Do the second example as well in order to check the meaning of *What does her husband do?* i.e. *What's his job?* Circulate, helping as needed. Students can check their answers before whole class feedback.

> **ANSWERS**
> 2 What does her husband do?   3 Does she like Britain?
> 4 What does she love?   5 Does she miss the USA?
> 6 Where does Catherine Zeta Jones come from?
> 7 Where does she live now?
> 8 Does she go back to Wales?
> 9 Why does she miss Wales?

b Do an example with two students in front of the class. Put the students in pairs to ask and answer the questions. Circulate and help as needed. Check that students are using short answers.

2 **a** Focus students on the photo of Sarinder and his friend. Elicit some ideas about them. *Where are they from? Are they brothers? Friends? Where do they live? How old are they? What do they do?*

Do the first example with the students. Make sure they realise it is written by the British young man. Students continue individually. Circulate and help as needed.

> **ANSWERS**
> 1 is   2 's   3 comes   4 lives   5 are   6 finishes
> 7 want   8 owns   9 want   10 go   11 stay
> 12 loves   13 's got   14 lives   15 misses   16 've got

b [T4.4] Students listen and check their answers.

3 **a** Ask students to think of someone from another country, city or culture. Have some suggestions of famous people, if the students can't think of anyone.

b Demonstrate so that students understand the activity. Choose a person and get students to form the questions to ask you. Put them in pairs. Allow them time to prepare. Circulate and help as needed.

4 Show an example of writing about the person you chose in 3b. Ask students to write about their person. This can be done in class or at home. If in class, circulate and help as needed.

ADDITIONAL PRACTICE

RB **Resource bank:** 4B *Three people I know*, page 127

Workbook: Short answers, page 23; Negatives, page 23; Positives and negatives, page 23; Questions, page 23

Language focus 3 (PAGE 38)

Activity verbs and adverbs of frequency

1 As an introduction, focus students on the picture. Ask students *Do you like reading? What do you read?* and try to elicit e.g. *newspapers, books, e-mails, magazines.*

Focus students on the spidergrams a, b, g and h. They then fill the empty circles with the six verbs. Encourage them to use their *Mini-dictionaries*. They can work individually and then compare answers in pairs. Check answers with the whole class. Pronunciation to check: radio /ˈreɪdiːəʊ/, newspaper /ˈnjuːs.peɪpə/.

> **ANSWERS**
> c play   d write   e listen to   f watch   i do   j have

2 **a** Ask students where they could put *shopping*. Students can then add the other words from the box. Circulate and help as needed. Pronunciation to check: magazine /mægæziːn/, guitar /gɪtɑː/, relatives /relətɪvz/.

> **ANSWERS**
> a   read   a magazine, an e-mail
> b   go   shopping
> c   play   the guitar, computer games
> d   write   an e-mail
> e   listen to   CDs
> f   watch   a video
> g   go to   the cinema, a restaurant
> h   visit   your relatives
> I   do   your homework

> **Language note:**
> Point out that we use *the* in *listen to the radio* (but not in *watch television*) and we talk about *the cinema* (also *the theatre / the pub*) and play *the guitar* (*piano, flute,* etc.). Students can learn these as fixed phrases.

b Drill students by saying the words in the box in 2a and students provide the full collocation. Put students into pairs. One student in each pair closes their book. The other student tests him/her. Then they swap roles.

3 **a** Students can work in pairs to place the adverbs on the line. Or you could draw the line on the board, write the adverbs on cards and invite the class to stick them in the correct place.

> **ANSWERS**
> Always (100%) > usually (90%) > often (70%)
> > sometimes (30%) > not ... often (10%) > never (0%)

b Tell students about yourself, for example *I often go shopping on Saturday*, and put a tick next to it on the board. Then say *I always read the newspaper in the morning* and put a cross by it. Students then tick the statements which are true for them.

Grammar

Focus students on the questions in the *Grammar* box. Students work individually to look back at the sentences and discover the rule.

> **ANSWERS**
> Adverbs of frequency come <u>before</u> the verb in positive sentences and <u>after</u> *don't* in negative sentences.

Refer students to *Language summary C* on page 152 of the *Students' Book*, where position with the verb *be* is also covered (or you can leave this point till later).

Language note:

Sometimes, usually and *often* can also go at the beginning and ending of phrases, but at this level it is better to start with a simple rule of position. *Not often* can be separated as in *I don't go there often*, but again we have started with the simpler rule.

PRACTICE

1 Demonstrate the activity by writing some examples about yourself on the board. Students can work individually and then compare their sentences in pairs.

2 Students could start by asking you the questions. Check they understand that *ever* means at any time. Also point out that if they answer using *always* or *usually*, they need to give more information. So *Do you play football?* cannot just be answered by *usually* or *always*. We have to say *I usually/always play on Saturday*. Encourage students to use *How about you?* to continue the conversations instead of repeating the question.

Stronger students might ask you how to say things like *once a week, every Thursday*, which you could teach them. Collect examples of good language and any errors for analysis and correction later.

ADDITIONAL PRACTICE

RB **Resource bank:** 4C *Always, sometimes, never*, page 128; 4D *Verb dominoes*, page 129

Workbook: Adverbs of frequency, page 26; Activity verbs, page 26; Word order: frequency adverbs, auxiliaries, page 26

Task: Find an e-mail friend
(PAGE 39)

See *Teacher's tips: making tasks* work on pages 7–8.

Preparation: reading

Start by asking students *Have you got any hobbies?* Focus students on the photo of Teresa and ask *Where is she? What is she doing?* Set the situation: she wants to find friends from different countries and elicit ideas as to how she can do so.

Ask students to read about Teresa and answer the questions.

ANSWERS
a Cork, in Ireland b Yes, she's a music student.
c twenty-one d Yes, she does. e Yes, she does.
f Yes, she does. She likes going to the cinema, reading, the Internet, driving her car, going out with friends, travelling and speaking Spanish.

Task: reading and speaking

1 Check students understand the situation. Focus students on the table on page 39. Ask them to give you the

questions for Peter, for example: *Nationality? Where is he from? Age? How old is he? Occupation? Is he a student? What does he do / What's his job?* etc. Build up the questions gradually. When you have finished, students can look at the *Useful language* box, part a to compare their ideas with the suggested language.

Divide the class into A/B pairs. Student B turns to page 140 and looks at the information about Peter and Sofia. Student A asks questions about Peter and Sofia and writes the answers in the table. Ask two students to start the activity in front of the class.

Then Student A turns to page 138 and looks at the information about Marina and Joao. Student B asks questions and completes the table for each person.

Circulate and help as necessary. Note down any common errors for correction later.

You may need to check the following before they start or help them as you monitor: *hockey, basketball, softball, rock music, classical music, receptionist, movies.*

ANSWERS

	Peter	Sofia
nationality/city	Singapore	Santander in Spain
age	twenty-six	twenty-two
occupation	a hotel receptionist	a music student
interests	writing and listening to music, playing softball, going to the movies, going out with his friends, cooking	playing the guitar, football, tennis, going to the cinema, going out with friends, animals
languages	English Mandarin Chinese	French, English, Spanish

	Marina	Joao
nationality/city	Tachov in the Czech Republic	Bela Horizonte in Brazil
	eighteen	twenty-five
occupation	an engineering student	a language student
interests	all types of sport, especially hockey and basketball, reading and computers, dogs	rock music, sport, tennis
languages		Portuguese, English, Spanish

2 Ask students to decide who is the best e-mail friend for Teresa. They put the people in order and write a few notes particularly on their first and last choices. Focus them on b in the *Useful language* box and drill the phrases, giving choral and individual repetition.

Put students in small groups and get them to discuss their answers and come to a group decision. Someone from each group then reports back to the class. Give each group time to choose their spokesperson and prepare what they are going to say.

Real life (PAGE 40)

Asking politely

1 [T4.5] Ask students for the names of local cafés and ask them which ones they like and why.

Focus students on the pictures in the cafés and check *customer* and *waiter/waitress*. Ask some questions about the relationships to encourage the students to look more closely: *Look at b. Who are they? Mother and children*, etc. Pre-teach *the bill*.

Ask students to try and put the sentences in the correct place in the conversations. Check that students can work out the meanings of the sentences. Do the first one as an example.

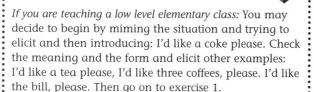

Exercise 1: alternative suggestion

If you are teaching a low level elementary class: You may decide to begin by miming the situation and trying to elicit and then introducing: I'd like a coke please. Check the meaning and the form and elicit other examples: I'd like a tea please, I'd like three coffees, please. I'd like the bill, please. Then go on to exercise 1.

ANSWERS
a   Do you want a drink?
b   Excuse me, I'd like three cokes, please.
c   Do you want milk?
d   I'd like one of those, please.
e   Excuse me. I'd like the bill, please.

Highlight:
the form of *I'd like = I would like*
the meaning = *I want*; it's polite; we are talking about now.
the use of *the* with bill.
the question with *Do you want*

Language note:

At this stage teach these phrases as useful 'chunks' of language rather than going into the grammar. It is easier to teach *Do you want* instead of *Would you like* at this early stage. You can point out the difference between *I like* and *I'd like*: the first is about something always true and the second about something you want now.

ADDITIONAL PRACTICE

Workbook: Asking politely, page 27

Pronunciation

See *Teacher's tips: helping students with pronunciation* on pages 7–8.

1 [T4.6] Play the tape or give the models yourself and help students to hear the polite intonation.

2 Get students to copy the intonation on the tape. Encourage students to exaggerate and 'sound English!'

2 Students act out the conversations. Circulate and focus particularly on whether they remember to include 'd in *I'd like* and also how polite they sound. You can set it up so that the other student only replies if they think their partner sounds polite enough.

3 Set the situation: they are in a café. Demonstrate using two students in front of the class. Students work in pairs or small groups to act out the conversations. Encourage them to develop the conversations further. Circulate, helping where needed and collecting examples of good language and errors for feedback later.

Study ... (PAGE 41)

Finding spelling in a dictionary

1 Write on the board *he/she/it*. Ask students to give you the third person singular form of some verbs, e.g. *work*, *fly*, *watch*, *play*. Focus them on the dictionary entry for *work* and show them where to find the third person form.

2 Students use their *Mini-dictionaries* to find the third person forms of the verbs.

ANSWERS
a runs   b finishes   c swims   d misses   e works
f flies   g says   h watches

3 Do the first example with them and then get students to work out the rules for the other ones. Check they understand *vowel* and *consonant*.

ANSWERS
a take 's'   b take 'es'   c take 'ies'   d take 's'

4 Students use the rules to work out these verbs. They then check in their *Mini-dictionary*.

ANSWERS
a eats   b leaves   c studies   d stays   e catches
f carries

Practise ... (PAGE 41)

Students can do this section independently to monitor their own learning. Or use it for further practice of the language covered in Module 4, or as a test. Make sure students do not look at the *Language summaries* until after they have finished all five exercises. Students can do this section for homework.

1–6 Make sure students read the instructions carefully. Provide the answers either by checking as a whole class or by giving them a copy from the *Teacher's Book*.

1 Present simple *he/she* forms

You could do this as a dictation; you say the verb and the student writes the third person singular form.

ANSWERS
b studies c listens d watches e does f hates
g goes h works i has

2 Present simple auxiliaries

ANSWERS
a don't b does c Do, do d does e Does, doesn't

3 Words that go together

Put the words onto sets of cards. Students, in pairs or groups, match the collocations.

ANSWERS
b	visit	your aunt
c	have	dinner
d	do	your homework
e	go	shopping
f	go to	a restaurant
g	listen to	a CD
h	read	the newspaper

4 Adverbs of frequency

Cut up each sentence into its individual words and students, in pairs or groups, unjumble the sentences.

ANSWERS
b You never listen to me.
c I don't often catch the bus.
d My sister usually visits me on Sunday.

5 Activities

ANSWERS
b cooking c running d swimming e driving
f reading

6 *Do you want...? / I'd like...*

ANSWERS
b 4 c 1 d 3

Pronunciation spot

a [T4.7] Model and drill the three different sounds. Get students to place their hands over their throats to feel the difference between the voiceless /s/ and the voiced /z/. Play the tape so that students can notice the difference.

Explain: /s/ follows a voiceless consonant, for example,

likes /laɪks/, /z/ follows a voiced consonant or a vowel or diphthong, for example *loves* /lʌvz/ *Anna's* /ænəz/, and /ɪz/ follows the sounds /tʃ/ /dʒ/ /ʃ/ and /ʒ/.

b [T4.8] Play the tape. Students decide which sound is at the end and write the word in the correct category.

ANSWERS
/s/ flats hates waits
/z/ pens cousins enjoys
/ɪz/ boxes misses

c Students practise saying the sounds. Get students to add future third person singular examples to the three pronunciations.

Remember! (PAGE 41)

Get the students to look back over the *Practise* section and tick those they understand and got correct. Encourage them to do extra study of the areas they are weak in.

Students do the *Mini-check* on page 161 and tell you their scores.

ANSWERS
1 read 2 goes 3 listen 4 watches 5 has
6 goes 7 play 8 does 9 My brother lives in Berlin.
10 Where do you work? 11 What does Erica study?
12 I never go to bed early.
13 He doesn't often speak English.
14 Does your wife work for a big company?
15 My mother doesn't like spiders.
16 Do you want a drink?
17 I'd like three coffees, please. 18 shopping
19 reading 20 driving

module 5

Getting from A to B

Vocabulary and reading (PAGE 42)

Transport

1 Students work in pairs to find the types of transport in the pictures. Explain that they will not find all of them. Check pronunciation of motorbike /məʊtəbaɪk/, scooter /skuːtə/, aeroplane /eərəpleɪn/, bicycle /baɪsɪkəl/, bus /bʌs/, underground train /ʌndəɡraʊnd treɪn/, a subway train /sʌbweɪ treɪn/.

> **ANSWERS**
> a an aeroplane
> b a bus
> c a scooter   a car   a taxi
> d a bicycle
> e a train
> f a ferry
> g an underground (British English) / a subway train (US English)
> h a tram

2 Write *fast* at the top of the board and *slow* at the bottom. Check students understand and then ask them where to put *aeroplane*. Write it at the top and number it 1, then ask them for number 12 at the bottom (*bicycle*). Students work individually to put the rest of the words in order and then compare with a partner.

> **ANSWERS (SUGGESTED)**
> 1 an aeroplane   2 a train   3 a bus
> 4/5 a car / a taxi   6 a motorbike
> 7 an underground / subway train   8 a ferry
> 9/10 a tram / a bus   11 a scooter   12 a bicycle

3 Ask a student *How do you usually travel to school?* Check that he/she uses the correct preposition: *by bus, by train*. Highlight the use of by for all the types of transport and the use of *on foot* when we walk. Students work in pairs to talk about how the various people travel.

4 Focus students on the vocabulary box. Encourage them to use their *Mini-dictionary*, if necessary. They can then find the vocabulary in the pictures.

> **ANSWERS (SUGGESTED)**
> people waiting in a queue – b
> passengers – b, c, g, h
> a crowded train – g
> travelling fast – a, e
> travelling slowly – b, c, d
> bad traffic – b, c, g

5 [T5.1]

Ask students *Do people drive on the right or the left in your country? What about in Britain? Which countries drive on the left?* Then get students to read the first fact and decide which number should go in the gap. They then work individually and put the numbers in the other gaps. Encourage them to guess the meaning of unknown words and use their *Mini-dictionary* if necessary. A *Mag Lev* (*Magnetic Levitation*) *train* is not in the *Mini-dictionary*, so check this. Check how to say numbers with *thousand* and *million*, *per cent* and the meaning of *more than + number*. Point out that we don't say *thousands* and *millions*. Play the recording for students to check their answers.

> **ANSWERS**
> a 59   b 740   c 100,000,000   d 5   e 77,000,000
> f 8   g 9,000,000   h 1,000,000   i 3   j 500,000

6 **a** Get students to find the answer to 1 and write it on the board: *drive a car*. Then students do the exercise individually.

> **ANSWERS**
> 1 drive   2 ride   3 wait for   4 on   5 off
> 6 to   7 by   8 take   9 to

b Students, in pairs, take it in turns to test their partner, by saying the verbs only. Get a strong pair to demonstrate the activity in front of the class.

7 First check *most, a lot of* and *not many*. Use *Language summary A* on page 152. Do the first example on the board and ask students if it is true. If it is false in relation to their country show students how to change it. If it is true, then choose another example which is false and do this instead.
Refer students to *Language summary A* on page 152.

ADDITIONAL PRACTICE

Workbook: Vocabulary, page 28; Prepositions, page 28; *most, a lot of, some, not many*, page 30; Listen and read, page 30

Language focus 1 (PAGES 44–45)

can and *can't*

> **Language note:**
> *Can* and *can't* for possibility is introduced before ability because this use is more common. The ability use is covered in Module 11.

1 Focus students on the photos and identify the city. Ask if they know New York. Where is the airport? Students read about Karen and answer the questions. Check the time at present and the time she needs to be at JFK Airport: She only has 1 hr and 20 mins to get there.

2 Students work individually to complete the table. Check: *shuttle bus*.

ANSWERS

type(s) of transport	time (in hours/ minutes)	cost
1 taxi	about an hour	$35 + a tip of 15–20%
2 subway and bus	90 minutes	$2
3 walk, subway and AirTrain	1 hour 32 minutes	$7
4 subway and New York Airport Express Bus	1 hour 5 minutes	$15

3 Give students time to think individually first and then get them in pairs to choose. Encourage them to talk about each way. Circulate and check if they use *can/can't*.

4 [T5.2] Play the recording for students to check their answers. Elicit their ideas on number 1. Then compare with what the speakers say about it and so on.

ANSWER
4 is the only possibility

Grammar

Write the gapped sentences on the board and ask students to complete them, in pairs. Check that we are talking about something that is possible (+) or impossible (–).

Highlight:
• that after *can* we use the base form of the verb and we don't change it for *he/she/it*
• that *can't = can not*
• that we make questions by inverting *can* and the subject

Refer students to *Language summary B* on page 153 of the *Students' Book*.

Pronunciation

[T5.3] Start by saying a positive sentence yourself, for example *I can go*. Ask students where the stress is (on *go*). Show them how *can* is weakened to /kən/ and let them listen to your example again. Then give the negative *I can't go* and ask about the stress. Stress both *can't* /kɑːnt/ and *go* /gəʊ/. Then say the two sentences several times, randomly, and ask students to say positive or negative until they become more confident. Play the recording for students to complete the activity.

ANSWERS
1 You can't take the bus.   –
2 Can we take a train?   ?
3 Can I park here?   ?

4 We can walk.   +
5 They can wait over there.   +
6 You can go by car.   +
7 We can't drive there.   –
8 You can take the ferry.   +
9 You can't ride your bicycle up there. –
10 Can you fly there?   ?

PRACTICE

1 [T5.4] Check that students understand the sentences. Explain the meaning of: *find a taxi easily, safely, it depends*. Play the first question and answer and show the cross. Students listen to the rest of the recording and mark the sentences.

ANSWERS
b X   c ✔   d ?   e X   f X   g ?   h ?   i X

2 Demonstrate with a student. They can either talk about New York or their own cities/towns. Drill the question so that students stress the main verb and weaken *can*: Can /kən/ *you travel by tram?* short answers, *Yes, you can* /kæn/, *No, you can't* /kɑːnt/ (Or US pronunciation /kænt/) and *It depends* /dɪpendz/. Explain that *you* here means *people*.

3 Write a couple of examples on the board or focus students on the examples in the book. Students individually write eight sentences about their own town/city.

ADDITIONAL PRACTICE

RB **Resource bank:** 5A *The Perfect Holiday* page 130
Workbook: *can / can't*, page 28; Short answers, page 29

Listening and vocabulary (PAGE 45)

At the airport

1 Karen Davis is now at JFK airport. Focus students on her travel itinerary and get them to find the answers to the questions. Check: *arrival* and *departure*.

ANSWERS
a 18.30 and 9.35.
b London Heathrow and Milan Malpensa
c Flight AA100 and BA0572 (Help students with the pronunciation of these to help them with the listening)

2 Students match the phrases and meanings. The phrases are commonly heard in all international airports. Check the meanings and give choral and individual practice of the phrases. This will help students to hear them in the recording.

ANSWERS
b 5   c 6   d 1   e 4   f 2

When doing feedback on *delayed/late*, check reasons why and introduce *bad weather*, which is useful for the next listening.

3 a 📼 [T5.5] Focus students on the first three questions and play the first announcement. Ask students *Is this for Karen? (No)*. Then play the other announcements and students write the answers.

ANSWERS
1 Desk 4
2 Delayed by one hour.
3 Gate 12

b 📼 [T5.6] Explain that Karen is now at Heathrow Airport, London. Elicit that she is now *in transit*. Focus students on the questions and then play the next set of announcements.

ANSWERS
1 To the transit desk
2 Gate 12

ADDITIONAL PRACTICE

Workbook: Vocabulary booster: on a plane, page 32; Improve your writing: Completing an immigration form, page 33

Language focus 2 (PAGES 46–47)

Articles (2): *a/an*, *the* and *zero*

📼 [T5.7] Focus students on the pictures. Ask them to read the information about Salem and complete the gaps with the words in the box. They then listen and check.

ANSWERS
a engineer
b Dubai
c the United Arab Emirates
d Saturday
e Wednesday
f weekend
g golf

TAPESCRIPT
Salem Al-Romeithi is twenty-six years old. He's an engineer and he lives with his family in a large house in Dubai, a large city in the United Arab Emirates. He works for an international company from Saturday to Wednesday but at the weekend he spends all his time playing golf.

Grammar

1 Ask students to underline all the examples in the text and draw their attention to the use of articles.

ANSWER
We use *an* before a vowel sound, for example *an engineer*.

2 Do example a with the students. Students, in pairs, discuss and help each other with the gaps. They can refer back to

the text to find a relevant example. Then they begin to work out 'rules'.

Go through the answers with the class and ask or guide them to giving reasons for their choices. At this early stage of the course we have not included the idea of countable/uncountable nouns or shared knowledge. If you are working with students whose language does not have articles, you should give the students more information.

ANSWERS
a	an, a	(a singular noun to mean 'one')
b	–, –, -	(names and titles and names)
c	a, a, an	(jobs)
d	the, the, the	(fixed phrases)
e	–,–,–	(towns, cities and most countries)
f	the, the, the	(irregulars – in each case a group of states)
g	the, the, the	(fixed time phrases cf *at night*)
h	–, –, –	(with times and days)
i	–, –, –	(fixed phrases of place)
j	–. –. –	(types of transport)

Refer students to *Language summary C* on page 153 of the *Students' Book*.

PRACTICE

1 a Students complete the gaps individually and compare with a partner.

b 📼 [T5.8] Play the recording for the students to check.

ANSWERS
2 a 3 a 4 – 5 the 6 the 7 the 8 –
9 an 10 a 11 – 12 the

📼 [T5.8] I live in Dubai. It's a fantastic city but we have a real problem with traffic. Most people come to work by car so it's very busy in the morning when they come into the city centre and in the evening when they go home. I'm an engineer and I have a company car. My journey to work takes about twenty-five minutes. I also use my car at the weekend when I play golf.

2 a Demonstrate with question 1 and check students are using *a/an* correctly. Students work individually. They do not have to write long sentences, for example for 5 they can just write *By bus and on foot*.

b Students, in pairs, ask and answer the questions.

3 a Students, in small groups, answer the *Quiz*. They all write down the group's answers, paying attention to the use of the article. Allow ten minutes for the answers. Get students to check their answers on page 147.

If students do not use articles in their own language, draw attention to the use or non-use of articles, for example by always including the appropriate article when you introduce new vocabulary (e.g. a tram) and particularly lexical phrases (e.g. near the city centre).

ADDITIONAL PRACTICE

Workbook: Articles: *a* and *the*, page 29

Task: Complete a survey about transport (PAGE 48)

Preparation: reading and writing

1 Tell the students they are going to ask and answer questions about *transport* /trænspɔ:t/. Check the meaning of this. Students work in pairs with two As together and two Bs together and can help each other form the questions. Tell the Bs to look at the questions on page 141.

2 a Students work together to write the full questions for their survey. They can use the *Mini-dictionary* or ask you vocabulary questions.

ANSWERS
Student A
1 How far do you walk every week?
2 How often do you travel by car?
3 What do you think of the roads in your town?
4 Do you ever take taxis?
5 Do / Can you ride a scooter?
6 Do / Can you ride a motorbike?
7 How do you usually travel when you go on holiday?
8 Which of these types of transport do you like best?

Student B
1 Do / Can you drive a car?
2 Do / Can you ride a bicycle?
3 How far do you travel every week?
4 How often do you use public transport?
5 What do you think of public transport in your town?
6 How do you travel to school or work every day?
7 How long is your journey?
8 Which of these types of transport do you like best?

b Students in their pairs practise reading the questions out loud. Get them to stress the main verb and noun in each question. Do a couple of examples on the board.

Task: speaking

1 Students, in A/B pairs, ask and answer the questions, filling in the circles for their partner. Refer students to the *Useful language* box a and drill these possible answers.

2 Students in small groups of As and Bs report back on their partner. Demonstrate with an example in front of the class and refer students to the *Useful language* box b. Remind students to use the *he/she* forms: *likes / doesn't ride* etc.

Follow up: writing
Focus students on the example and ask them to write a paragraph about how they use public transport.

Real life (PAGE 49)

Buying a ticket

1 Focus students on the photos and check they understand Florence's situation. Waterloo International Station is the terminus for the Channel tunnel trains from London to Paris. Students work individually to put the conversation in the correct order. They can compare in pairs before they listen. Words to check: *platform*, *ticket*, *single*, *return*, *sign*.

2 [T5.9] Students listen and check their answers.

ANSWERS
The correct order is:
M: A ticket to Paris, please ... the six o'clock train.
F: Single or return?
M: Single.
F: That's £94.50.
M: Here you are.
F: Thank you. Sign there, please.
M: Thanks. Which platform is it?
F: Platform eighteen.

Before students practise the conversation, drill some of the phrases. Then they repeat after the recording, or after you. Highlight the intonation of *Single or return?* Make sure the customers sound friendly and polite when they ask questions.

3 [T5.10] Focus students on the questions and make sure they understand the activity. Play conversation 1 and students write their answers, then they compare in pairs. Circulate. Play the conversation or part of the conversation again, if needed. Then play conversation 2. The tasks practise listening for specific information.

ANSWERS
Conversation 1
a Heathrow airport
b a single
c twenty to six (5.40)
d platform 7
e five to six (5.55)

Conversation 2
a Oxford
b a return
c twenty-four minutes to ten (9.36)
d platform 12
e nineteen minutes to eleven (10.41)

4 Students work in pairs, two As and two Bs. Focus them on the relevant text on page 49 and they write out the questions they need to ask. Circulate and help as needed.
Reorganise the students into A/B pairs. Ask student Bs to turn to page 144 and explain that they are ticket clerks. Ask two fairly strong students to start the conversation in front of the class. Then students act out the conversation in pairs and Student A writes down the information.

5 When they have finished the first conversation, ask Student As to look at the information on page 138 and have the second conversation. Student B writes down the information.

ADDITIONAL PRACTICE

RB **Resource bank:** 5B Transport crossword, page 132; *Learner-training worksheet A* (using the *Mini-dictionary*)

Workbook: Catching planes and trains, page 31; Asking questions, page 32

Consolidation, Modules 1–5 (PAGES 50–51)

A Listening and speaking: Personal information

1 Students work in pairs to complete the gaps.

2 [C1] Students listen to the recording and check their answers.

ANSWERS
1 b 's c lives d a e the f works g is
h married i got j haven't k don't l ride
m likes/loves n going o 's

3 Give students two minutes to think about a friend, making notes if they wish.

4 Students work with a partner, speaking for one minute about their friend.

B Question words

1 Students complete each question of the quiz, using the words from the box. The question words can be used more than once. They then choose the correct answer a, b or c.

ANSWERS
1 Where
2 What
3 How old
4 When
5 Where
6 How old
7 Who
8 What

2 Students work in groups thinking of questions they could ask about their own country.

3 Students answer each others questions, then check their answers to the quiz.

C Listening: Information about times and prices

1 a [C2] Students listen to the conversations and tick the topics they hear.

ANSWERS
Conversation 1 travelling by train
Conversation 2 the zoo
Conversation 3 television programmes

b Students put the words in the correct order. Then check in pairs, before checking as a class.

ANSWERS
2 When does it arrive in Dublin?
3 How much is it?
4 What time does the zoo open?
5 What time does it close?
6 How much does it cost for a ten-year-old child?
7 How can you travel there?
8 When does the football start?
9 When does it finish?
10 What time is the film?

c Students listen again and write the answers to the questions.

ANSWERS
1 Six thirty
2 Eight forty
3 £21
4 ten a.m.
5 five thirty
6 £8
7 by underground
8 seven
9 about nine to nine thirty
10 at nine o'clock

D *can* and *can't*

Students work in groups, making sentences about their school using *can* and *can't*.

E Alphabet quiz

Students complete the sentences in pairs. Check answers as a class.

ANSWERS
b brother c close d diary e engineer/electrician
f favourite g garden h have i identity
j Japanese k know l law/languages
m musician n night o open p police q queue
r ride s single t travel u uncle v visits
w wait y years z zoo

module 6

Eating and drinking

Vocabulary (PAGE 52)

Food (countable and uncountable nouns)

1 Elicit the names of the *meals: breakfast, lunch, dinner* and ask students which is their favourite.
Focus students on the picture and ask the question.

> **ANSWER**
> breakfast

2 Students, in pairs, find the food in the picture. Check with the whole class. Drill the words, particularly fruit /fruːt/, juice /dʒuːs/, cereal /sɪərɪəl/, banana /bənɑːnə/, oranges /ɒrɪndʒɪz/, toast /təʊst/, jam /dʒæm/, yoghurt /jɒgət/, biscuits /bɪskɪts/, sausages /sɒsɪdʒɪs/.

3 **a** Use the examples of *eggs* and *milk* to demonstrate countable and uncountable nouns. Or bring in some real food to make this clear. Students work individually or in pairs to categorise the words. Circulate and monitor, then check with the whole class.

> **ANSWERS**
> **Countable nouns:** eggs, oranges, an apple, bread rolls, sausages, grapes, a banana, biscuits
> **Uncountable nouns:** milk, butter, cereal, jam, toast, meat, cheese, yoghurt, orange juice, coffee, water, tea, fruit

> **Exercise 3: alternative suggestion**
>
> Put the names of the foods on cards or have pictures of each. Students, in small groups, categorise them into countables and uncountables.

b Check that students realise that countable nouns can be plural. Focus students on the *s* at the end of *eggs, biscuits*, etc.

> **Language notes:**
> * *In a mono-nationality class* pay particular attention to words which are countable in the students' language but uncountable in English, or the other way round.
> * Point out generalities, for example that liquids and meat are uncountable in English: *water, tea, chicken, beef,* etc.
> * With drinks, point out that we can ask for a *coffee,* meaning *a cup of coffee,* and a *tea,* a *beer,* a *water,* a *coke,* etc.
>
> Refer students to *Language summary A* on page 153.

ADDITIONAL PRACTICE

Workbook: Countable and uncountable nouns, page 34; Vocabulary: Food, page 34

Language focus 1 (PAGE 53)

There is and *There are*

[T6.1] Write the numbers 1–8 on the board. Play the first sentence and ask students to look at the picture. Is it true (✔) or false (✘)? Play the rest of the recording.

> **ANSWERS**
> | | | |
> |---|---|---|
> | a | There's an apple. | ✔ |
> | b | There are a lot of grapes. | ✔ |
> | c | There are five sausages. | ✘ |
> | d | There's a lot of toast. | ✘ |
> | e | There's some tea. | ✔ |
> | f | There are six bread rolls. | ✔ |
> | g | There are no bananas. | ✘ |
> | h | There's no yoghurt. | ✘ |

Grammar

1 Write the sentences on the board and ask students to choose the correct alternatives.

> **ANSWERS**
> There's a banana.   There are eight eggs.
> There's some butter.

Highlight:
the meaning of *There's / are*
the use of *There's* with singular and uncountable nouns
the use of *There are* with plural nouns
The use of *some* for a relatively small quantity compared with *a lot of* for a large quantity.

2 Elicit this negative form onto the board by asking about *apple juice*. This is one negative form. *Any* is looked at in Language focus 3.

Refer students to *Language Summary B* on page 153.

Pronunciation

See *Teacher's tips: helping students with pronunciation* on pages 7–8.

[T6.1] Focus students on the tapescript of recording 1 on page 168. Play the first two examples and write them on the board. Use another colour to show the linking (often between final consonant sounds and following vowels or diphthongs). Drill the students on each sentence.

PRACTICE

1 **a** Focus students on the hotel breakfast picture. Write the example sentences on the board and ask if they are true or false. Students then write their own sentences, five true and four false. Circulate and monitor.

b Students work in pairs. Student A closes their book and Student B reads out their sentences. Student A says if they are true or false. Circulate and note any errors for feedback.

2 Write the example on the board and help the students to correct it so that it is true for them. They continue individually. Circulate and help where needed.

ADDITIONAL PRACTICE:

Workbook: *there is / there are*, page 35; Short answers, page 35

Listening

Breakfasts around the world

1 [T6.2] Focus students on the photos and ask: *What do you think he/she/they have for breakfast?* Before listening, introduce/check: *glasses, tropical fruit, rice, hot/spicy food, lemon, omelette*. Also write the words *mango, guava, kim-chi, tortilla* on the board and tell the students they will hear these but you will check them later. Play the first extract and elicit the answers. Play the remainder of the recording, stopping after each extract to allow students time to write and compare with a partner. Circulate and monitor.

ANSWERS
Kemal: Two or three glasses of black tea, cheese, eggs, tomatoes, bread, butter, jam and sometimes yoghurt
Mi-Kyung: White rice and Kim-chi (a dish of mixed Korean vegetables)
Dimitry: Black tea with lemon and sugar, bread, cold meat, cucumber and sometimes a small cake or some biscuits
Sonia: Tropical fruit (guava, mango), coffee, maybe bread and jam
José: a coffee but no breakfast. At 11 o'clock, a coffee and some tortilla (Spanish omelette with potatoes and eggs)

2 Demonstrate a by telling students about your breakfast, and remind them how to use the adverbs *always, usually, often, sometimes, not often, never* from Module 4. Students discuss these questions in pairs. Circulate and monitor.

3 Write on the board: *I usually have breakfast. ...* and elicit possible answers: *at home, at work, with my family, at 7 o'clock*. Then *I have ...* and elicit possible answers. Other starter phrases are *For lunch I always/often/usually have ... I don't usually / never have ....* Students work individually to write three or four paragraphs about breakfast, lunch and dinner and also about snacks. Circulate and help as needed. Or set this for homework.

Reading and speaking (PAGE 54)

1 **a** Focus students on the illustrations and ask them to match these with the words in the box.

b Students use their *Mini-dictionaries* to check the meanings of the words. Or elicit the words. For example, *fish, meat, cheese, nuts. What is the same = protein*. Show a picture of fruit and vegetables and name some vitamins: A for carrots, C for fruit and green vegetables, and elicit *vitamins*. Students look at the pictures again and make the matches.

ANSWERS
vitamins: carrots, green vegetables, lemons, melon
protein: grilled fish, nuts
minerals: carrots, green vegetables, grilled fish, lemons, melon, nuts
a lot of calories: chocolate, nuts

2 Introduce/check *healthy* /ˈhelθiː/ and *unhealthy* /ʌn ˈhelθiː/ and write these as headings to two columns on the board. Elicit ideas of healthy and unhealthy food. Then students, in pairs, write eight foods that are healthy and eight unhealthy. They start with ideas from the pictures as this will help them when they read the text. In the feedback, introduce *X is/are good / bad for you*, which is more natural than saying *X is/are un/healthy*. Write students' ideas on the board and make sure you include *fruit juice* here.

3 **a** Focus students on the list of ideas. Discuss the first item with the class as a whole, and then put students into pairs to discuss the others. They can use their *Mini-dictionary* for unknown words. Have a whole class discussion at the end. Encourage freer speaking without worrying too much about accuracy.

b Allow students one and a half minutes to read the text quickly and write the ideas at the head of each paragraph. Encourage their skill of skimming for overall meaning without getting blocked by unknown vocabulary.

ANSWERS
2 It's okay not to eat breakfast.
3 Coffee and tea are bad for you.
4 Vegetarian food is always healthy.
5 Carrots help you see in the dark.
6 There are 'good' foods and 'bad' foods.

4 As an example, refer back to students' lists of what is healthy and unhealthy and then focus them on *fruit juice*. Write on the board: *Were you right/correct in exercise 3a? What information is surprising?*
Ask them to read Fact 1 slowly and then check. If they said *fruit juice* was healthy, then put a tick and a cross next to question 1 as it is partly true and partly false. Then ask *Is this information new for you? Is it surprising?*
Then students work individually and then check their answers in pairs.

5 To demonstrate, get the students to ask you the two questions. Answer using phrases such as *I love, I really like, I don't like, I hate* and develop it into a mini-conversation rather than just short answers. Students then discuss the questions with their partner. Circulate and collect examples of good/bad language for feedback.

Language focus 2 (PAGE 55)

some and *any*

Grammar

1 Write the four sentences on the board, in two columns: the first two in one column and the second two in a second column. Ask students to search the Facts 1 and 2 in the text for the answers.

ANSWERS
some   any   any   some

Ask if the nouns are singular, plural or uncountable and title the first column *Uncountable nouns* and the second column *Plural nouns*.

Get the students to think about the examples and circle the correct alternative:

ANSWERS
some   any

Ask students to find two examples of *some* and two examples of *any* in the text and underline them.

POSSIBLE ANSWERS
* Don't drink any coffee before you go to bed.
* don't put any milk or sugar in it!
* some apples contain a lot of sugar
* some rice, pasta, bread or noodles

2 Highlight:
* the meaning of *some* (an amount, not usually big) and sometimes a part of something, e.g. *some cake*, *some melon*; and *any* (none)
* that we use *some* with positive and *any* with negatives (we can also use *a lot of* if it is a large amount)
* We use *any* with questions. Show 2 as an example.

Refer students to *Language summary C* on page 153.

Language note:
With the questions *Do you want…?* or *Would you like…?* we often use *some*. You can deal with it later in the Real life section.

PRACTICE

1 a Make sure students realise these sentences are not all true. At this stage they should simply concentrate on the correct grammar. Do the first example with the class and then students work individually. Then, in pairs, they compare their answers.

ANSWERS
1 some   2 any   3 some, some   4 any   5 some
6 any   7 some   8 any

b Students, in pairs, say whether the sentences are true. They can look back at the text to check their answers.

ANSWERS
1 False   2 True   3 True   4 True   5 False   6 False
7 True   8 False

Pronunciation

See *Teacher's tips: helping students with pronunciation* on pages 7–8.

[T6.3] The main focus here is on keeping *some* and *any* weak and putting the stress on the verb and the noun. Play the tape or model the examples yourself and write them on the board. Ask *Where's the stress?* and mark the stress as in the examples. Ask students to look at the tapescript on page 168. Play the tape. Students repeat the sentences, paying attention to stress.

2 a Focus students on the picture of Katie and her fridge. Ask *What does she want? (to eat healthy food)*. Allow them two minutes to read and memorise her shopping list on page 147.

b Students, in pairs, write down the things she wants to buy. Then get students speaking in full sentences: *She wants to buy some…* and check the sentence stress.

ANSWERS
She wants to buy… some nuts, some orange juice, some mineral water, some oranges, some grapes, some apples, some bananas, some green vegetables, some fish, some yoghurt, some pasta and some bread.

3 a Focus students on the picture of Katie and the food she actually bought. Students, in pairs, answer questions a and b. Do the example together. Circulate and check students are using *some* and *any* correctly.

b Students, in pairs, answer the question. Encourage them to use *There's / are some*.

ANSWERS
a She's got some nuts, some mineral water/a bottle of mineral water, some yoghurt, some grapes and some apples.
b She hasn't got any orange juice, oranges, bananas, green vegetables, fish, pasta or bread.
c Unhealthy food: There's some pizza, some jam, some chocolate, and some Cola / a bottle of Cola.

ADDITIONAL PRACTICE

RB **Resource bank:** 6A *Food battleships*, page 134; 6B *The recipe game*, page 135

Workbook: *some* and *any*, page 35; *some, any, a(n)* and *no*, page 35; Vocabulary booster: Vegetables and other things to eat, page 36

Language focus 3 (PAGE 56)

How much and *How many*

Students, in pairs, choose the correct answers. New words: *blood, rain, desert, miles*. They can use their *Mini-dictionary* or you can introduce them.

Refer students to page 143 for the answers.

Grammar

Write the content of the *Grammar* box on the board. Get them to look at the quiz and work out the answers in pairs.

> **ANSWERS**
> *how many* with countable nouns (in the plural)
> *how much* with uncountable nouns

Refer students to *Language summary D* on page 154.

PRACTICE

a Do the first example with the whole class and then ask students to complete the gaps individually. Early finishers can check with a partner. Circulate and help with *time* [U] and *times* [C].

> **ANSWERS**
> 1 How much   2 How many   3 How much
> 4 How much   5 How much   6 How much
> 7 How many   8 How much   9 How many
> 10 How many   11 How much   12 How many
> 13 How much   14 How many   15 How many

b Write on the board: *Is your teacher's lifestyle healthy or unhealthy?* Get students to ask you the questions and note down the answers. In pairs, they decide how healthy your lifestyle is. Then they interview their partner. Circulate and help as needed. Get some whole class feedback and find out who has the healthiest lifestyle!

ADDITIONAL PRACTICE

RB **Resource bank:** 6C *Sports stars*, page 137

Workbook: Questions with *how much* and *how many*, page 37

Task: Describe the differences between two pictures (PAGE 57)

Preparation: listening

1 Focus students on the picture and ask: *Where are the people? What is it?* Introduce/elicit *a carnival*. Ask students: *What can you do there? What can you see/hear?* The picture is suggestive of the Notting Hill Carnival held in London every summer. Students, in pairs, try and find all the items in the picture. Circulate and help as needed. Check the pronunciation particularly of *prawns* /prɔːnz/, *sunglasses* /sʌnglɑːsɪs/, *feathers* /feðəs/, and *balloons* /bəluːnz/. Check their answers on an overhead transparency, if possible.

2 [T6.4] Play the beginning of the recording and show students how to number the first item. Play the remainder of the tape and students number the things as she describes them. Students check in pairs.

> **ANSWERS**
> 1 the mother   2 the boy's hat   3 the drums
> 4 the soup   5 the plate of rice   6 the plate of prawns
> 7 the knives, forks, spoons

Task: speaking

1 Divide the class into A/B pairs. Student B turns to page 148. Make sure the students cannot see each others' pictures.

2 Explain that the pictures are different and that they have to find ten differences between them. Focus them on the language in the *Useful language* box. See how much they already know by writing the phrases with gaps and eliciting the missing words:

a In my picture
_____ 's a small boy.
There's _____ soup.
There aren't _____ balloons.
___ the left there's a ...
____ the middle there's a....

b Elicit different question forms as in the box. Write up the starting words:

In your picture,

Is there a.. / Are there any...?
Has the man got a ...?
How many ... are there?
What colour is the ...?

3 Allow students ten minutes to find the ten differences. Ask them to make brief notes. They should not look at each other's pictures, so ask them to turn facing each other with their books up or work back to back. Circulate, helping where needed and make a note of good language use and errors for feedback later. After ten minutes students have some time to practise what they will say to the class. Refer them to *Useful language* box c. After a few minutes, have a whole class feedback, with different students each identifying one difference.

> **ANSWERS**
> The differences in picture B are:
> • the woman hasn't got a spoon in her hand
> • the plate of rice has changed to a plate of noodles
> • there isn't a container with knives on the table
> • there are no balloons decorating the stall
> • the boy only has six feathers in his hat
> • the boy is carrying a cup of soup
> • the man is playing on four steel drums
> • he isn't wearing any sunglasses
> • there are four spoons in the container
> • the woman is wearing a green dress

Real life (PAGE 58)

Ordering food and drink

1 Ask students the questions or get them to ask each other. You can also tell them about your preferences.

Pronunciation

[T6.5] Focus students on the meaning of food words. Get students individually to tick any that are similar to their own language. Play the tape, word by word and if the word is similar, get the students to compare the pronunciation. Drill any that seem to be difficult.

2 **a** Ask students their favourite restaurants, and if they ever order *take-away* food (for example, in the UK, pizzas, Chinese food and Indian food are popular *take-aways*). Focus students on the three photos and ask them to match the food and the restaurants.

> **ANSWERS**
> 1 hamburgers 2 pizzas 3 coffee and cakes

b [T6.6] Play the recordings and get students to answer the first question: which restaurants are they in? Words to check before listening again: *burgers*, *fries*, *take away*, *deliver*, *change*, *lemonade*. *Also* check British money, for example, how to say *£4.30 (four pounds thirty)*. Then they listen again to answer the next two questions.

> **ANSWERS**
> **Conversation 1**
> 1 Picture 1
> 2 Two Super King Size Burgers, large fries, two lemonades 3 £8.50
> **Conversation 2**
> 1 Picture 3
> 2 Two coffees and a piece of chocolate cake 3 £6.60
> **Conversation 3**
> 1 Picture 2
> 2 A large Cheese Supreme pizza and a bottle of diet lemonade 3 £11.85

3 [T6.7] Ask students to read the conversations and predict which word goes in each gap. Then play the recording for them to check individually or in pairs.

> **ANSWERS**
> b Can c Anything d away e else f have
> g Keep h order i What j much

Pronunciation

[T6.8] Students read the transcript on page 168 and listen at the same time. Pause the recording after each sentence and get the students to repeat, paying attention to polite intonation.

Students could also practise reading the extracts in exercise 3. Circulate and help with the pronunciation as needed.

4 Divide the class into A/B pairs. Ask one pair to demonstrate in front of the class, using the menu on page 138. Pairs continue with their own roleplays, swapping roles when they have finished the first conversation. Circulate, collecting examples of good language and any errors for feedback later.

ADDITIONAL PRACTICE

Workbook: Ordering food and drink page 37; Improve your writing: Describing food, page 38

Study ... (PAGE 59)

Finding grammar in a dictionary (1)

1 This study section is designed to develop the students' use of the *Mini-dictionary*, in this case researching countability and plurals. Focus students on the entries for *grape* and *cereal*. If possible, use an overhead transparency to show the C and U.

2 Students look in their dictionaries to find whether the words are countable or uncountable. These words come from previous Modules and extend the idea of countability beyond food vocabulary. You could decide to put students in A/B pairs here and have A research half and B the other half and then teach each other.

> **ANSWERS**
> | | | | |
> |---|---|---|---|
> | job | C | music | U |
> | money | U | coin | C |
> | traffic | U | game | C |
> | flight | C | transport | U |
> | platform | C | work | U |
> | economics | U | chewing gum | U |
> | tennis | U | traffic jam | C |

3 Show the entry for *grandchild*, if possible on an overhead transparency. Elicit the fact that it is countable. Show students how to find the plural form.

4 Ask the students to write the plural form of the words and then check in the *Mini-dictionary*.

> **ANSWERS**
> CDs, knives, matches, people, women, tourists, glasses, offices, ways, meals, babies, wives

Practise ... (PAGE 59)

1 Food and drink

> **ANSWERS**
> b butter c toast d fruit e biscuits f orange juice
> g vegetables h yoghurt i noodles

2 *There is* and *There are*

In class, dictate each item and students write the full sentence: you say *restaurants* and students write *There are a lot of restaurants.*

3 *Some* and *any*

ANSWERS
b some   c any   d some   e any   f any

4 *How much* and *How many*

In class, students choose the correct alternatives and then they ask and answer the questions with their partner.

ANSWERS
b How many, are   c How much   d How many
e How much   f How much, is

5 Ordering food and drink

ANSWERS
B: Yes, can I have some chicken soup, please?
A: Anything else?
B: Yes, I'd like a cheese sandwich.
A: Would you like anything to drink?
B: A mineral water, please.

Pronunciation spot

This section focuses on some international words where there may be a difference in pronunciation between English and the students' languages.

a Get the students to tick any words which are the same or similar in their language.

b [T6.8] Play the tape and after each item students say the word in their language and everyone can decide what is the difference in pronunciation.

c Play the tape again and students mark the stress. Drill the words, giving choral and individual repetition. If the problem is with a sound rather than the stress, pay attention to the sound.

ANSWERS

●   ●   ●   ●   ●   ●
airport   hospital   café   hotel   university   snack bar
●   ●   ●   ●   ●
platform   terminal   college   information desk

Remember! (PAGE 59)

Ask students to tick the items which they understand and got correct. Students do the *Mini-check* and tell you their scores.

ANSWERS
1 carrots
2 rice
3 lemons
4 noodles
5 Is
6 are
7 is
8 is
9 a
10 any
11 some
12 no
13 How many sons have you got?
14 How much water do you drink every day?
15 How much money do you want?
16 How many people are there in your office?
17 Hello, can I have a coke, please?
18 I'd like some tea, please.
19 Can I have the bill, please?
20 How much is that?

module 7

Extraordinary lives

Language focus 1 (PAGE 60)

Past simple: *was* and *were*

1 Write the words on the board and ask students to think of a famous person for each one. Encourage them to look up the words in their *Mini-dictionary*. Drill, giving choral and individual repetition. Pay particular attention to the word stress and sounds in: *scientist* /saɪəntɪst/, *political* /pəlɪtɪkəl/, *comedian* /kəmiːdiːən/, *composer* /kəmpəʊsə/.

2 a Students, in pairs, look at the photos and answer the questions. Because of the context, was and were should not present a problem. Students can check new words in their *Mini-dictionary*. Words to check: *legend* /ledʒənd/, *born* /bɔːn/, *originally* /əˈrɪdʒɪnəli/, *blind* /blaɪnd/, *deaf* /def/. Also check *the 1950s, 1960s* etc.

b [T7.1] Play the recording for students to check their answers. Play each answer separately, check the answer, then see if they understood any other information about each person.

ANSWERS
1	b	he died in 1963.
2	b	she was Polish, born in Warsaw.
3	c	Their first film was in 1926.
4	c	They were schoolfriends.
5	b	He was deaf from the age of thirty.
6	b	He was the leader of China from 1949 to 1976.
7	b	Tolstoy's most famous books were Anna Karenina and War and Peace.
8	a	He was born in the sixteenth century.

Grammar

Write the examples and do the gap fill exercise on the board. Or focus students on the *Grammar* box. Refer students to the present form of be and the examples from the quiz. Then they complete the gaps.

ANSWERS
+
you/we/they were

–
I wasn't
he/she/it wasn't
you/we/they weren't
?
was I?
was he/she/it?
were you/we/they?

Refer students to *Language summary A* on page 154 of the *Students' Book*.

PRACTICE

1 Demonstrate the example on the board and then get students individually to write seven more sentences. Circulate and monitor.

Pronunciation

See *Teacher's tips: helping students with pronunciation* on pages 7–8.

1 [T7.2] Play the recording and students write down the ten sentences in the past.

ANSWERS
a	He was born in New York.
b	Where were you born?
c	He wasn't French.
d	They weren't from London.
e	She wasn't happy.
f	They were very late.
g	You were right.
h	He wasn't in.
i	They were sorry.
j	You weren't ready.

2 Play the first example again or model it yourself. Ask students *Where's the stress? (born, York)* and how *was* sounds /wəz/. Drill all the sentences. Students should concentrate on the stress rather than trying to over-emphasise the weak forms of was and were. Highlight the fact that the negatives are pronounced more strongly.

3 Play the recording again and students repeat the sentences.

2 a Do the first example with the students and then they continue individually. They then compare in pairs.

ANSWERS
1	were
2	were, were
3	were
4	were
5	were
6	was, were
7	was, were
8	was
9	Were, were

b Demonstrate by getting students to ask you the questions. Help them with the pronunciation of the questions. Introduce *I'm not sure* and *I think*. Then students, in pairs, interview each other. Circulate and collect examples of good language use and errors for feedback.

ADDITIONAL PRACTICE

Workbook: Past simple: *was/were*, page 39; Short answers, page 39

Vocabulary

Years, decades and centuries

1 [T7.3] Do the first example on the board with the whole class. Play the remainder of the recording and students circle the correct answer.

> **ANSWERS**
> a 2006 b 1985 c 1990 d 1989 e 1878
> f 1914 g 1804 h 1917 i 2030

Pronunciation

1 Replay the recording or model the examples yourself. Write the dates on the board, elicit and mark the stresses. Drill students.

2 Play the recording again and get students to repeat, focusing on correct stress.

2 [T7.4] Introduce/check the following: *the _____th century, the 90s/the 1990s, and from ___ to ___.* Highlight: the use of *the + s* to talk about a decade and the use of *the* with *centuries*.

The vocabulary in this exercise is not all in the *Mini-dictionary*. Get students to use bilingual dictionaries or you could introduce the words. Ask students to read the sentences and ask you or the other students: *What does X mean?* Words to check: *popular* /pɒpuːlə/, *emperor* /empərə/, *President* /prezɪdent/, *Revolution* /revəluːʃn/, *landing* /lændɪŋ/, *hit single* /hɪt sɪngəl/.

Students check individually or in pairs.

> **ANSWERS**
> b from 1804 to 1815
> c in the 90s
> d in the sixteenth century
> e in 1917
> f in 1969
> g from 1939 to 1945
> h in the eighteenth century
> i in the 80s
> j in the fifteenth century

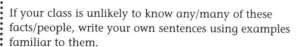

Exercise 2: alternative suggestion

If your class is unlikely to know any/many of these facts/people, write your own sentences using examples familiar to them.

3 This gives simple written practice with decades.

> **ANSWERS**
> b the nineteen-thirties
> c the nineteen-sixties
> d the nineteen-twenties
> e the seventeenth century

4 *In a mono-nationality class:* students, in pairs, write five sentences about famous people or events in their countries. *In a multi-nationality class*, students of the same nationality could work together and others could work individually. Encourage students to use at least one example of a century and one of a decade. Put students in new pairs to tell each other about the dates they have chosen.

Refer students to *Language summary C* on page 155 of the *Students' Book*.

ADDITIONAL PRACTICE

Workbook: 3 Vocabulary: years, decades and centuries, page 40

Reading (PAGE 62)

An ordinary life ... an amazing idea

Reading: additional suggestion

In a low elementary class: The text on Tim Berners-Lee is used to introduce regular and irregular past tense verbs. You could introduce regular past tense verbs first, using a different context and including verbs such as *lived, liked, loved, finished, started, worked*. Tell them about your own life and ask them to remember the verbs you used. They then do exercise 4 on page 47 of the Workbook, before going on to the Reading activities and *Language focus 2*.

1 Focus students on the photo of Tim Berners-Lee. Check the meaning of *invent* and see if anyone knows what he invented.

2 Get students to check the meaning of the words in their *Mini-dictionary*.

3 Ask students to look at the Fact file before they read. Check they understand each category. At this stage, stop them using their dictionaries and emphasise that they don't need to understand every word in order to do the activity. Students read silently and complete the file. They then check answers with a partner.

> **ANSWERS**
> | | |
> |---|---|
> | His important idea | The world wide web (www) |
> | Place of birth | England |
> | Place(s) of study | London and Oxford |
> | Place(s) of work | Dorset, England, Switzerland, the USA |
> | Personal details | About 50 with brown hair; he lives in Massachusetts |

Language focus 2 (PAGE 62)

Past simple: regular and irregular verbs

Teacher's Note: We introduce regular and irregular past forms together so that students can work with interesting texts rather than ones which have been specially written to avoid all irregular verbs. The rule about regular verbs is very simple, and the irregular verbs focused on here are very common.

1 a Students, in pairs, find two sentences about Tim's life now and four about his life in the past. Ask them to look for verbs other than *be*; for example *Tim B-L looks ordinary ... has long hair / Tim had a very important idea. He invented the World Wide Web / Tim went to school / Both his parents worked with computers / he loved computers*. Write the sentences on the board. Get students to help you to underline the verbs on the board. Focus on the past tense verbs: *had, invented, went, worked, loved*.

2 Get students to underline the remainder of the past verbs in the text.

> **ANSWERS**
> *left, went, studied, became, made, graduated, got, had, decided, decided, went, wrote, said*

Write these on the board and ask students to tell you which ones are regular and which are irregular.

> **ANSWERS**
> (Including the original four examples)
> Regular: *invented, worked, loved, studied, graduated, decided*
> Irregular: *had, went, became, made, got, wrote, said*

Grammar

1 Students simply write the regular and irregular forms in the *Grammar* box.

> **ANSWERS**
> invented, worked, loved, studied, graduated, decided

Highlight that:
• for most verbs we add *-ed*.
• for verbs ending in *-e*, we add *-d*.
• for verbs ending in *-y*, we change this to *-ied*.

2 Students can write the irregular verbs in the *Grammar* box.

> **ANSWERS**
> had, went, left, became, made, got, wrote

Refer students to *Language summary B* on page 154 of the *Students' Book*.

> **Additional suggestion**
>
> Refer students to the Study Section of Module 7 which goes further into the rules and shows how to find the past form in the *Mini-dictionary*.

PRACTICE

1 Do the first example on the board and then students write the others individually. They should cover the text about Tim Berners-Lee so that they do not simply copy some of the answers. They check with a partner and then with the whole class. Circulate and monitor.

> **ANSWERS**
> b He went to school in London.
> c When he was 18 he went to Oxford university.
> d At university he became interested in computers.
> e He made his first computer from a television.
> f He graduated in 1976.
> g He got a job with a computer company in England.
> h He went to Switzerland in 1989.

2 Students close their books and work in pairs to tell each other what they remember. Circulate and help as needed.

3 a If you have not already shown students how to find the past forms in the *Mini-dictionary*, you need to do so now. Use part 1 of the Study section of Module 7 as an example. Students use their *Mini-dictionary* to find the past forms. Check the meaning of any new words.

> **ANSWERS**
> arrived began believed could took shared
> needed died described stole wanted won

b [T7.5] Ask students: *Who invented the telephone? Who invented the radio?* Play the recording and students listen and read initially to see if their ideas were correct. Words to check: *ill, poor, patent office, invention, toy, inventor, an invention*.

Teacher's Note: In this Module they have already practised reading and will be going on to practise listening. This activity mainly gives practice with past forms, so it isn't necessary to treat the text as primarily a listening or reading. However, you could ask the students initially only to read or listen.

c Do the first example with the students and then ask them to complete the gaps with the past forms. Students check in pairs. Circulate and check for spelling.

> **ANSWERS**
> 1 invented 2 was 3 shared 4 made 5 could
> 6 wanted 7 took 8 needed 9 took 10 arrived
> 11 believed 12 described 13 decided 14 invented
> 15 stole 16 wrote 17 described 18 took
> 19 began 20 won 21 died 22 decided

Students listen again and check their answers. Stop the recording and, where necessary, check the spelling. You could have the text on an overhead transparency with the words written in and uncover it as you check the answers.

Teacher's Note on Pronunciation: Traditionally, coursebooks have made a distinction between past simple forms which end in /t/, /d/ or /ɪd/. We believe that the important thing to focus on is when we *don't* pronounce the e in -ed. So for example, we don't say *worked* /wɜːked/. It's best if you focus on the number of syllables in the verb rather than the sounds /t/ and /d/, which will often come naturally.

Pronunciation

1 [T7.6] Focus students on the tapescript on page 169 or write the first two examples on the board. Play the first two, get the students to count the number of syllables and write these on the board.

ANSWERS

●   ● ●
worked   *studied*

Play the recording and students mark the stresses. Stop after each word, if necessary.

ANSWERS

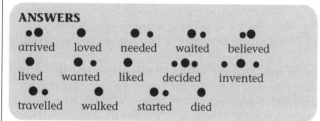

2 Write on the board: *wanted, waited, needed* and *decided* and model these. Underline the final /t/ or /d/ sound and highlight that this is the only case in which we pronounce the e in *ed*.

3 [T7.7] Do the first two examples with the whole class. Play the recording and students write 1 or 2 depending on whether they hear the Present simple or the Past simple.

ANSWERS

a	We wanted the bill.	2
b	I needed some money.	2
c	They lived in Spain.	1
d	I liked her.	1
e	They arrived at eight o'clock.	1
f	We worked hard.	1
g	I loved chocolate.	1
h	I believed you.	1

4 Students look at the tapescript on page 169, listen and repeat. Focus on the pronunciation of the correct number of syllables.

ADDITIONAL PRACTICE

Workbook: Past simple spelling of -ed endings, page 40; Regular verbs, page 40; Irregular verbs, page 41; Pronunciation: Past tense endings, page 41; Past simple regular and irregular verbs, page 42

Listening (PAGE 64)

A true story

1 Focus students on the photos of David's Russian grandmother. They then answer questions a and b. Explain that his grandmother moved to London and they are going to listen to her story.

2 a [T7.8] Students read the statements and use their *Mini-dictionary* to check the meanings of the words and phrases in bold. This will help their predicting skills and will give them support in their listening.

Play the beginning of the recording and decide together whether 1 and 2 are true or false. Then play the full Part 1 and students work individually and then compare with a partner. Check the answers for each part so that students build up a clear picture of the story. Do the same for Parts 2 and 3. Circulate whilst the pairs are working together. Replay any sections that students are finding difficult.

ANSWERS

Part 1
1 False: they met in London
2 False: she worked for a rich family
3 True
4 True
5 True

Part 2
1 True
2 True
3 True
4 False: she was sixteen years old
5 False: she spoke no English

Part 3
1 False: she found some Russian people
2 True
3 True
4 False: he was forty-eight years old
5 False: they had two children

b Ask students to read the tapescript on page 169 at the same time as they listen to the story again. Then ask them *What do you think of this story?*

3 Talk about your grandparents or an older relative. Students look at the instructions and, in pairs, discuss the questions. This is freer speaking practice so circulate but don't correct.

Real life (PAGE 64)

Dates and other past time phrases

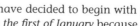

Language note:

We have decided to begin with *January the first rather than the first of January* because, in our experience, learners at this level have difficulty remembering to use *the* and *of*. In the US January first is correct.

1 **a** Focus students on the dates and students practise the pronunciation of the months. Drill any difficult months.

Exercise 1: alternative suggestion:

Play a game to check if students know the months of the year: students stand in a circle/circles and throw the ball to each other. The person catching the ball has to say the next month.

b Ask for today's date to see if students are able to pronounce dates and ordinal numbers. Or ask them to match the dates and the numbers either individually or in pairs. The numbers have been chosen to focus on particularly difficult sounds. Then students, in pairs, test each other by covering b and pointing to different dates to see if their partner can say them.

ANSWERS

the third	3
the second	2
the twelfth	7
the thirty-first	12
the twenty-second	11
the fifteenth	8
the twenty-first	10
the first	1
the fifth	4
the tenth	6
the seventh	5
the twentieth	9

Refer the students to the *Language summary E* on page 155 of the *Students' Book*.

Pronunciation

See *Teachers's tips: helping students with pronunciation* on pages 7–8.

1 [T7.9] Write 7th May on the board and try to elicit the two ways of saying it. Ask students *Where's the stress?* and work on this and the pronunciation of /θ/ and /ð/. Give choral and individual repetition. Play the recording and students repeat the dates. Focus particularly on the pronunciation of *th*.

2 [7.10] Students, in pairs, say the dates using the form *the ___th of _____*. They then listen and check and repeat the pronunciation.

3

ANSWERS

a the first of February 1943
b the third of September 1993
c the thirty-first of December 1963
d the thirteenth of September 2002
e the twenty-third of July 1933
f the thirtieth of December 2004

2 Introduce and drill the question forms: *What date is your birthday? When's your ___'s birthday?* Students, in pairs, practise this or mingle and collect dates from the rest of the class. Circulate and check they are saying the dates correctly.

3 Demonstrate on the board what students have to do. They should write the time phrases in their notebook individually and then compare with a partner.

Exercise 3: alternative suggestion

Write the time phrases on cards, either large ones which students can put on the board, or small sets for different groups. Students work together to put the phrases in order. In this case you would have to decide that the information would be based on the age and birthday of one member of the group.

ANSWERS
(these will vary, depending on the ages of the students and the month and day of the week. These answers are for a 21-year-old doing the activity on a Thursday in November).

now

ten minutes ago
last night
yesterday morning
last Tuesday
last weekend
two weeks ago
last month
last August
your last birthday
last year
ten years ago
when I was twelve
when I was eight
twenty years ago
when I was born

past

Highlight:

- the use of ago after a specific period of time – a time-line showing this could help:

30 years ago   Now

- the use of *last* with days, months and year
- that we don't use *last* to talk about a previous day's evening, afternoon or morning; here we have to use *yesterday*
- the pronunciation of *when* I was /wɒz/.

Refer students to *Language summary D* on page 155 of the *Students' Book*.

4 This board game practises: *When was the last time you...?* and gives practice with the past time phrases. Demonstrate in front of the whole class: a student throws the die, lands on a square and asks you the question; in your answer include a time phrase. Then get the student to ask some other people to show a range of answers. To do this activity, students need to know the past forms of each of the verbs. Check this by calling out the verb and students reply with the past. Words to check particularly: *ate, swam, spent, cooked, rode.*

Put students in small groups of three or four to play the game, each with counters and a die. Make sure they realise they can choose the person who answers the question. Circulate and monitor, collect errors for feedback later.

ADDITIONAL PRACTICE

RB **Resource bank:** 7A *The History Quiz*, page 138

Workbook: Ordinal numbers, page 42; Dates, page 43; Time phrases, page 43

Task: Tell your life story (PAGE 66)

Preparation: listening

See *Teacher's tips: making tasks work* on pages 11–12.

1 Introduce Marlene and focus students on the pictures of her life. Ask them *What can you see in the pictures?* Words to check: *played the piano, mum, dad, professional singer, toy piano.*

2 [7.11] Play the first extract and do the example together. Play the remaining extracts. Students write in the numbers.

> **ANSWERS**
> Extract A 3   Extract B 1   Extract C 2
> Extract D 6   Extract E 4   Extract F 5

Task: speaking

1 Tell students they are going to talk about their lives. *Either:* Show them simple pictures about your own life and use them to talk for about a minute. It is important that students see that your pictures are very basic (you can draw them quickly on the board), the pictures are just to act as prompts and something for the listener to look at. If your students won't draw, they could write simple key words. *Or:* show them some notes you have prepared about the same events.

2 Students spend a few minutes thinking about what they are going to say. They look at the phrases in the *Useful language* box and practise saying them quietly in combination with their notes/pictures. They then cover the phrases and try again. Help them with any vocabulary they need to talk about their lives. Ask them to make notes for their talk.

> **Exercise 2: additional suggestion**
>
> Let students look at the *Useful language* box, then put up on overhead transparency of the phrases, with the prepositions or other words missing, for example: *I was born ___ 1987; ___ a child I liked playing tennis.* and see if students can complete them. Drill the phrases you think are most useful.

Students then talk to a partner about their lives, this time just using the notes/pictures without looking at the *Useful language* box. Circulate, monitor and collect examples of good language and errors for feedback later.

> **Additional suggestion:**
>
> Choose a strong student to start talking to you about his/her life. Pretend that you are bored and give no encouragement to the student. Stop and ask the students if you are a good listener, and why not.
>
> Start again and this time keep eye contact, look interested, say things like *Mmm, Right, Really?* Stop and have a discussion on the effect of showing interest. Ask students if this is different in their own cultures, and what sort of sounds or words they use to show that they are interested. Students then work on being an encouraging listener during the activity.

3 Students tell the rest of the class three interesting things about their partner. In a large class, students work in small groups.

> **Follow up: writing**
>
> Before writing, students do Workbook exercises 15 and 16 on page 45, which focus on writing life stories. Give students a copy of your own life story, highlighting the use of linkers such as *before, after,* and *then.* Students write their own story either in class or for homework. If in class, circulate helping students with accuracy.
>
> Put the biographies up around the class, numbered, and the students go round with their notebooks writing a name next to each number.

ADDITIONAL PRACTICE

RB **Resource bank:** 7B *Past tense bingo*, page 139

Workbook: Vocabulary: Life stories, page 45; Improve your writing, page 45

Study ... (PAGE 67)

Finding grammar in a dictionary (2)

1 This study section helps students to find past forms of verbs in a dictionary. If possible, put the dictionary entry for *know* on an overhead transparency, or focus students on it in the book and show them how to find the past form *knew*.

2 Students research the past forms of the verbs in their *Mini-dictionaries*. Circulate and help as needed. Write the past forms on the board.

> **ANSWERS**
> saw   opened   lived   read   stopped   studied
> played   bought

3 This is a guided discovery activity where students notice the rules for themselves. Do a with them and then get them to look at the list on the board and work out the rules.

ANSWERS
a 2   b 1   c 4   d 2   e 3

4 Do the first example with the students, eliciting from them which rule *watch* follows. Students use the rules to work out the past forms of the verbs and then check in their *Mini-dictionary*.

Practise ... (PAGE 67)

Students can do this section independently to monitor their own learning. Or use it for further practice of the language covered in Module 7, or as a test. Make sure students do not look at the *Language summaries* until after they have finished all five exercises. Students can do this section for homework.

1–5 Make sure students read the instructions carefully. Provide the answers either by checking as a whole class or by giving them a copy from the *Teacher's Book*.

1 *was* and *were*

a In class, ask students if they remember the page at the beginning of the Module with famous people in it. In pairs they complete the gaps.

b Students write the answers individually or with a partner.

ANSWERS
1   were
2   was, wasn't, was
3   were
4   Was
5   weren't, was, was

2 Dates

ANSWERS
b   eighteen sixty-nine to nineteen forty-eight
c   in 1946
d   December the twenty-fifth (or the twenty-fifth of December)
e   the nineteen-nineties
f   the nineteenth century

3 Past simple

In class, dictate the verbs and students have to write the past forms.

ANSWERS
b went   c made   d began   e had   f wanted
g became   h left   i got   j decided   k took   l died

4   Past time phrases

ANSWERS
b   The concert started half an hour ago.
c   I telephoned Jim yesterday morning.
d   We were in class together last year.
e   She came to Spain in 2003.
f   We took the photograph when we were on holiday.
g   My birthday is on May 16th.

Pronunciation spot

a ▭ [T7.12] Play the recording of the two sounds or model them yourself and drill the students. Play the words and get students to repeat. Write the words on the board in two lists. Do some minimal pairs practice with *walk/work*. For example, say *walk, walk, work, walk, work, work* and students have to identify which sound they hear. A student can then say the words in front of the class whilst their classmates decide which sound they hear. Students can then do the same in pairs.

b Get the students to write two lists from a and then look at the words and decide which list they should go in.

ANSWERS
/ɔː/   daughter   morning   law   quarter
/ɜː/   girl   learn   third   Turkey

c ▭ [T7.13] Students listen, check and then repeat the words.

Remember! (PAGE 67)

Get students to look back over the *Practise* exercises and tick those they understand and got correct. Encourage them to do extra study of areas they are less confident about. Students do the *Mini-check* on page 161 and tell you their scores.

ANSWERS
1 were   2 wasn't   3 was   4 was   5 weren't
6 My husband worked for ICI from 1998 to 2004.
7 We left Shanghai in 2002.
8 People first used computers in the twentieth century.
9 My birthday is on January the twenty-second.
10 I watched television last night.
11 The Berlin wall came down in the (19)80s
12 We went to Chicago when I was fifteen.
13 made   14 wrote   15 became   16 bought
17 took   18 got   19 went   20 started

module 8

Fact or fiction

Vocabulary (PAGE 68)

Describing films

1 Check if students already know any words to describe types of film, then focus students on the photographs of the films. In pairs they ask *Do you know this film? What's its name in your language?* Students then match the films to the vocabulary in 1.

> **ANSWERS**
> (including the names of the films)
> 1 a science fiction film   Star Wars
> 2 a musical   Singing in the Rain
> 3 a cartoon   Toy Story
> 4 a historical film   Titanic
>   or a romantic film
> 5 an action film   Terminator
> 6 a horror film   Frankenstein
> 7 a comedy   A Charlie Chaplin film
> 8 a love story   Devdas: A Bollywood film

Drill the types of film paying particular attention to *science fiction* /ˈsaɪəns fɪkʃən/, the stress in *cartoon* /kɑːˈtuːn/, *historic* /hɪˈstɒrɪk/, *romantic* /rəʊˈmæntɪk/ and *horror* /ˈhɒrə/.

2 a Encourage students to find the meanings of the words in their *Mini-dictionary* or introduce them yourself. Ask students which word describes a comedy to elicit *funny* and then get them to match the other adjectives with films. They can work alone and then compare their answers in pairs.

Pronunciation

🖭 [T8.1] Write the four patterns on the board and do a couple of examples with the whole class. Students then listen and complete the table. Drill the words, focusing on the word stress.

> **ANSWERS**
>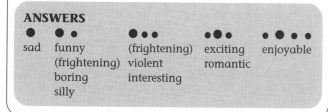
> sad funny   (frightening) exciting   enjoyable
>   (frightening) violent   romantic
>   boring   interesting
>   silly

---

b *In a mono-nationality class*, students can say the names of films in their own language.

In a multi-nationality class, write some famous films on the board, encourage students to use the films in the photos on page 68, and/or bring in some adverts for films currently showing.

ADDITIONAL PRACTICE

Workbook: Vocabulary: Types of film, page 46; Adjectives to describe films, page 46

Reading (PAGES 68–69)

1 a Focus students on the questions. Get them to check the words in bold in their *Mini-dictionary* or introduce them yourself. Others to check: *successful, popular*.

b Students, in groups of three or four, try to find the answers in the text as quickly as possible.

> **ANSWERS**
> 1 1937   2 $200 million   3 1889   4 India   5 Eleven
> 6 $20 million   7 1996   8 Thirty-five times every year
> 9 20   10 1895, café

2 Ask students *Have you seen The Jazz Singer?* (the first example) If someone says yes, then ask *Was it good?* Do the same for *Singing in the Rain*. Then ask a student to ask you about *West Side Story* and see if they can remember the questions. Write them on the board and drill them. Teach *Have you seen* as a phrase without going into the grammar for now. Students, in pairs, ask and answer about each film in the text.

In a mono-nationality class, check that students know the films in their own language.

Language focus 1 (PAGE 70)

Past simple negative forms

1 Introduce the verbs in the box. Elicit their past forms or get students to find the meaning and past form in their *Mini-dictionaries*. Check pronunciation, for example *create/created, drink/drank*.

> **ANSWERS**
> sleep   slept   find   found
> create   created   drink   drank
> follow   followed   fall in love   fell in love
> give   gave

2 a 🖭 [T8.2] Focus students on the photos, get them to cover the text and tell each other what they know about the films.

Ask students to read the text about Dracula and tell you the two mistakes. Or read the text aloud and ask students to tell you (as the mistakes have already been underlined). Students continue in pairs, finding the mistakes in the texts.

b Play the recording so that students can check their answers.

> **ANSWERS**
> a Poland ✗ Transylvania ✔; Vodka ✗ blood ✔
> b cat ✗ rabbit ✔
> c China ✗ England ✔; his girlfriend ✗ poor people ✔.
> d handsome ✗ ugly ✔; loved ✗ were frightened of it
>   – they hated it ✔.
> e forty ✗ fourteen ✔; pleased ✗ angry ✔;
>   lived happily together ✗ they killed themselves ✔.

3 Write the sentences on the board and ask students to complete the gaps. They listen again to the first extract to check.

> **ANSWERS**
> lived, didn't drink, drank

Grammar

Highlight:
- that we didn't + the base form of the verb: *didn't live* not *didn't ~~lived~~*
- the short (contracted) form *didn't*
- that it is the same for all persons

Point out that the structure is similar to the present simple:
he lives > *he doesn't live*
he lived > *he didn't live*

Refer students to *Language summary A* on page 155.

PRACTICE

1 Demonstrate with *rabbit*, eliciting onto the board *Alice didn't follow a white cat. She followed a white rabbit.* Students work individually using the words in the box.

2 **a** Ask students to find twelve mistakes. You could do the example of the rollerblades with them. Students work individually or in pairs. Words to check: *baseball cap, sunglasses, MP3 player, trainers*.

b Students write sentences, using the verbs in the box. Circulate and help as necessary.

c [T8.3] Play the recording and students check their answers.

> **ANSWERS**
> 1 People didn't wear/have rollerblades 500 years ago.
> 2 People didn't ride scooters.
> 3 People didn't use mobile phones/mobiles.
> 4 People didn't listen to music on an MP3 player.
> 5 People didn't read newspapers.
> 6 People didn't have clocks.
> 7 People didn't wear trainers.
> 8 People didn't eat burgers.
> 9 People didn't drink cola/coke.
> 10 People didn't have aeroplanes.
> 11 People didn't wear baseball caps.
> 12 People didn't wear sunglasses.

Pronunciation

See *Teacher's tips: helping students with pronunciation* on pages 7–8.

[T8.4] Play the example or model it yourself and write it on the board. Ask students where the stress is and mark this on the sentence. Drill the sentence, giving choral and individual repetition. Students listen and repeat the other sentences from the recording.

3 **a** Students now have the opportunity to personalise the language. Do the first example with the whole class and emphasise that they should put the verb into the positive or negative past form so that it is true for them. Students work individually, then write three or four more sentences about yesterday evening or last Sunday. Circulate and help as needed.

b Students compare their answers in pairs.

ADDITIONAL PRACTICE

Workbook: Common verbs in the past tense, page 46; Past simple: Negative, page 47

Listening (PAGE 72)

The author behind the legend

1 Focus students on the photo and ask them to discuss the questions in pairs.

2 See if students know anything about the films. Introduce *author* and *director* and ask, *Who is the author of the Lord of the Rings? Who was the director of the films? Where did he make the films? Were the films successful?* Then students read the fact-file to check their answers. Encourage them to use the *Mini-dictionary* for unknown words.

3 **a** Find out if they know anything about Tolkien, for example: *Where was he from? What was his job? When did he write the books?* Then focus them on the statements about his life. Encourage them to use the *Mini-dictionary* for the words in bold or introduce these yourself. Other words to check before the listening: *adult, religious, hippies*.

b [T8.5] Tell students that this is a radio programme about Tolkien. Play the beginning of the recording and do the first example together. Then play the remainder and students tick or cross the statements. This practises the skill of listening for specific information. Students check their answers in pairs and have feedback with the whole class.

c Play the recording again. Students listen for further detail and correct the false information. Students check their answers in pairs. Replay the relevant part of the recording again.

> **ANSWERS**
> 1 False. He didn't have a happy childhood.
> 2 True
> 3 True
> 4 False. He wasn't a professor at Cambridge University. He was a professor at Oxford University.
> 5 True
> 6 True
> 7 False. They loved his stories.
> 8 False. They didn't appear in 1974. They appeared in 1954.
> 9 False. Adults liked his stories. Hippies especially.
> 10 False. He didn't see the films before he died.
> 11 False. His family didn't make a lot of money from the films.
> 12 True

Language focus 2 (PAGE 73)

Past simple questions

Do the example on the board and then get students to reorder the questions. They can check their answers by looking at the tapescript on page 170.

Grammar

Elicit the rules onto the board: Students tell you how to make the question by looking at example 1 above. Try to elicit the short answers.

Highlight:
- that we don't use the past form of the verb in the question, i.e. not ~~When did he died?~~
- we use a short answer, for example *Yes, they did* and not ~~Yes, they made a lot of money.~~

Remind them of the Present simple question forms:
he lives > does he live?
he lived > did he live?

Refer students to *Language summary B* on page 155 of the *Students' Book*.

PRACTICE

1 **a** Do an example with the whole class. Then students work individually and tick or cross the sentences. They use the *Mini-dictionary* to look up any unknown words. Words to check: *abroad, fashionable, instrument, work hard*.

b Introduce the activity by answering the questions about your own childhood. If possible bring in a photo of yourself when you were about ten. Help the students form and pronounce the questions, giving choral and individual practice as necessary. Work on stressing the verbs and nouns and linking the *did you* /dɪd juː/.

In your answers include *I can't remember*. Students, in pairs, ask and answer the questions.

c Students report back on one or two interesting facts they found out about their partner.

ADDITIONAL PRACTICE: YES/NO QUESTIONS

RB **Resource bank:** 8A *Looking back*, page 140

Workbook: Past simple: Questions, page 47; Short answers, page 47

2 Focus students on the picture and establish the situation: *Anna and Helena are talking about Helena's weekend*. Demonstrate the first example, writing the full question and eliciting the answer. Students complete the questions individually and, in pairs, compare their answers Circulate and monitor.

ANSWERS
a   4
b   Who did you go with? – 7
c   How did you get there? – 2
d   Why did you go there? – 3
e   What did you think of it? – 6
f   What did you do there? – 1
g   When did you come back? – 5

Language notes:
- We say *think of* when we are talking of a place or person or film, etc. We use *think about* when we are talking about something more complex, for example *What do you think about the situation in ...?*
- *How did you get there?* is more commonly used than *How did you go there?*

3 Get students to ask you questions about one of the times. If the questions are too general, you could make them more specific, for example *Where did you go on holiday last year / what was your favourite holiday?* Students continue the activity in pairs. They should make brief notes about their partner.

4 Refer students to the example. They then use their notes to write about their partner. Circulate and help as necessary.

ADDITIONAL PRACTICE

RB **Resource bank:** 8B *John Wayne*, pages 141–142; 8C *Safe at last!*, page 143

Workbook: Question words, page 48; Past simple: Positive, negative and questions, page 48; Listen and read: National heroes and heroines, page 50

Task: Interview students about arts and entertainment
(PAGES 74–75)

Preparation: listening

1 [T8.6] Play the recording and ask *What is this about? Sports? Studying? Arts and Entertainment?* (you will need to check these) *Travel?* to help students listen for gist. Words to check before listening: *concert, ballet*. Do these as part of checking the meaning of *entertainment*.

Then focus students on the questions and play extract 1. Ask what the question is and show them that it answers f. Play the other extracts one by one. Allow students time to choose their answers. They check their answers in pairs.

ANSWERS
a 4   b 2   c 5   d 3   e 6

Then ask students to listen again and write the speakers' answers to the questions.

ANSWERS
a   Cameron Diaz   b   three weeks ago
c   it was okay, not fantastic
d   different types, favourite group = Red Hot Chilli Peppers
e   She loves it. Her favourite is *Swan Lake*
f   *His Dark Materials* by Philip Pullman

2 Students work in pairs or small groups. Explain that they are going to write a questionnaire about arts and entertainment. Remind them of the questionnaire they wrote in Module 5 on Transport.

Start with the questions in the *Useful language* box a. Write the following on the board or on an overhead transparency:

Who / favourite / actor?
What kind / books / like?
When / last go / cinema?
What / see?
Who / in it?
enjoy / it ?
Who / by ? (in relation to a book)

Elicit full questions, then look at the questions written in full in the *Useful language* box a and drill them as needed to help build students' confidence.

Students work together and write a questionnaire of seven or more questions.

Task: speaking

1 Regroup students so that they are working with two other people from different groups/pairs. Get one student to ask you some questions and use some of the phrases in the *Useful language* box b. Focus students on this and give them choral and individual practice as needed. Encourage them to add further information to their answers. Students interview each of the other two students and make a note of their answers.

2 Students tell the class three pieces of information they found out about the other students.

Follow up: writing

Focus students on the example and get them to write about three things they enjoy/ed doing. In class, circulate and help as needed. Or they can do this for homework.

Real life (PAGE 76)

Arranging a night out

1 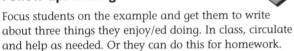 [T8.7] Focus students on the photo. *Where are they? (in the cinema) Who are they?* (friends: Anna and Tara). Play the first three sentences and ask *What is it about? Yesterday? Tonight? Tomorrow night? (tomorrow night) What does Anna want? (to go to the cinema).*

Focus students on the questions. Allow them time to read and understand. Then play the recording and students answer the questions. Make sure they have covered the right hand side of the page. They can compare answers in pairs.

ANSWERS
a   the new Johnny Depp film
b   9.30 (and also 7.30)
c   At Macy's for a drink. At about 8.00.

2 Students work with a partner and put the conversation in order. Circulate but only help if students get really stuck. Early (and successful) finishers can go and help other pairs.

ANSWERS
a 3   b 11   c 1   d 6   e 9   f 8   g 7   h 2   i 5
j 4   k 10

Students listen again and check their answers.

3 a ▭ [T8.8] Ask students to cover the conversation. Play the recording of sentences from the dialogue and students complete the gaps. Or they predict what is in the gaps and then listen to check.

ANSWERS
1 Let's go the cinema!   2 What's on?
3 Why don't we go and see that?
4 How about the new Johnny Depp film?
5 What time is it on?
6 Why don't we have a drink first?
7 That's a good idea.
8 Let's meet at about eight o'clock.

b Play each sentence again and students copy, focusing particularly on the stressed syllables.

4 a Students, in pairs, write their own dialogue. Circulate, helping as needed.

b Students practise reading their dialogues together. Then they can read them out to the class.

ADDITIONAL PRACTICE:

Workbook: Arranging a night out, page 51

Study ... (PAGE 77)

Checking and revising

Point out to students how important it is to revise regularly. Ask them what they do to revise. This study section revises all the negative verb forms from Modules 1–8.

1 Students write the negative forms of the verbs.

ANSWERS
b aren't   c wasn't   d weren't   e doesn't work
f don't come   g didn't live   h didn't get
i hasn't got   j haven't got

2 ▭ [T8.9] This practises distinguishing between positive and negative sentences. Play the recording and students tick the sentence they hear.

ANSWERS
a She wasn't married.   b He doesn't speak English.
c They weren't at home.   d I haven't got a pen.
e I don't like sport.   f She hasn't got a car.

3 Students listen and repeat the sentences.

Practise ... (PAGE 77)

Students can do this section independently to monitor their own learning. Or use it for further practice of the language covered in Module 8, or as a test. Make sure students do not look at the *Language summaries* until after they have finished all five exercises. Students can do this section for homework.

1–5 For each exercise, make sure students read the instructions carefully. Provide the answers either by checking or by giving them a copy from the *Teacher's Book*.

1 Describing films *(or is it film?)*

ANSWERS
a enjoyable b horror, frightening c comedy, funny
d love story, romantic e musical, silly
f action, violent g science fiction, exciting
h historical, interesting, boring

2 Past simple forms

ANSWERS
b found c fell d slept e gave f earnt/earned
g drank h cost

3 Past simple negatives

ANSWERS
b didn't listen to c didn't drive/have d didn't eat
e didn't watch/have f didn't wear

4 Past simple questions

ANSWERS
b Where did you go? c Who did you go with?
d How did you get there? e What did you do there?
f What did you think of it?

5 Arranging a night out

ANSWERS
Paras: Do you want to go to the cinema on Saturday?
Joe: That's a good idea! What's on?
Paras: There's a new Bollywood musical.
Joe: I don't really like that sort of thing. Why don't we go to the new Will Smith film?
Paras: OK. Let's meet (at eight) outside the cinema (at eight).

Pronunciation spot

Stressed syllables

a If possible, use an overhead transparency of the example with *interesting* to show students how the ' symbol shows that the following syllable is stressed. They do not need to understand all the phonetics. Write *interesting* on the board and mark the stress with a circle. Write *romantic* on the board, ask students to find it in their *Mini-*

dictionary and decide where the stress is. Write the phonetics with the ' symbol on the board to help them. Then get one of them to draw a circle over the stressed syllable.

b Students look in their dictionaries, decide where the stress is, and transfer this to the words by marking the stressed syllable with a circle. They work in pairs so that they sound out the words to each other. Circulate, helping as needed. Write the words on the board and get individual students to come up and mark the stress. See if the rest of the class agree but don't confirm or correct yet.

c ▭ [T8.10] Play the recording for students to check the answers on the board. Then they listen and repeat the pronunciation.

ANSWERS

●   ●   ●   ●   ●
cartoon comedy historical average successful
●   ●   ●   ●
popular create appear romantic

Remember! (PAGE 77)

Get the students to tick the ones they understand and got correct and encourage them to do extra study for the ones they were weak at. Students do the *Mini-check* on page 162 and give you their scores.

ANSWERS
1 science fiction, love story 2 comedy, cartoon
3 horror, action 4 frightening 5 exciting
6 violent 7 interesting 8 enjoyable
9 Meg didn't fall in love with Tom.
10 I didn't sleep very well last night.
11 She didn't give me the parcel.
12 The camera didn't cost $500.
13 He didn't find his keys. 14 did you go
15 did you get 16 did you do 17 Did you have
18 Do you want to go to see a movie?
19 Let's meet at seven o'clock.
20 Why don't we go to that new café?

module 9

Buying and selling

Language focus 1 (PAGE 78)

Comparative adjectives

1 a Bring in pictures of cars to stimulate discussion. Begin by asking *Have you got a car? What make is it? Why do you like it?* or *What car would you like? Why?* In pairs, they discuss the questions. Listen and check which adjectives they are already using.

Focus students on the list of adjectives and ask them to think of a car for each category. They work in pairs. Encourage them to look up any new adjectives in their *Mini-dictionary*.

b Ask students to cover the box and see if they already know the opposites. They then look at the box and check.

Students then tell a new partner about their car or the car they would like to have, using the adjectives to explain why.

> **ANSWERS**
> expensive – cheap
> small – big
> comfortable – uncomfortable
> ugly – attractive
> old – new
> easy – difficult

> **Language note:**
> The opposite of *ugly* can also be *beautiful*, but *attractive* is given here because it can be used with objects, and with both men and women.

See also *Teacher's tips: helping students with pronunciation* on pages 7–8.

2 Focus students on the pictures of Juliana, and the Micro /ˈmaɪkrəʊ/ and Victa Deluxe /vɪktə dɪlʌks/. Ask them to read the short text about Juliana and answer the questions.

> **ANSWERS**
> a She wants to buy an old car because she wants to drive to university with her three friends.
> b She wants to spend about €900.

3 Focus students on the advertisements and the pictures. Do the first example with the whole class. Then they tick or cross the remaining sentences. They work out the meaning of the comparatives without an explicit language focus at this point. *In a low elementary level class*, do a brief analysis of the grammar first.

> **ANSWERS**
> b ✗ c ✔ d ✔ e ✗

> **Language note:**
> if your students speak a language which does not have articles, point out that we use *the Micro* and *the Deluxe* here because we are talking about a particular Micro and Deluxe – the ones in the pictures.

Grammar

1 Write the sentences on the board and ask students to complete the gaps, using the language from the activity they have just done. Check that they understand the meaning of the comparative form.

> **ANSWERS**
> a than
> b more, than

2 Write *old* on the board and ask students how many syllables it has, then add *-er*. Gradually build up the information in b and c in the same way, asking students questions until you have elicited/introduced all the rules.

Students then add all the adjectives from exercise 1 onto your table on the board.

> **ANSWERS**
> a faster, smaller, older, cheaper, newer, slower, bigger
> b uglier, easier
> c more expensive, more comfortable, more uncomfortable, more difficult, more attractive

3 Point out the irregular forms of *good* and *bad*.

Refer students to *Language summary A* on page 155 of the *Students' Book*. You may also decide at this point to do the *Study* section on page 85 (Finding spelling in a dictionary).

PRACTICE

1 Do the first example on the board. Students then work individually to make comparative sentences. They compare in pairs before checking with the whole class. Check the meaning of *in good/bad condition*.

> **ANSWERS**
> b The Micro is cheaper than the Deluxe.
> c The Deluxe is more comfortable than the Micro.
> d The Micro is smaller than the Deluxe.
> e The Deluxe is more difficult to park than the Micro.
> f The Deluxe is in better condition than the Micro.
> g The Micro is in worse condition than the Deluxe.

2 a Focus students on the photos and ask them to check the meanings of any new adjectives in their *Mini-dictionary*. Or introduce and check: *smart, sweet, healthy, nice*
b Demonstrate using the example. Encourage students to use *I'm not sure; I think; No it isn't!* when they disagree with their partner.

Circulate and monitor. If necessary, help with pronunciation, particularly of *mineral water* /mɪnərəl wɔːtə/ and *healthier* /helθɪə/.

Pronunciation

See *Teacher's tips: helping students with pronunciation* on pages 7–8.

1 [T9.1] Play the recording or model the sentences yourself. Students write them down and then mark the stresses. Then write the sentences on the board and mark the stresses. Drill with choral and individual practice as needed.

2 [T9.2] Ask students to look at the tapescript on page 170. Play the recording sentence by sentence and students mark the stress. They then repeat, working on the stresses.

ANSWERS

a A Vespa is slower than a Harley-Davidson.

b A Vespa is easier to ride than a Harley-Davidson.

c A Swatch is better for children than a Rolex.

d A Rolex is smarter than a Swatch.

e Cola is sweeter than mineral water.

f Mineral water is healthier than cola.

Exercise 2: additional suggestion

In a strong elementary level class: students can talk about other topics as a follow-up, for example: *laptops and PCs, two different TV channels, vegetables and French fries, two famous actors,* etc.

ADDITIONAL PRACTICE

RB **Resource bank:** 9A *New Year's Eve*, page 144

Workbook: Adjectives: opposites, page 52; Comparative adjectives, page 52

Language focus 2 (PAGE 80)

Superlative adjectives

Focus students on the photos and ask: *What are these? Why are they famous?*

Students read and check if their ideas were correct. They can look up unknown words in the *Mini-dictionary*, or ask you.

Grammar

1 Write the sentences on the board and ask students to complete the gaps. They can look in the reading text to find the language. Check they understand the meaning of the superlative form.

ANSWERS

a the biggest

b the most

2 Refer students to the text to complete the table.

ANSWERS

the fastest   the biggest   the busiest
the most expensive   the best

Ask students to tell you the rules about syllables and spelling for comparative forms. Point out that the rules are the same for the superlative forms.

Highlight:
• the use of *the* in front of the superlative form.
• that we say the ... -est in the world (not of).

Refer students to *Language summary B* on page 156 of the *Students' Book*.

PRACTICE

1 [T9.3] Do this with students individually. They check in pairs before listening to the answers. Or conduct it as a quiz by putting students into groups of three or four to write the superlative form and to select the correct answer. Get a group to give the answer in each case and then play the relevant part of the recording to check if they are correct.

ANSWERS

1	the tallest	a
2	the richest	c
3	the most expensive	a
4	the oldest	b
5	the most successful	b
6	the highest	b
7	the most common	c
8	the most popular	c

2 a Students select one of the topics and find the relevant card on page 147. They complete the card with the correct superlative form. They can then compare their answers with someone who was working on the same card. Circulate and help as needed. If you have enough people who worked on different cards, put students into A/B pairs to talk about their answers to the questions. Circulate and collect examples of errors for feedback.

ANSWERS
Your town and country
a the best
b the busiest
c the prettiest
d the worst
e the most beautiful
f the biggest
g the highest

People you know

a   the tallest
b   the fastest
c   the oldest
d   the youngest
e   the richest
f   the untidiest
g   the longest

b Students write sentences about five of the questions. Circulate and monitor.

ADDITIONAL PRACTICE

RB **Resource bank:** 9B *A superlative survey*, page 146

Workbook: Superlative adjectives, page 53; Comparative and superlative adjectives, page 54; 7 Pronunciation, comparatives, page 54; Listen and read, page 55

Reading (PAGES 80–81)

1 Ask students to answer the questions and explain why/why not.

2 **a** Focus students on the photographs and get them to ask and answer the questions in pairs. They can use their *Mini-dictionary* to check any of the adjectives or ask you.
b Focus students on the words in the box and ask them to find them in the pictures. They can use their *Mini-dictionary* or ask you.

ANSWERS

a rug	a herb
a flower	a decoration
a toy	medicine
a gift	

In the feedback stage, introduce *floating market* and *boats*.

3 Get students to copy the following table from the board into their notebooks.

ANSWERS

What is the name?	Where is it?	What can you buy there?	When is it open?
1			
2			
3			
4			
5			

Students read the text and complete the table. Encourage them to guess the meanings of unknown words.

ANSWERS

What is the name?	Where is it?	What can you buy there?	When is it open?
1 The Grand Bazaar	Istanbul, Turkey	almost anything rugs and carpets	we don't know
2 Floating market Damnoen Saduak	100 km from Bangkok, Thailand	tropical fruit and vegetables	six in the morning till midday, everyday
3 Campo de' Fiori	Rome, Italy	flowers, fruit and vegetables	seven in the morning to midday but not on Sunday
4 Christmas market	Nuremberg, Germany	toys, hand-made gifts, Christmas decorations, food, drink	from the end of November until Christmas
5 The Sonora Market	Mexico City	toys, birds, herbs, natural medicine	every day from early in the morning till late at night.

Exercise 3: additional suggestions

- Tell the students they are going to write about a market. They can choose one they often visit, one that is famous in their country, or one they visited on holiday. Show some sentence starters to help them organise their writing:

  The market is called … It's in … It's open from … It sells a lot of … and … I often go there … I like(d) it because …

- Get students to roleplay a situation in a Tourist Information Office, telling a tourist about a famous market in their city/country.

Vocabulary (PAGE 82)

Shops and shopping

1 Students match the pictures to the shops in the box. They work individually and then check in pairs. In the feedback, drill the pronunciation as needed.

ANSWERS

a a bakery   b a butcher's   c a clothes shop
d a dry-cleaner's   e a gift shop   f a hairdresser's
g a local shop   h a pharmacy   i a post office

Language note:

Explain that the apostrophe is there because we once said a *butcher's shop*. A *baker's* is an alternative to *a bakery*. A *chemist's* is an alternative to *a pharmacy*.

2 Students, in pairs, write the answers to the questions. Demonstrate with the first one. They can use their *Mini-dictionary* to check any unknown words in bold. Circulate and help as needed.

ANSWERS
b a hairdresser's   c a bakery   d a clothes shop
e a gift shop   f a post office   g a butcher's
h a local shop   i a pharmacy

3 Students, in pairs, think of one more thing you can do or buy in each place. They then give feedback to the class. *In a pharmacy you can...*

Exercise 3: additional suggestions

- *In a multi-nationality class*, write on the board: *a newspaper, potatoes, a dictionary, toothpaste, bread, a pair of jeans, aspirin, cigarettes, flowers, fruit, stamps.* Ask students *Where do people normally buy these things in your country?* Students interview people from a different country.

- *For further speaking practice:* establish the situation of a tourist needing to find a shop and see if the students can suggest a question. Introduce *Excuse me. Can you help me? Where is / Where's the nearest ...?* and get students to ask and answer in pairs. Circulate and help as needed.

ADDITIONAL PRACTICE

Workbook: 9 Vocabulary: Shops and shopping, page 54; Improve your writing: Describing a place, page 55; Vocabulary booster: a supermarket, page 56.

Real life (PAGES 82–83)

Asking in shops

1 **a** Ask for some names of famous department stores in the town/city where students are studying. Focus students on the store directory and the pictures of Anna. In pairs students decide which departments she is in. Students can use their *Mini-dictionary* to check unknown words or ask you.

ANSWERS
a   The Food hall (the bakery section) in the basement.
b   The DVD/Video/Music department on the second floor.
c   The Books department on the third floor.
d   The Stationery department on the ground floor.
e   The Ladies' clothes department on the first floor.

b [T9.4] Play the first extract and decide which picture it is with the whole class. Then play the remainder of the recording, if necessary pausing after each conversation.

Students can compare their answers in pairs. Circulate to see if you need to replay any parts.

ANSWERS
1 b   2 e   3 c   4 d   5 a

Exercise 1: additional suggestion

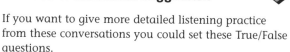

If you want to give more detailed listening practice from these conversations you could set these True/False questions.

1 Anna wants to buy a CD.
2 She pays £15.20.
3 Anna likes the colour of the top.
4 She doesn't buy the top.
5 The book about Greece is in the travel section.
6 They sell diaries in the books department.
7 She buys a pen.
8 She buys a diary.
9 She buys a plain muffin.
10 There's a restaurant on the fourth floor.

ANSWERS
1 True
2 False; she pays £50.20.
3 False; she wants blue.
4 True
5 True
6 False; she needs the stationery department
7 True
8 False; they only sell diaries in November and December
9 False; she buys a chocolate muffin
10 True

2 **a** Ask students to match the questions and answers. They then check in pairs.

b Play the recording for students to check their answers.

ANSWERS
2 f   3 h   4 a   5 b   6 c   7 d   8 e

Pronunciation

See *Teacher's tips: helping students with pronunciation* on pages 7–8.

1 [T9.5] Play question 1, write it on the board and ask *Where's the stress?* Explain that it is on the important words.

2 Play the remainder of the recording. Stop after each item and get students to mark the stresses working in pairs. Feedback to the whole class.

3 Students listen again and copy the pronunciation, focusing on the stress and a polite/friendly intonation. Use a back-chaining drill, for example *these > these please > one of these please > have one of these please > Can I have one of these please?*

Students work with a partner and test each other on the questions. They should cover the questions and use the answers to try and remember the questions. Circulate, checking their pronunciation is clear and polite.

3 **a** Set the situation: Peter is Canadian and he's on holiday. Ask *What do you buy when you are on holiday?* Use students' suggestions to revise vocabulary from the shopping list, for example, *sunglasses, baseball cap* and to introduce/check *batteries*.

b 📼 [9.6] Play the recording. Students listen and tick the things Peter buys. They work individually and then check their answers in pairs. If necessary, replay some parts of the recording.

ANSWERS
T-shirt	✔
stamps	✔
fruit	✘
batteries for camera	✔
sunglasses	✘
toothpaste	✘
bread and cake	✔

c Refer students to the tapescript on page 171 and get them to practise the conversations. See also an additional idea for using dialogues in Module 8: Real life, page 62 of the *Teacher's Book*.

4 Divide the class into A/B pairs and refer them to page 142 (As) and page 145 (Bs). Ask them to look at the first situation. Demonstrate the opening of the activity with two students in front of the class: A is buying things from B's shop. Then students roleplay the situation in their pairs. Circulate and help with problems, noting use of language for feedback later. When they have finished, they move on to the second situation and swap roles.

ADDITIONAL PRACTICE

RB **Resource bank:** 9C *Shopping crossword*, page 146
Workbook: Asking in shops, page 57

Task: Choose souvenirs from your country (PAGE 84)

Preparation: listening

1 **a** Bring in or talk about a souvenir from a place you have visited. Students ask you questions about it, and about your holiday. Then ask students to match the pictures with the words in the box.

ANSWERS
a a silk scarf   b a CD   c cheese   d a leather bag
e a lamp   f a doll

b Students discuss the question in pairs and then report back to the class.

2 📼 [T9.7] Play the first person and ask: *Which souvenir is it?* Then play the remainder of the recording and students write in the numbers.

ANSWERS
a 6   b 4   c 5   d 3   e 2   f 1

Task: speaking

1 Ask the students to read about the people on page 143. Words to check: *ethnic, folk music, poetry.* Elicit some ideas for Mark and Lena with the whole class. Then students think of their own ideas for each person. If they are studying abroad, they can think of souvenirs from the country where they are, or things from their own country (see alternative suggestion below).

2 Students, in small groups, choose the best souvenir(s) for each of the people. Help them to present their ideas and prompt them to use the phrases in the *Useful language* box. Students work in their groups to choose the best souvenir. Circulate, collecting examples of good language and any errors for feedback later.

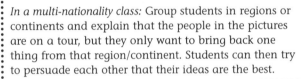

Task: alternative suggestion

In a multi-nationality class: Group students in regions or continents and explain that the people in the pictures are on a tour, but they only want to bring back one thing from that region/continent. Students can then try to persuade each other that their ideas are the best.

3 Each group can choose a spokesperson to report back on their decisions. Focus the groups on part c of the *Useful language* box. Allow time to prepare and rehearse. Let students speak without interrupting them and deal with any language points after everyone has spoken.

Study ... (PAGE 85)

Find spelling in a dictionary (2)

1 This section focuses on the spelling of comparative and superlative forms and dictionary use. Focus students on the dictionary entry for *cheap.* If possible, use an overhead transparency to show students how to find the comparative and superlative forms.

2 Students form rules for one-syllable adjectives and adjectives ending in *-y* by matching the beginning from Box A and the ending from Box B.

ANSWERS
a 2   b 4   c 3   d 1

3 Students use the rules to write the comparative and superlative forms of the adjectives and then check in their *Mini-dictionary.*

ANSWERS

sillier	silliest
greater	greatest
truer	truest
hotter	hottest
younger	youngest
thinner	thinnest
older	oldest
friendlier	friendliest

Practise ... (PAGE 85)

Students can do this section independently to monitor their own learning. Or use it for further practice of the language covered in Module 9, or as a test. Make sure students do not look at the *Language summaries* until after they have finished all five exercises. Students can do this section for homework.

1–4 Make sure students read the instructions carefully. Provide the answers either by checking as a whole class or by giving them a copy from the *Teacher's Book*.

1 Comparative adjectives

In class, students complete the gaps and then talk about their answers in pairs or groups.

ANSWERS
2 younger   3 better   4 easier   5 more important
6 hotter

2 Superlative adjectives

In class, students complete the gaps so that they are true for them. Then they talk about their ideas in pairs or groups.

ANSWERS
b best   c worst   d most violent   e saddest
f most exciting   g most boring

3 Shops

ANSWERS
b butcher's   c bakery   d clothes shop
e dry-cleaner's   f hairdresser's

4 Asking in shops

ANSWERS
a   Do you take credit cards?
b   Can I have one of those please?
c   Have you got this in a large?
d   How much is this?
e   What time do you close?

Pronunciation spot

The sound /ɪ/

a   [T9.8] Play the recording or model the first couple of superlatives yourself. Students identify the sound /ɪ/ before *st*. Drill the sound in isolation. Play the recording and students repeat the words.

b   [T9.9] Play the recording or say the words yourself. Students listen and underline the /ɪ/ sound. In some cases the spelling is very different from the pronunciation. They then listen again and repeat.

ANSWERS
this   English   tissues   business   married   places
matches   lived   women   dictionary   minute

Remember! (PAGE 85)

Students tick the exercises they understand and got correct and do extra study of any weaker areas. Students do the *Mini-check* on page 162 and give you their scores.

ANSWERS
1   bigger than
2   smaller than
3   cheaper than
4   more expensive than
5   better than
6   worse than
7   the hottest
8   the coldest
9   the most popular
10 the friendliest / the most friendly
11 the most famous
12 butcher's
13 clothes shop
14 hairdresser's
15 local shop
16 Do you take credit cards?
17 Have you got / Do you have this in blue?
18 How much is it?
19 Can I have one of those, please?
20 What time do you close?

module 10

Street life

Language focus 1 (PAGE 86)

Present continuous

1 Ask students to talk about the following questions with a partner: Do you like mobiles? When do you use them? Then get students to answer the questions.

2 [T10.1] Make sure students understand *say* versus *tell the truth*. Play the first conversation and elicit the answers from the whole class, then play the rest of the recording and students write their answers.

> **ANSWERS**
> Conversation 1:
> a his girlfriend or his wife
> b He says he's waiting for a bus.
> c Yes, he is.
> Conversation 2:
> a her husband
> b She says she's at work.
> c No, she isn't.
> Conversation 3:
> a Her mother (mum)
> b She says she's walking to the library and then home.
> c Yes, she is.

3 [T10.2] Write the sentences on the board, play the recording and elicit what should go into the gaps.

> **ANSWERS**
> a 'm waiting   b 'm finishing   c 'm walking

Grammar

1 Ask the students about the three sentences *What are the verbs?* and underline. See if anyone knows the name of the tense. Tell them it is the Present continuous and ask them to look at the sentences and say when we use it.

Highlight:
- that we use the Present continuous for speaking about an action happening now or around now. A time line will help to show this:

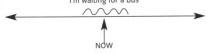

- the form of the tense: *be + -ing*

2 Ask students to complete the gaps, or build up the tables with them on the board or on an overhead transparency, to show the positive, negative and question forms.

> **ANSWERS**
> + 's, 're   – isn't, aren't, telling   ? is, are

Refer students to *Language summary A* on page 156.

Pronunciation

1 [T10.3] Play the recording and students decide which picture they refer to. Words to check: *standing, chatting, carrying, moving.* They compare their answers in pairs.

> **ANSWERS**
> 1 b   2 a   3 c   4 c   5 b   6 b   7 b   8 c   9 a
> 10 c

2 [10.4] Play the recording or model the words yourself. Drill the /ɪŋ/ sound and the full -ing forms.

3 Ask the students to look at the tapescript on page 171. Students listen and repeat the sentences.

PRACTICE

1 Focus students on the *Mini-dictionary* entry for *eat* or put it on an overhead transparency and show the students how to find the *-ing* form. Students try writing the *-ing* forms of the verbs and then check in their *Mini-dictionaries*.

> **ANSWERS**
> a eating   b buying   c reading   d playing
> e sitting   f drinking   g driving   h getting
> i riding   j cleaning

ADDITIONAL PRACTICE

RB **Resource bank:** Learner training Worksheet B: spelling the *-ing* form, page 147

2 Ask students about the first photo. *What's he doing? (He's cleaning windows.)* Then ask them to repeat the question form and drill it if needed. Elicit and drill the question form for one of the pictures with more than one person: *What are they doing?* Students, in pairs, ask and answer the questions.

> **ANSWERS**
> a He's cleaning windows.   b She's eating a croissant.
> c He's sitting and reading a newspaper.
> d They're getting off a train.
> e They're playing football.   f He's riding a bicycle.
> g They're jogging.   h She's buying fruit (apples).
> i He's driving a taxi.

3 Do the first example with the whole class. Students then make each sentence true for them.

ADDITIONAL PRACTICE

RB **Resource bank:** 10A *What's Sam doing?* page 148

Workbook: Spelling *-ing* forms, page 58; Present continuous, page 58; Question words, page 58; Short answers, page 59; All forms, page 59

Vocabulary (PAGE 88)

Clothes

1 **a** Students, in pairs, ask and answer questions about the other people.

b Students, in pairs, tick the things they can see in the pictures. Go through the answers, checking meaning. Students write two columns in their notebooks titled *S/he's wearing* and *S/he's carrying...* and decide in each case whether we say *He/she's wearing a ....* or *carrying a ....* In the feedback, highlight the plural words.

Note: there are no *shorts* in the pictures so check this.

> **ANSWERS**
> **S/he's wearing**
> trousers   jeans   sandals   tights   a hat   a tie
> a coat   a belt   a skirt   shorts   a scarf   boots
> trainers   a jumper   socks   gloves   a dress   earrings
> shoes   a shirt   a suit   a jacket   a T-shirt
> **S/he's carrying**
> a briefcase   a handbag   a backpack   a sports bag

2 Demonstrate an example and the students have to guess who it is. Students, in pairs, describe and guess the person.

3 Students, in pairs, describe someone in the class for their partner to guess.

Pronunciation

See *Teacher's tips: helping students with pronunciation* on pages 7–8.

1 ▣ [T10.5] Focus on the pronunciation of the items. Do the first two examples on the board. Students decide if the vowel sounds are the same or different. Play the first two examples and students listen and check. They then work in pairs to decide on the rest of the items, then listen and check.

> **ANSWERS**
> c S   d S   e D   f D   g D   h S   i D   j D

2 Play the recording again or model the words yourself and give choral and individual practice.

ADDITIONAL PRACTICE

Workbook: Vocabulary: clothes, page 60; Listen and read: Street style, page 61

Listening (PAGE 89)

People who wear uniforms

1 **a** Focus students on the pictures of Andy and Michelle and ask *What are they wearing?* to elicit/introduce a *uniform*. Ask *What are their jobs? Andy is a guard* /gɑːd/ *and Michelle is a police officer.*

b Ask students the questions. The Present simple is used in the first question as it refers to normal routine (not just in the

picture now). Students discuss the questions. They check the adjectives in their *Mini-dictionary* if necessary. In the feedback, elicit from students that it is difficult for Andy to *move his head* (a phrase that is needed in the listening).

c ▣ [T10.6] Focus students on the photos again and get them in pairs to decide who wears what in their jobs. Play the recording for them to check their answers.

> **ANSWERS**
> **Andy**
> a hat that is 300 years old   leather trousers   tights
> **Michelle**
> a white shirt   black trousers   a black and white hat
> very big shoes

2 Students read the questions first. Play the recording again for students to listen in more detail. Students, in pairs, check their answers. If necessary, play any parts again.

> **ANSWERS**
> a   Because it's small and very heavy; you can't move your head.
> b   Because the trousers are leather and uncomfortable.
> c   No.
> d   Yes, because it's smart.
> e   The shoes because they are big and ugly.

3 Students discuss the questions in small groups. The emphasis is on freer practice here, so encourage students to communicate without worrying if they are completely accurate.

Language focus 2 (PAGE 89)

Present simple or continuous?

Ask students to read the text and do the first question with them. They write the answers to the questions. Words to check: *getting ready, dark, bright, a top (a general word which covers anything which isn't obviously a T-shirt or a blouse or shirt – for women), make-up.* Students look these up in their *Mini-dictionary.* Circulate and help as needed.

> **ANSWERS**
> a   She's getting ready to go out.
> b   She's wearing a new pink top, a blue skirt and quite a lot of make-up.
> c   She usually wears dark colours.
> d   She wears bright colours.
> e   No, she doesn't.
> f   Yes, she is.

Grammar

1 Students underline the correct explanations. demonstrate the difference visually by drawing two timelines:

> **ANSWERS**
> usually true   happening now

2 Draw students' attention to the two sets of words. Or write the words on the board, in random order, and ask students to tell you which go with the Present simple and which with the Present continuous.

Refer students to *Language summary B* on page 156.

PRACTICE

1 **a** Focus students on the example in the book. Students choose the correct form and compare their answers in pairs. Words to check: *casual* /kæʒuel/, *aftershave* /ɑːftəʃeɪv/, *jewellery* /dʒuːəlri/.

> **ANSWERS**
> 1 Do you usually wear; are you wearing
> 2 Are you wearing; do you normally wear
> 3 Do you usually wear   4 Do you wear
> 5 Do you normally; Are you wearing
> 6 Do you ever wear   7 Are you wearing
> 8 Do you wear
> 9 Are you wearing; Do you normally wear
> 10 Do you ever wear

b Demonstrate by getting students to ask you some of the questions. Answer naturally and give more information than the bare minimum. Students, in pairs, ask and answer the questions. Encourage them to speak freely.

2 **a** Get students to read each extract and match it with a question from 1a.

> **ANSWERS**
> 1 Question 9   2 Question 1
> 3 Question 8 or possibly the second half of Question 1

Do the first two examples with the whole class. Then students complete the gaps with the Present simple or Present continuous. They compare their answers in pairs. Help the students with writing the forms, especially the negative.

b 🔊 [T10.7] Students listen and check their answers.

> **ANSWERS**
> a wear b go c go d 'm not wearing
> e 'm working f wear g doesn't wear
> h 'm wearing i 'm not wearing j 'm wearing
> k 'm going l don't normally wear m hate

3 Students work in small groups of three or four, but not with the person they did exercise 1 with. They discuss the items. Remind students to pay attention to the use of the Present simple.

ADDITIONAL PRACTICE

RB Resource bank: 10B *A letter home*, page 150

Workbook: Present continuous and Present simple, page 60

Vocabulary and writing (PAGE 90)

Describing people

See *Teacher's tips: working with lexical phrases* on pages 9–10.

1 Students, in pairs or individually, write in the names of the people. They can use their *Mini-dictionary* for unknown words or ask you. Words to check: *moustache, beard, slim, shaved head, good-looking, well-built*. Check if students can work out some of these as they go along, using the pictures.

> **ANSWERS**
> b Paolo, Kamilla and Martha   c Martha
> d Sheena and Mike   e Paolo and Mike   f Mike
> g Kamilla, Paolo, Sheena and Martha   h Mike
> i Mike   j Pedro   k Kamilla and Martha   l Mike
> m Sheena and Pedro   n Sheena   o Paolo
> p Paolo and Kamilla   q Kamilla and Paolo

2 Do one example with the class. Then students, in pairs, write alternatives, referring back to exercise 1.

> **ANSWERS AND LANGUAGE NOTE**
> a dark, long, short, brown, red, white, grey, etc. Teach: *He's bald.*
> b green, brown, grey, etc.
> c a beard, a shaved head, a pony-tail, side-burns, etc.
> d in her twenties, in her early forties, in her late sixties, etc.
> e not very tall, not very slim, good-looking, well-built, (very) smart, attractive, etc.
>
> Point out that we say: *He isn't very tall* rather than *He's short.* And *She isn't very slim* rather than *She's fat.* The use of *short* and *fat* are considered too direct/rude.

3 Students, in pairs, write descriptions of the six people's appearance based on pictures on page 91. The students could read out one or more of their descriptions and the other students guess who they are talking about.

4 Focus students on the example and ask them to write about themselves or a famous person. This could be done for homework.

ADDITIONAL PRACTICE

RB Resource bank: 10C *Identity parades*, page 151

Task: Complete and describe a picture (PAGE 92)

Preparation: listening

See *Teacher's tips: making tasks work* on pages 11–12.

1 Focus students on picture A and get them to ask and answer the questions in pairs. They write their answers for feedback later.

ANSWERS

a It's morning
b It's growling at the cat. Black and white.
c She's listening to some music on her headphones and she's eating and drinking. She's wearing a black dress and blue trainers. She's got a cup of coffee or tea.
d He's wearing an orange jumper or T-shirt, brown trousers, grey shoes, a baseball cap and sunglasses.
e The man's got a moustache. He's wearing a purple jacket or jumper, a gold medallion, blue trousers, and brown shoes. The woman has got long blonde hair and she's wearing a pink dress and black shoes.

2 [T10.8] Play the recording for students to find the mistakes. They put crosses on the picture where there are mistakes.

ANSWERS

1 The girl is wearing a black dress, not a white skirt.
2 The dog isn't running.
3 There are a man and woman sitting at the café, not two women.
4 The woman has got long blonde hair, not short dark hair.

Task: speaking

1 Focus students on picture B and tell them it is the evening. Make an overhead transparency of the picture and give them examples of changes they could make. Refer them to the box for ideas and check the meaning of: *accessories*, *unhappy* and other unknown words.

2 Put students in A/B pairs. Student B should ask Student A questions about their changes, and draw these in on the blank picture on page 146. Demonstrate this with a student. When Student B has drawn the ten changes, they swap roles.
Students check their questions with *Useful language* box a and read the answers in b. Drill any phrases as needed.

3 When students have both finished drawing, they compare their pictures to see how successful they were.

Real life (PAGE 93)

Street talk

1 a [T10.9] Do the example with the whole class. Students do the others individually and then compare their answers with a partner. Play the recording for students to check their answers.

ANSWERS

1 a 2 b 3 c 4 b 5 a 6 c 7 b

b Students listen again and write the answers.

ANSWERS

1 Yes, it's ten o'clock. 2 No, take it. 3 Yes I think so.
4 Yes, it's fine. 5 No, sorry, I haven't.
6 Yes, it's over there. 7 At about five thirty.

Pronunciation

See *Teacher's tips: helping students with pronunciation* on pages 7–8.

1 [10.10] Play the recording and get students to notice the polite intonation. Give a model of rude/flat intonation yourself to compare. Then students copy each question sounding as polite as they can.

You could write the questions on the board or use an overhead transparency, and use arrows to show a polite intonation pattern for requests. The voice tends to start quite high and moves after the main stress.

ANSWERS

1 Excuse me have you got the time please?
2 Is anyone sitting here?
3 Is this bus going to the city centre?
4 Is it okay to park here?
5 Excuse me, have you got any change, please?
6 Is this the way to the station?
7 What time do the shops close on Saturdays?

2 Students practise the conversations with a partner. They start by reading aloud but then encourage them to cover the actual language and try to remember them.

2 Students choose five questions that they think are most useful to them or which are new/most difficult for them. They take a minute to learn them by heart. Then they stand up and imagine they are in a main street, stop the other 'passers-by' and ask a question. Their partner answers and then they move on. Get them to use *Excuse me*, to attract the other's attention.

ADDITIONAL PRACTICE

Workbook: Street talk, page 62.

Consolidation, Modules 6–10

A Grammar: Present simple, Present continuous, Past simple

Students work alone or in pairs to choose the correct answers. Check answers as a whole class.

ANSWERS

2 'm sitting 3 got 4 comes 5 works 6 met
7 decided 8 didn't have 9 came back
10 're staying 11 wants

B Reading and speaking: Snacks around the world

1 Students work alone or in pairs to complete the gaps. Check answers as a whole class.

ANSWERS
1 2 a 3 a 4 some 5 any 6 a 7 some
8 some/an 9 some 10 some

2 Students discuss the questions in pairs. Circulate and supply any vocabulary needed.

C Speaking: Real life

1 Students work in pairs and decide what they would say in each situation.

2 [C1] Play the recording, pausing after each question to allow students to check their answers.

ANSWERS
a Can I have the bill, please?
b How much is this T-shirt?
c I'd like to order two large pizzas, please.
d I'm sorry, I don't understand. Can you say that again, please?
e Do you sell shampoo?
f Have you got this in a bigger size?
g No, thanks, I'm just looking.

3 Students practise the situations in pairs.

D Listening: Song: *Return to Sender*

[C2] Students turn to either page 143 or 144. Play the recording. Students then compare their answers with their partner.

E Reading and speaking: Comparatives and superlatives

1 Students read about the four holidays, then work in pairs to answer the questions.

ANSWERS
a African safari
b Courchevel
c Greece
d Ölüdeniz

2 Students make comparative sentences using the adjectives in the box. Check answers as a class.

3 a If you do this in the class, you could set up a roleplay either between the people described or between a travel agent and the people. Alternatively, put the students in small groups to discuss the best holiday for the two sets of people.

ANSWERS
1 Courchevel is the best for them. It's busier and more exciting than the Pelion Peninsula and they can ski and swim, and dance in clubs.
2 Ölüdeniz is the best for them. It's quieter and nearer the sea than the Pelion peninsula. There's an old town 15 km away.

F Vocabulary

Students work alone to find the words. Check answers as a class.

ANSWERS
a nuts, cereal
b orange juice, wine, beer
c trousers, suit, jeans
d decide, believe, graduate
e fell, bought, wrote
f busy, new, young
g butcher's, bakery, clothes shop

module 11

The world around us

Vocabulary (PAGE 96)

Animals and natural features

a Students, in pairs, write down as many different animals as possible. The first group to reach twelve is the winner. Then focus students on the vocabulary box and the pictures on page 96 and 97. Get them to tick the pictures they can see. In the feedback check the meanings of the words that are not in the pictures: *a human being, a kangaroo, a mountain, a lake, a river, the moon, an ant*.

Students copy the table into their notebooks on a new page and write the words in the correct categories. Get them to add extra words. Check the meanings of the categories first.

ANSWERS
(ticks means that the items are in the pictures)

animals/ living things	geographical features	planets, etc.
a bird ✔	a volcano ✔	
an insect ✔	a mountain	the earth ✔
a chimpanzee ✔	a lake	the moon
a snail ✔	a river	
a human being		
an elephant ✔		
a donkey ✔		
a kangaroo		
a dolphin ✔		

b Students, in small groups, try to add any words to the categories. Circulate and help. Elicit their ideas onto the board.

Reading (PAGE 96)

1 Students read the text and decide which fact is not true. They can look up words in their *Mini-dictionary* or ask you for help. Encourage students to guess the meanings and then check with you *(Does ..... mean ....?)*. Students discuss which one is not true and then check on page 143. Other phrases to check: *up to (= maximum)* and *at least (= minimum)*.

2 Do the first example with the class and then get them to look for the other numbers. They then check by re-reading the text, where the numbers are written out in full. Either ask them to copy out full sentences or just underline the answers. Do the first example together.

ANSWERS
- Snails can sleep for 3 years.
- The average person eats around 8 kilos of dirt during their lifetime.
- About 10% (ten per cent) of people in the world are left-handed.
- Chimps can learn up to two hundred and forty different signs.
- The earth rotates at around 1,500 kph (one thousand five hundred kilometres per hour).

- The Arctic Tern flies 40,000 km (forty thousand kilometres) every year.
- You share your birthday with 18,000,000 (eighteen million) other people in the world.
- There are at least 10,000,000,000,000 (ten thousand billion) ants in the world.

3 Students in pairs discuss the questions, then have a whole class feedback.

Language focus 1 (PAGE 97)

can and *can't* for ability

Grammar

1 Get the students to underline three examples in the text. Do the first example with them.

POSSIBLE ANSWERS
Snails can sleep for up to three years.
Dogs can't see colours.
Chimpanzees can't talk but they can learn sign language.

2 Write the sentences on the board and elicit what should go in the gaps. Students have already studied *can* for possibility in Module 5, so the form shouldn't be a problem for them.

ANSWERS
+ can   – can't   ? Can

Refer students to *Language summary A* on page 156.

PRACTICE

1 Refer students to the example and elicit any other ideas about dogs. Students then work individually to write six sentences. They can use the *Mini-dictionary* to check the verbs or you could introduce these. Circulate and help as needed.

Pronunciation

[T11.1] Write the two sentences on the board and get students to listen to the recording and mark the stresses. Remind them of the pronunciation of *can* /kæn/ and *can't* /kɑːnt/ here. Drill the sentences. Refer students to the tapescript and play the remainder of the recording. After each example, elicit the stresses and ask students to repeat. Check: *newborn babies*.

2 This is an opportunity to personalise the questions. Students stand up with the questions, mingle and ask as many different students as possible. They try to find at least one person for each ability. Get two students to demonstrate in front of the group and drill the questions: *Can you......?* Remind them of the short answers: *Yes, I can* and *No, I can't* and introduce *Yes, but not very well*. Circulate and collect examples of errors for feedback later.

ADDITIONAL PRACTICE

RB **Resource bank:** 11A *Can you or can't you?* page 152

Workbook: *can/can't* for ability, page 63; Questions and short answers, page 63

Language focus 2 (PAGE 98)
Question words

1 a Students, in pairs, refer to the Animal Quiz and write the answers without looking back at the text.

b They look back at the text and check.

2 Students look back at the quiz and circle each question word.

Grammar

1 Identify and introduce any new *wh-* words to students. Ask them match the question words and the answers.

> **ANSWERS**
> b How tall...?   Ten metres.
> c How often...?   Every day.
> d How long...?   Three hours.
> e How fast...?   Forty kilometres an hour.
> f Which city...?   Los Angeles.
> g Which animals...?   Lions.
> h What kinds of music...? Rock and pop.

Highlight particularly:
– the use of *How long?* as students often say *How long time?*
– that we don't say *Which kind of?*
– a range of adjectives we can use after *How (how big, expensive, cold, hot, near etc.)*

2 Check that students remember the difference between *How much* and *How many*. Elicit some examples in relation to food.

> **ANSWERS**
> How many – countable nouns
> How much – uncountable nouns

3 Focus students on the explanation or write the two examples on the board and elicit the difference between *what* and *which*.

Refer students to *Language summary B* on page 157.

PRACTICE

1 Do the first example together. Then students work individually to choose the correct question word.

> **ANSWERS**
> a What   b How much   c Which   d How many
> e How long f How often   g How fast h How far
> i How often j What

2 a Demonstrate some examples from the table. Explain that students do not have to use column D in each case and that they can add extra items, for example: *How often do you read a newspaper?* Ask students to write a question for each item in column A.

b You could drill some of the questions before students talk to each other. Elicit some onto the board, and ask students to mark the stress. They then copy you, saying them as fast as possible so that they weaken the auxiliary verbs and pronouns. For example:

> **ANSWERS**
> How far can you swim?
> Which languages do/can you speak?
> How often do you read a newspaper?
> How fast can you run?

ADDITIONAL PRACTICE

RB **Resource bank:** 11B *The Dinner Party*, page 153

Workbook: Question words, pages 64–65; Word order in questions, page 65; Questions with other verb forms, page 65

Real life (PAGE 99)
Saying quantities and big numbers

1 Start by dictating some simple numbers, and then more complicated ones, to give students some basic revision. Ask them to do the matching activity and then check in pairs.

> **ANSWERS**
> a fifty kilometres per hour
> b five hundred kilos
> c five hundred and five
> d five thousand
> e fifty thousand
> f five hundred thousand
> g five million
> h five billion
> i five point five
> j one metre fifty-five centimetres

Highlight:
• that we don't use plurals with hundred, thousand, million, billion
• the use of *and* in c
• the alternative: *fifty kilometres an hour* in answer a

2 📼 [T11.2] Play the recording and students write down the numbers. They compare with a partner whilst you monitor and see if any numbers need to be replayed. Then students listen again and copy the pronunciation.

ANSWERS
a 400 b 820 c 9,000 d 4.8 e 20,000
f 300,000 g 12,000,000 h 670,000,000
i 7,865 j 12.7

3 **a** Focus students on the questions and the question words in the box. Do the first example with them and then they continue individually. They can compare their answers in pairs. Circulate and help as needed.

ANSWERS
1 What 2 How fast 3 What 4 How many
5 How tall 6 How much 7 How far
8 How many 9 How old 10 How much

b Students, in pairs, ask and answer the questions. Remind them they can use *about* or *around* or say *I'm not sure* or *I've got no idea / I really don't know. I think...* Circulate and help as needed.

ADDITIONAL PRACTICE

[RB] **Resource bank:** 11C *The numbers game*, page 155

Workbook: More about numbers, page 68; Pronunciation: numbers, page 68

Listening (PAGE 100)

1 Focus students on the pictures. Students, in pairs, ask and answer the questions. Follow this up with a whole class discussion.

2 Focus students on the vocabulary in the box and do one example with them. Students, in pairs, work on the remainder of the vocabulary. They can use their *Mini-dictionaries*. Have feedback with the whole class.

3 **a** Students, in pairs, try and answer the questions. It doesn't matter if they have no ideas as the aim here is to orientate them to the topic and content of the recording and encourage predicting skills.

b 📼 [T11.3] Tell students they are going to listen to a radio programme about pets. Play the beginning of the extract and do question 1 with them. Then students listen and check their answers / answer the questions.

ANSWERS
1 about 500 million
2 cat food
3 about sixteen
4 about nine weeks
5 between two and five
6 over one hundred
7 they are hairless (they haven't got any hair)

Ask students *Did anything surprise you?*

4 📼 [T11.4] Tell students that the next part of the programme is about dogs. They can read the extract and predict the missing words. As above, it doesn't matter if they have no idea as this approach will help their listening skill. They listen to the recording and complete the gaps.

ANSWERS
b fifty-three million
c two billion dollars
d a hundred and fifty
e in many countries
f 65 kilometres per hour
g 1932
h making films
i forty-four thousand dollars

Language focus 3 (PAGE 101)

Use of articles (3)

1 In pairs, students read and tick anything they agree with and put a cross against anything they don't agree with. Words to check: *rabbit, cruel, balcony, owner, rub.*

2 Ask the students to underline all the animals in the text. They then circle all the examples of *a/an* and *the* associated with each one and write – where there is no article.

Teacher's note: The approach here helps students to notice differences in the use of articles between English and their language. *In a multi-nationality class*, students can work in groups of the same nationality and use their first language if needed.

Grammar

Do example 1 with students. If necessary, they can translate the examples to see if the rule is the same in their language. Circulate and help as needed. Have a whole class feedback at the end, exploring the difference between the different languages.

Highlight:
• the idea that we know which one. You could use examples from the classroom here, e.g. the door, the window.
• the use of the plural form in 3.

Refer students to *Language summary C* on page 157.

PRACTICE

1 This practises rule 3 from the *Grammar* box. Introduce or check *I don't mind* (i.e. *it's not a problem for me*). Students write a sentence about each item and then compare with a partner.

2 **a** Students complete the gaps individually and then check with a partner. Words to check: *area, allergic to.*

ANSWERS

1 a 2 a, a 3 the, – 4 – 5 a 6 The 7 –, a
8 The, – 9 –

In the feedback get students to tell you each time why the answer is correct.

b Demonstrate the activity, correcting the first two examples so that they are true for yourself or ticking ones which are already true. Students do the same. Students can talk about their answers in groups or in pairs. Encourage them to ask each other more questions about each answer.

Pronunciation

1 [T11.5] Play the recording or model the examples yourself and write the phonetics on the board. Drill the two different pronunciations.

2 [T11.6] Play the recording and students decide which pronunciation they hear.

ANSWERS

a	the east 2	the west 1
b	the left 1	the right 1
c	the beginning 1	the end 2
d	the morning 1	the afternoon 2
e	the president 1	the prime minister 1
f	the king 1	the queen 1
g	the EU 2	the USA 1
h	the Arctic 2	the Antarctic 2

Ask students about the sound following *the* in pronunciation 2. Elicit the rule: that if *the* is followed by a vowel or diphthong sound, it is pronounced /ðɪ/.

3 Students listen and repeat. Drill as necessary, focusing on the two pronunciations.

ADDITIONAL PRACTICE

Workbook: Articles, page 68

Task: Devise a general knowledge quiz (PAGE 102)

Preparation: listening

1 Students read the quiz individually and complete the questions with a question word. Then, in groups of three or four, check the correct question words.

ANSWERS

1 How many 2 What 3 How many 4 How far
5 Where 6 When 7 How many 8 Where
9 How many

2 [T11.7] Students answer the quiz in small groups, then they get a group representative to give you their answers before you play the recording. Award one point for each correct answer.

ANSWERS

1 c 2 a 3 b 4 b 5 c 6 b 7 c 8 a 9 c

Task: writing and speaking

1 a Students work in three teams, A, B and C and make sure they understand the categories in the box.

b Students work together to write at least eight questions. They can use their own ideas and/or ideas from the 'fantastic facts' files on pages 141, 142 or 143. Focus students on the *Useful language* box for examples of questions.

Exercise 1: additional suggestion

For further practice on questions: write the key words from the questions in the *Useful language* box on the board. Students then have to write the full questions. For example:

When / Italy / win / the European cup?
Where / Albert Einstein / born?
What / capital / Canada?
How far / be / Berlin / Warsaw?
Where / sushi / come from?
Who / write / War and Peace?

They then categorise the questions into topics, which will further check the meaning of the topics.

Language note:

Students might ask you why there is no auxiliary verb *did* in the question Who wrote War and Peace? This is a subject question, as opposed to an object question (What did Tolstoy write?). Tell students it is a different kind of question. They can just copy it for questions about authors and painters and questions with *who won...?* Alternatively, give a mini-lesson on how we form this type of question.

2 Students practise the pronunciation of their questions so that they are intelligible for the other groups. In each group, different students practise saying one of the questions and their colleagues can help correct them.

3 Conduct the Quiz in a lively way. Team A say what categories they have and Team B choose a category. A representative from Team A asks Team B the question.

Decide on a points system. For example, if a student answers correctly without asking the rest of their team, they get two points. If they have to confer, they get one point. If their answer is incorrect, Team C can then try and if they get the answer right, they get one point. Then Team B say what categories they have and Team C choose one, and so on.

Before they start, drill ways of answering by looking at the *Useful language* box b.

Study ... (PAGE 103)

Recording new vocabulary

1 This study section is intended to encourage students to start a vocabulary notebook and identifies different ways of recording vocabulary. Ask students if they have a special book for their vocabulary and elicit ideas for recording vocabulary effectively.

Show students the examples on page 103 or write these on the board or an overhead transparency.

2 Students divide the words in the box into three categories.

ANSWERS

potato	eye	walk	carrot
nose	jump	bean	head
run	mushroom	mouth	climb
fly			

3 Students can do this in their notebook or in a special vocabulary notebook. The reason they should write on three pages is so that they can later add to these lexical sets (*vegetables, parts of the body, verbs of movement*).

Students select a different method for each set and discuss which method they like best.

They could also write the pronunciation and grammar of each word. Encourage the use of more systematic recording of vocabulary and check this regularly.

ADDITIONAL PRACTICE

RB **Resource bank:** *Learner-training worksheet C:* Recording new vocabulary, page 156

Practise ... (PAGE 103)

Students can do this section independently to monitor their own learning. Or use it for further practice of the language covered in Module 11, or as a test. Make sure students do not look at the *Language summaries* until after they have finished all five exercises. Students can do this section for homework.

1–5 For each exercise, make sure students read the instructions carefully. Provide the answers either by checking as a whole class or by giving them a copy from the *Teacher's Book*.

ANSWERS

1 Animals and natural features
b a mountain
c an elephant
d a volcano
e a snail
f a chimpanzee

2 *can* for ability
b You can't drive.
c She can cook very well.
d They can't understand you.
e I can't read music but I can sing.

3 Question words
b Which
c How many
d How often
e How far
f How long
g How much

4 Saying quantities and big numbers
b twenty million
c forty kilometres per hour
d ninety-nine point nine
e twelve metres thirty centimetres

5 Articles
b a
c the
d a
e the
f a
g the
h –

Pronunciation spot

The sounds /w/ and /h/

a [T11.8] Play the recording or model the two sounds yourself. Help the students form the sounds and get them to listen and repeat. Then ask them to listen and repeat the words.

b [T11.9] Play the recording and get students to listen and repeat the words and phrases with /w/

Do you want some water?
Where were you last night?
What did you do at the weekend?

c [11.10] They do the same with /h/
a big hotel
Is there a hairdresser's near here?
He's got long hair
Have you got the time?

Remember! (PAGE 103)

Ask the students to tick the exercises they understand and got correct. Encourage them to do further study of areas they are still unclear about. Students then do the *Mini-check* on page 162.

ANSWERS
1 mountain 2 insect 3 human being 4 bird
5 earth 6 Can you play golf?
7 She can understand Chinese. 8 I can't cook.
9 How much 10 How fast 11 Which 12 Who
13 33.3 14 400,000 15 2008 16 14 m 62 cm
17 Sam loves dogs but he doesn't like the dog next door.
18 Money is a problem for most people.
19 I can see the moon. 20 There's a pen in my bag.

A weekend away

Language focus 1 (PAGE 104)

Future intentions: *going to*, *would like to* and *want to*

1 Ask students *What do you usually do at the weekend?* They discuss this in pairs. Then focus students on the photos of weekend activities and get them to match these with the vocabulary.

> **ANSWERS**
> a having a barbecue, having a family meal
> b going for a walk   c relaxing at home
> d at a wedding

2 **a** 🔲 [T12.1] Tell the students the recording is about people talking about next weekend. Students copy the table into their notebooks. Play the first extract and complete the information about Neela, showing students they only need to write notes. Don't focus them on the future forms. Then play the remainder and students complete the table individually. They then compare their answers in pairs.

> **ANSWERS**
>
> | | Plans for Saturday | Plans for Sunday |
> |---------|--------------------|------------------|
> | Neela | | lunch with her grandparents |
> | Phil | Not much; stay at home and relax; finish his book; sleep a lot ||
> | Megan | go shopping | have a barbecue |
> | Jamie | go away to the country ||
> | Anna | work on Saturday see a film | a friend's wedding |
> | Sharif | watch the football | do something with the children maybe take them swimming |

b 🔲 [T12.2] This exercise encourages more intensive listening. Do the first example with the whole class then play the recording and students complete the gaps. Pause the recording regularly to allow students to write. Students compare their answers in pairs.

> **ANSWERS**
> 1 big group   2 have lunch   3 be, birthday
> 4 do much   5 finish, book   6 get, camera
> 7 this weekend   8 friend's wedding   9 watch, football

Grammar

1 **a** Work directly with the *Grammar* box, getting students to read the rules. Or ask students to close their books and remember the sentences about Neela and her grandparents and Phil's plans. Elicit:

I'm going to have lunch with my grandparents.
I'm not going to do much this weekend.

Highlight:
- the meaning of *going to* for future intentions
- the form: *be + going to + verb*

Ask students to make the question form by giving the prompt: *watch the football tonight?*

b Ask students if they can remember about Neela on Saturday and elicit:

I'm going out with a group of friends.

Highlight:

We usually don't say *I'm going to go*.

2 Ask them to remember what Phil says about his book and what Sharif says about his children.
I want to finish my book.
I'd like to do something with the children.

Highlight:
- that basically they mean the same
- that *want to* is stronger and more direct than *I'd like to*
- the form: *'d like to + verb; want to + verb*

Refer students to *Language summary A* on page 157 *and B* on page 158. *Language summary B* covers future time expressions.

PRACTICE

1 Students individually write sentences about each person.

2 Focus students on the pictures and ask them to decide, in pairs, what the people are going to do. Encourage them to omit the second *go* in examples such as *he/she's going swimming/shopping*. Circulate and help as needed.

> **ANSWERS**
> a   She's going shopping.
> b   He's going to meet his girlfriend.
> c   They're going to take the dog for a walk.
> d   He's going to have a cigarette.
> e   He's going swimming.
> f   She's going to catch a plane.

3 🔲 [T12.3] Check the question forms: *Do you want to... Would you like to... and Are you going to ...?* Do a couple of examples, then students work individually and check their answers in pairs.
    Play the recording for students to check their answers.

> **ANSWERS**
> a are   b Are, are   c Do, Do   d Are, would
> e Are, are   f would   g Do   h Do, would

Pronunciation

See *Teacher's tips: helping students with pronunciation* on pages 7–8.

1 [T12.4]

Write the sentences on the board and play the recording or model them yourself several times. Students have to identify where the stressed words are. Add the stress blobs and show the weak form of *to*.

ANSWERS
● /t/ ● ● ●
Are you going to have a busy weekend?
● ● /t/ ●
What do you want to do?

2 [T12.3] Play the recording again for students to practise the questions. Work on *Would you like* /wʊd juː laɪk/ and *Do you want?* /duː juː wɒnt/ to help students say these questions more quickly and naturally.

4 Get the students to ask you the questions. Answer as fully as possible to encourage students to speak freely. Students, in pairs, ask and answer the questions. You could ask some of the students to tell the class one thing they learnt about their partner.

ADDITIONAL PRACTICE

RB **Resource bank:** 12A *Future Walkabout*, page 157

Workbook: Future plans: *going to*, page 69; *want to*, page 70; Short answers with *going to* and *want to*, page 70; *would like to* and *want to*, page 71; Future forms, page 71

Vocabulary and speaking (PAGE 106)

Going out and staying in

See *Teacher's tips: working with lexical phrases* on pages 9–10.

1 Get the students to ask you the questions and check they understand the adjectives. They then, in pairs, ask and answer about their weekend. Circulate and help, as needed.

2 Focus students on the quiz, check *spend weekends* and that they understand it refers to every weekend, not just last weekend. Revise the meanings of the frequency adverbs. Give them an example about your own weekends to show how to use the numbering system. Students work individually, using their *Mini-dictionary* to check any unknown words or phrases.

3 Students work in small groups of three or four. Focus them on the speech balloon and check they remember where to put the frequency adverbs in a sentence. Do a few examples with the whole class before students talk to each other.

Language note:
Point out the following common phrases using *the*: *at the weekend, do the housework, do the shopping, go to the gym, go to the cinema, go to the theatre.* Also the use of no article with: *go to bed, stay in bed.*

4 **a** Students do this exercise individually, then compare in pairs before looking in the text to confirm the answers.

ANSWERS
2 stay in bed 3 do the housework 4 have a party
5 go swimming 6 go to the gym
7 go to the country 8 go for a walk
9 go out with friends 10 go away for the weekend

b Students memorise the words and then test each other in pairs.

5 Students, in pairs, ask and answer the questions. Give them the sentence starter: *My idea of the perfect (Saturday) is to... get up late, ...* etc.

ADDITIONAL PRACTICE

RB **Resource bank:** 12B *Collocation snap*, page 158

Workbook: Word combinations, page 71

Language focus 2 (PAGE 107)

Suggestions and offers

1 [T12.5] Focus students on the picture or put this on an overhead transparency. Set the situation and ask students to listen with the single question *What do they decide to do?* This will encourage them to listen for gist. They check with a partner before whole class feedback.

ANSWER
They decide to go to a French restaurant, *The French Table*, with some friends.

2 Focus students on the gapped dialogue and do the first example with them. They work individually and then check in pairs. Circulate and help as needed.

ANSWERS
b 4 c 1 d 2 e 6 f 3

3 Students, in pairs, read the dialogue aloud. You could do this before looking at the grammar or afterwards.

Grammar

1 **a** Write the following on the board:
we all go out for a meal?
that new French restaurant?
phone and book a table?
book it for eight o'clock.

See if students can remember expressions to go before these. Add *Why don't we, How about, Shall* and *Let's*. Label these expressions making suggestions.

Highlight:
- the meaning of these three expressions.
- that *let's = let us*.
- that we use the base form after *Why don't we, Let's* and *Shall*

- that after *How about* we can use a noun or an *-ing* form
- the main stresses in each sentence and the pronunciation of *Shall we* /ʃæl wɪː/

Drill each expression as needed.

b Refer students back to the dialogue and elicit ways of answering the suggestions.

ANSWERS
Yeah, okay. That sounds (more) fun! *Yeah, it sounds good.*
Yes, please if that's okay. *Yes, good idea.*

2 a Try and elicit these two forms and label them Making offers.

Highlight:
- the meaning of the expressions
- the use of the base form after both expressions
- the sentence stress and the pronunciation of *Shall I...?*

b Elicit ways of answering.

Refer students to *Language summaries C and D* on page 158.

PRACTICE

1 a Students work individually to put the suggestions in order. Tell them to leave a gap after each answer.

b [T12.5] Students listen and check their answers. Students listen again and write down the answers. They check with a partner and decide if the person said yes.

ANSWERS
1	A How about a coffee?	
	B That sounds nice.	✔
2	A Shall I take your jacket?	
	B Oh, thanks.	✔
3	A Shall we ask for the bill?	
	B Yes, good idea.	✔
4	A I'll take you home.	
	B No, it's okay, I'll call a taxi.	✘
5	A Why don't we go to the cinema?	
	B Yeah, that's a good idea.	✔
6	A Let's have another drink.	
	B I'm okay, thanks.	✘
7	A Shall I call you tomorrow?	
	B Yeah, okay.	✔
8	A Why don't we meet at the station?	
	B That sounds fine.	✔
9	A I'll book the tickets.	
	B Great.	✔

Pronunciation

Focus students on the tapescript on page 173. Get them to listen to each suggestion and offer. *Are they polite and friendly or not?* (Yes) Play each sentence and get the students to copy. Encourage students to start quite high so that they sound friendlier.

2 Do example a with the students, then they continue in pairs. There may be more than one possible context for each of the sentences.

ANSWERS (suggested)
a 5, 9 (also possible: 8) b 1, 2, 6, 8, 4 c 1, 7
d 1, 3, 6

3 Students work in four groups or pairs and write a dialogue for one of the situations in exercise 2. Make sure that each pair/group works on a different situation. Circulate and help as needed. Then one or two groups act the dialogue in front of the class. See suggestion for using dialogues in the Real life section in Module 8.

ADDITIONAL PRACTICE

[RB] **Resource bank:** 12C *The school party*, page 159

Workbook: Suggestions and offers, page 72; Pronunciation *I'll, we'll*, page 72

Task: Plan a weekend away
(PAGES 108–109)

1 Ask students *Do you ever go away for the weekend? Where do you go?* Tell them about your own weekends away. Then explain that if you are in London there are some great places to go for the weekend and show them the photos of different places. Get them to try and match the words in the box to some of the photos, using their *Mini-dictionary* or asking you about the words. Check the meaning of words not in the photos. Drill as needed.

ANSWERS
1 a magnificent cathedral
2 cliffs and beaches, sailing, beautiful views
3 traditional live music, a lively bar
4 a castle, a lake with an island, a golf course
5 B & Bs

2 a Tell students the texts come from a guide book of England. Ask them to read the texts and match them with the photos.

ANSWERS
The Isle of Wight – 2   Canterbury and Leeds Castle – 1, 4
Dublin – 3, 5

b Get students to read more carefully and, for each text, to see whether it has any of the things in exercise 1. Students can write numbers (1 for the text on the Isle of Wight, 2 for the text on Canterbury etc.) next to the words.

ANSWERS
The Isle of Wight: beautiful views, cliffs and beaches, a castle, sailing, B & Bs
Canterbury and Leeds Castle: a magnificent cathedral, B & Bs, a castle, a lake with islands, a golf course
Dublin: a castle, traditional live music, beautiful views, B & Bs, lively bars, beaches.

c Put students in small groups of three or four and get them to discuss the question. This is an opportunity for freer practice so don't correct at this stage.

3 [T12.7] Set the situation of three friends, Julie, Sarah and Rob in London deciding where to go for the weekend after next. Give students a minute to read the questions. Do the first example with the class. Play the remainder of the recording and students tick the correct answer. They compare their answers.

ANSWERS
a 3   b 3   c 3   d 3   e 1   f 1   g 2

4 [T12.8] Refer students to page 173, where there are some sentences from the conversation. Get students to listen and repeat. Or ask students to close their books and write the questions they hear and then practise them.

Task: speaking

1 Students work in groups of three or four and try to plan a weekend away together. They make a list of possible places. You could then elicit a list onto the board.

2 a Students discuss the items. Each student suggests a different place. They try to make notes on why they want to go to that place, how they want to travel, etc. Encourage students to ask for any special vocabulary. They could use the *Useful language* box for help.

Each student proposes a place to the group and the group decide where to go, how to travel, etc.

b Each group plans how they will describe their plans to the rest of the class using *We're going to ... because ... We want to visit ... .* Circulate as before.

3 a Reorganise the class into new groups and each student presents their planned trip. Circulate as before.

b The whole class can decide which weekend sounds the most interesting. Ask them to write out their plans for homework.

Real life (PAGE 110)

Talk about the weather

1 *In a mono-nationality class*, ask the questions to check students know the names of the seasons and practise using them. *In a multi-national class*, put students from different countries into pairs or small groups to discuss the questions. Vocabulary to include: *spring, summer, autumn (UK) or fall (US), winter, the rainy season, the monsoon season, the dry season*, depending on where your students are from.

2 a Ask students *What's the weather like today? What was the weather like yesterday?* to see if they know any vocabulary already. Then students, in pairs, match the phrases with the pictures.

b [T12.9] Students listen and check their answers then listen and repeat the pronunciation. Drill any words the students are finding difficult to pronounce, for example *cloudy* /ˈklaʊdi/, *windy* /ˈwɪndi/.

ANSWERS
1 It's cloudy.   2 It's cold.   3 It's cool.   4 It's foggy.
5 It's hot.   6 It's icy.   7 It's raining.   8 It's snowing.

9 It's sunny.   10 It's warm.   11 It's wet.
12 It's windy.

3 Ask some questions to help students predict the content. For example, *Where is the coldest/hottest/wettest/driest place you know / in the world?* Students read the place names in the box. *Where are they?* You could use a map here to see how many of them students know. Students read the text and make brief notes about each place. Do the first example with them.

ANSWERS
Brazil – it never snows
Chicago – is called 'the Windy City'
El Azizia – the hottest place in the world
Malaysia – has only two seasons a year
Mawsynram – the wettest place in the world
Vostok – the coldest temperature in the world

4 a [T12.10] Introduce the two people and ask students what they know or can guess about the weather in Thailand and Canada. Students read the statements about each country, then listen to the recording and tick the statements which are correct. In pairs they compare their answers.

ANSWERS
Thailand: 1 ✔   2 ✘   3 ✔   4 ✘   5 ✔   6 ✔
Canada: 1 ✔   2 ✘   3 ✔   4 ✘

b Play the recording again for students to correct the statements that were untrue.

ANSWERS
Thailand
2   The cool season is from November to February.
4   It usually lasts about two hours.
Canada
2   The winters aren't really bad. They're cloudy and wet but not cold.
4   The summers are usually sunny and warm.

5 *In a mono-nationality class*, you could do this as a writing activity. If you do it in class, circulate, helping students as needed.

In a multi-national class, students, in pairs or small groups, tell each other about their countries. Focus them on the sentence starters in 5 to help their speaking. Circulate, collecting examples of good language and errors for feedback later. Then you could set the writing task.

ADDITIONAL PRACTICE

Workbook: Listen and read, page 74; Vocabulary: the weather, page 75; Talking about the weather, page 75

Study ... (PAGE 111)

Remembering collocations

1 Write the following on the board and ask students to match the words in the two columns. Introduce the idea of collocation. Ask students how they say these phrases in their own language and if they use the same verbs.

stay	breakfast
do	at home
have	my homework

2 Emphasise how important it is to record collocations where possible and show them two possibilities. You could build up the two methods on the board with them, eliciting the verbs from them. Students then copy these into their vocabulary book on two different pages.

3 Students write their answers in their notebook under the columns page. They work individually and then compare their answers with a partner.

ANSWERS
b study   c play   d do   e listen to   f get / start
g start / finish / leave / go to   h go / travel
i send / get   j ride   k go   l get

Pronunciation spot

Short forms

a 📼 [T12.11] Play the recording or say the sentences yourself and get students to write down what they hear. Then ask them what *I'll / I'd /* and *Let's* mean (*I will, I would, Let us*). Ask the students if they find these short forms easy or difficult to hear.

b 📼 [T12.12] Continue the dictation using the recording. Students check their answers in pairs. They then repeat the sentences, paying attention to the short forms.

ANSWERS
1 <u>I'm</u> coming!   2 We're going to stay at home.
3 <u>I'll</u> post it for you.   4 <u>I'd</u> like to drive.
5 <u>It's</u> raining and I'm really wet!   6 <u>Let's</u> take a taxi.

c Students write down the sentences, then practise them.

Practise ...   (PAGE 111)

Students can do this section independently to monitor their own learning. They can do this section for homework.

1–5 For each exercise, make sure students read the instructions carefully. Provide the answers either by checking as a whole class or by giving them a copy from the *Teacher's Book*.

1 Future intentions

ANSWERS
b   What do you want to do tonight?
c   What would you like for your birthday?
d   Miko wants to visit us next month.
e   I'd like to go for a long walk tomorrow.
f   Where are you going on holiday?
g   I'm going out for a meal.

2 Going out and staying in

ANSWERS
a sport   b a party   c relatives   d the gym
e school

3 Suggestions and offers

ANSWERS
b Good idea.   c Where shall we go?
d How about the beach?   e OK, shall I ring Steve?
f Maybe he'd like to come.
g Yeah, and let's take some food.
h Right, I'll make some sandwiches.

4 The weather

ANSWERS
a sunny   b foggy   c raining   d snowing   e cool
f cloudy   g warm   h windy

Remember!   (PAGE 111)

Ask the students to tick the items they understand and got correct and encourage them to do extra study of any they are unclear about. Students do the *Mini-check* on page 163.

ANSWERS
1 going   2 'm   3 want   4 like   5 do   6 to
7 make   8 go to   9 watch   10 make
11 I'll make some coffee for us.
12 Shall I telephone Pete?
13 Let's have some chocolate.
14 Why don't we stay at home tonight?
15 How about watching that new DVD?
16 sunny   17 cloudy   18 raining   19 snowing
20 windy

module 13

Learning for the future

Note to teachers: At this point in the course, you could decide to do the last three Modules in any order that you want, depending on the time available and your learners' needs.

Vocabulary and speaking
(PAGE 112)

Education and careers

1 **a** Ask students, in pairs, to write down as many school subjects as they know. They then look at the list of subjects and interview each other: *Did you study X at school?* They tick if their partner says *yes*. They can use their *Mini-dictionaries* to check any unknown subjects or ask you. Circulate and help as needed.

b Demonstrate by telling students about yourself. Introduce and drill the following: *I'm very interested in..., I'm not very interested in..., I'm quite interested in..., What about you?* Students in pairs talk about each subject. Circulate and help with pronunciation as needed.

Pronunciation

See *Teacher's tips: helping students with pronunciation* on pages 7–8.

1 🔲 [T13.1] Play the recording or say the subjects yourself. Do the first four examples with the class, showing them the silent vowel in history. Play each word and pause after it. Get students to say the vowel sounds and decide if there is a silent vowel or not.

> **ANSWERS**
> The following words have silent letters:
> history   literature   business studies   languages
> design   medicine   geography

2 Play the recording again and students mark the stressed syllable. Then drill the words as needed. Build up the words gradually, starting with the stressed syllable, to help students with the pronunciation, for example *ca > cation > fication > qualification.*

> **ANSWERS**
> •   •   •   •
> politics   management   science   history
> •   •   •
> literature   business studies   languages
> •   •   •   •
> economics   law   design   medicine
> •   •
> information technology   geography   maths
> •
> engineering

2 Focus students on the photographs and get them in pairs to discuss what is happening. Have class feedback and

---

then ask students to categorise the vocabulary in their notebooks. Students can use their *Mini-dictionary* or ask you. Circulate and help as needed. In the feedback check the meaning and pronunciation of the phrases.

> **ANSWERS**
>
> | school | university | work |
> |---|---|---|
> | go to primary/ secondary school | do a course | choose a career |
> | pass/fail an exam | have an interview | have an interview |
> | take an exam | apply for a course | earn money |
> | do a course | apply for a job | train to be (a chef) |
> | | pass/fail an exam | be unemployed |
> | | get a degree | do a course |
> | | get into university | |
> | | take an exam | |

> **Exercise 2: alternative suggestion**
>
> Put the phrases on sets of cards and ask students to organise them into three categories. They could work as a whole class or in small groups.

ADDITIONAL PRACTICE

RB **Resource bank:** 13A *Education crossword*, page 160

Workbook: Vocabulary: Education and learning, page 76

3 Students in pairs ask and answer the questions. This is an opportunity for freer speaking so circulate and collect examples of good language and errors for feedback later.

Listening (PAGE 113)

My career

1 🔲 [13.2] Focus students on the four photos and explain they are going to listen to people talking about their careers. Ask them to listen and write down any courses or jobs they talk about. Words to check: *qualifications, financial company, journalist, politics.* Play the recording and students work individually and then check in pairs. Circulate and see if you need to replay any parts.

> **ANSWERS**
>
> | | Subjects | Jobs |
> |---|---|---|
> | Will | a course in Information Technology | a van driver; a computer sales company. |
> | Vicki | training to be a maths teacher | worked for a big financial company; a maths teacher. |
> | Francine | French, Spanish, Portuguese | a job where she can use languages, maybe in an international company. |
> | Josh | history and politics at university | a journalist |

2 a Students work in pairs to answer the more detailed listening questions.

ANSWERS
1 Will   2 Francine   3 Vicki   4 Josh   5 Francine
6 Vicki   7 Will   8 Will   9 Josh   10 Vicki

b Play the recording again for students to check their answers.

Language focus 1 (PAGE 114)

Infinitive of purpose

Ask the students to match the beginnings and endings and identify who they refer to. Words to check: *to look after children*, *to get some experience*

ANSWERS
1   He went back to college to get some qualifications.
     Will
2   She stopped work to look after her children.
     Vicki
3   He's writing for his school magazine to get some
     experience.
     Josh
4   She's going to Lisbon to study Portuguese.
     Francine

Grammar

Write on the board: *She's going to Lisbon because she wants to study Portuguese.* Ask students how to say this in a different way. Cross out *because she wants* to show the infinitive of purpose. Students underline the other examples in sentences 1–3. Then they answer the question: *Why are you studying English?* to have some personalised practice.

Highlight:
• that *for study* is incorrect

Refer students to *Language summary A* on page 158.

PRACTICE

1 Do the first example with the students with their books closed, and elicit some ideas. Students write sentences in their notebooks and then compare with a partner. Circulate and help as needed.

POSSIBLE ANSWERS
(there may be other acceptable matches)
b   to find some information; to do some studying;
    to get a book; to check something
c   to check my e-mails; to do some studying; to get
    a book; to check something
d   to meet some friends; to study French; to train as
    a nurse; to do some shopping
e   to look up a word; to find some information;
    to check something
f   to study French; to train as a nurse

g   to meet some friends; to buy a train ticket; to get
    a book; to do some shopping
h   to pass his exams
i   to buy a train ticket
j   to buy a train ticket; to get a book; to do some
    shopping
k   to check my e-mails; to find some information;
    to check something
l   to check my emails; to find some information;
    to check something

2 Students in pairs can suggest other ideas. Circulate and help as needed and then have a whole class feedback.

Exercise 2: additional suggestion

For further practice of infinitives of purpose: Put students into small groups. Tell them they have a lot of money (give them an amount in your currency) and four weeks to visit any four places in the world. They have to decide where to go, why/what they want to do there, and in which order. They nominate a representative who practises how to tell the rest of the class: *First we're going to Paris to climb the Eiffel Tower and to go shopping, then we're going to the south of Spain to relax on the beach...* etc. Let them speak using a map of the world.

ADDITIONAL PRACTICE

Workbook: Infinitive of purpose, page 77

Reading (PAGE 114)

1 Ask students to discuss the questions with a partner or in small groups. *In a multi-nationality class*, ensure each group is composed of students who speak different languages. This is an opportunity for some freer speaking so circulate and listen but don't correct.

2 Ask students to read a–e and check they understand all the words. Then ask them to read the text silently and to match paragraphs 1–5 to a–e. Encourage students to guess the meanings of unknown words in the text. Or they can check in the *Mini-dictionary* or with you. New words: *global, basic/simple, explain, sadly, even (easier)*. Students work individually and then compare their answers.

ANSWERS
a 2   b 3   c 1   d 5   e 4

3 Students, in pairs, ask and answer the questions, which encourages them to read in greater detail. Circulate and help as needed.

ANSWERS
a   In 1930. It had 850 words.
b   To make spelling simpler. It never became popular.
c   It uses a few simple phrases for every possible situation. It has no grammar!
d   The language that people use in e-mails.
e   People don't use Anglic, so it isn't a good idea to learn it. If you are a ships' captain then it's a good idea to learn Seaspeak. If you aren't, then no!
f   Students' own ideas.

In the feedback encourage students to speak freely about their ideas for making English simpler.

Language focus 2 (PAGE 116)

might and *will*

Do the first example with the whole class. Encourage students to work out the meaning of *will/won't*, *might* and *might not* from the context. Students talk about the questions in pairs.

Grammar

1   Ask students to look back at sentences 1–4 and match them with the meanings a–d. They should try and work out the meaning for themselves.

ANSWERS
a   will   b   might   c   might not   d   won't

Highlight:

• the meaning of the verbs – the idea of prediction. As a contrast, refer back to Module 12 – about plans and intentions; ask students to organise these on a cline: *will*, *might*, *might not*, *won't*.
• the use of the base form of the verb after these modal verbs.
• the short (contracted) forms.
• the fact that we don't usually contract *might not*.

2   Drill the four sentences, paying particular attention to a tentative intonation for *might* and *might not* and the diphthong sound in *won't* /wəʊnt/ to make sure it doesn't sound like *want* /wɒnt/.

Refer students to *Language summary B* on page 158 of the *Students' Book*.

PRACTICE

1   Students complete the gaps in the sentences. They then check their answers together. More than one answer is sometimes possible depending on the students' opinions. Circulate and help as needed.

ANSWERS
a   will
b   won't / might not; will / might
c   might, might
d   might
e   will
f   will / might

2   Personalisation task: Introduce the activity by making predictions about your own life and then elicit a few more examples for example a. Highlight and drill some examples with the short form *I'll* which we use when speaking. Students write their ideas. Circulate and check for accuracy.

Pronunciation

1   ▭ [T13.3]   This activity is to practise hearing the presence of *'ll* or *won't*, which can be difficult in natural speech. It focuses on the confusion between *won't* and *want*.

Start with practice of this: write up *won't* and *don't* on the board. Say both and show how the pronunciation is the same. Drill the two words. Then write up *want* and show students how this is different from *won't*. Say *want* and *won't* several times in a different order and ask students to identify which one you are saying. They can then try this with a partner.

Say the sentences below. Students listen and copy you.

I won't live here.   *He won't get married.*

They won't have children.   *I won't be rich.*

Get the students to write a–j down the page in their notebook and write P or F against each one. Play the recording and do the first two examples with the class. They continue and then compare with a partner. Circulate and identify any examples you need to play again.

ANSWERS
a F   b F   c P   d F   e F   f F   g P   h F   i P   j P

2   Students listen to the sentences and copy them. Focus particularly on the pronunciation of *'ll* and *won't*.

ANSWERS
a   I'll see her at work.
b   I won't wait for you.
c   I want to go home.
d   I'll phone him at the weekend.
e   She won't arrive early.
f   I'll get up early.
g   I go to the gym in the morning.
h   We won't walk home.
i   I want to speak to her.
j   I have two children.

ADDITIONAL PRACTICE

[RB]   **Resource bank:** 13B *Looking into the future*, page 161
Workbook: *might*, *might not*, page 79; *will* and *won't* (*probably*), page 79; 9 *might* (*not*), *will* and *won't*, page 80

Task: Find the right course
(PAGES 116–117)

Preparation: reading and speaking

1   Ask students if they want to go, or if they have been, to college or university. Then ask them to read the college

brochure and answer questions a and b. Check: *full-time* and *part-time*. Students can look up unknown words in the *Mini-dictionary* or ask you. Then they compare their answers with a partner.

ANSWERS
a **Leisure and Tourism:** a career in tourism
Information technology: for business or industry
Childcare: for people working with pre-school children in nurseries or at home.
Sports studies: for working in sports centres and swimming pools, etc.
Performing arts: for any career in music, dance or drama, including the theatre and film (this is not explicitly stated)
Fashion design: for fashion and media
b **Full-time:** Leisure and tourism; Performing arts
Part-time: None
Both: Information technology; Fashion design; Sports studies; Childcare
2 years: Fashion design; Performing arts; Sports studies; Childcare

2 **a** Put the students into groups of three (A, B and C) and get each student to read about one of the people. They make notes about the main points (*What job do they want? What type of course do they want? What are their interests?*) and practise explaining these to their classmates.

b Students tell each other about the three people and make notes about each one.

Task: speaking

1 **a** Students read the course information again individually, and choose which courses would be suitable for each person.

b They predict which course each person will choose and why. Circulate and help as needed.

2 Students work in their groups and discuss their ideas. Focus students on the *Useful language* box. You could write up each phrase with an error, for example:

I think best course for Gaby is ...
Oliver will/might to choose ...
Taka might enjoy Sports course

Students try to correct the sentences in pairs and then check in the *Useful language* box; they also read the language for agreeing and disagreeing. Drill the sentences as needed. Students try and agree on the best course. Circulate and collect examples of good language use and errors for feedback later. Get the groups to tell the whole class what they decided.

3 [13.4] Play the recording. Students listen to the choices made by the three people and see how they compare with theirs.

ANSWERS
Taka: Basic information technology course
Oliver: Leisure and tourism
Gaby: None of them. She's going to find a shorter sports studies course at a different college.

4 Students discuss the questions with their group.

Real life (PAGE 118)

Applying for a course

1 *In a mono-nationality class*, ask students if they'd like to go to an English-speaking country to do an English course and why/why not. Also, how they would find a good school.

In an English-speaking country with a multi-nationality class, ask them why they chose your institution, and how they found out about it.

Focus students on the photo of Adriana and check they understand her situation. Ask them to complete the application form, Section A, using the information about Adriana.

ANSWERS
1 Ms
2 Farinelli
3 Adriana Paola
4 20-11-1987
5 female
6 Italian
7 Via Ezio 60, 04300 Latina, Italy
8 a) 02426439 b) the same
9 n/a
10 farinelli@bellquel.lat.it
11 7-53-58-285
12 a) no visa b) n/a

Students, in pairs, invent answers to Section B. Check students' answers to Question 3 to see if they have used the infinitive of purpose.

3 Set the situation and get two students to demonstrate the beginning of the roleplay. For example: *Good morning, can I help you? Yes, I want to register for an English course. I sent you my application form. What's your name? Adriana Farinelli. Okay, can I check the information? How do you spell your surname?... and what's your date of birth?* The administrator can mostly ask questions so that 'Adriana' has more to say than just *'that's right.'* Circulate, collecting examples of good language and errors for feedback later.

4 Students now complete the application form on page 147, using information about themselves. Encourage them to invent any information that they don't have. Circulate and check their writing. They can then act out a similar roleplay with a different partner. Circulate, collecting examples of good language and errors for feedback later.

ADDITIONAL PRACTICE

Workbook: 12 Improve your writing, page 81.

Study ... (PAGE 119)

English outside the classroom

1 Talk to students about how important it is to improve their English outside class; get students to read the examples and try to think of any others.

2 Focus students on the marking system and get them to mark the ideas.

3 Put the students into small groups to discuss the ideas and to choose one to try. Have a whole class discussion about their plans. Set a date for giving feedback on their experiment. Check how students are doing after a week and show interest and encouragement before the 'official' feedback date.

Practise ... (PAGE 119)

Students can do this section independently to monitor their own learning. Or use it for further practice of the language covered in Module 13, or as a test. Make sure students do not look at the *Language summaries* until after they have finished all five exercises. Students can do this section for homework.

1–4 For each exercise, make sure students read the instructions carefully. Provide the answers either by checking as a whole class or by giving them a copy from the *Teacher's Book*.

1 Subjects you study

ANSWERS
b engineering   c design   d economics   e science
f history   g medicine   h literature   i geography

2 Phrases related to study and jobs

If you are doing this in class, put the beginnings and endings on cards and ask students to match these.

ANSWERS
b go to university   c take an exam   d do a degree
e earn money   f apply for a job   g pass an exam
h get a degree   i train as a nurse   j fail an exam

3 Infinitive of purpose

POSSIBLE ANSWERS
(Students may think of different answers)
b   to buy toothpaste, shampoo, etc., to get medicine
c   to swim/go swimming, to play games, to sunbathe, to relax
d   to watch a film, to relax
e   to buy/get petrol, to get water, to get air, to buy sweets, newspapers, etc.
f   to borrow/take back a book, to study, to read, to use a computer
g   to have/drink a coffee, to meet a friend, to have/eat a cake

4 *will* and *might*

Answers depend on the students' opinions.

Pronunciation spot

The sounds /ɒ/, /əʊ/ and /ɔː/

a 🖭 [T13.6] Write the three sounds on the board as titles of columns 1, 2 and 3, and write the three words under them. Play the tape to see if students can hear the difference between the sounds and drill them.

b 🖭 [T13.7] Play the recording and students write 1, 2 or 3 after each word. Or they write the word in the correct column in their notebooks, or you write the words on cards and get students to sort these as they listen.

ANSWERS

course	3
college	1
office	1
home	2
go	2
show	2
more	3
short	3
shop	1
both	2
know	2
perform	3

Remember! (PAGE 119)

Ask the students to tick the exercises they understand and got correct. Encourage them to do extra study on areas they are not so clear about. Students then do the *Mini-check* on page 163 and tell you their scores.

ANSWERS
1 Information technology   2 Geography   3 History
4 Economics   5 Literature   6 passed   7 degree
8 train   9 applied   10 get   11 course   12 money
13 might   14 will   15 might not   16 won't
17 I'm going to the supermarket to buy a few things.
18 We went to the hospital last weekend to visit Rosa.
19 I'm going to meet my boss to talk about my new job.
20 Chris is going to the bank to get some money.

module 14

Keeping in touch

Reading (PAGE 120)

1 Ask students *What is your favourite way to keep in touch with friends?* Elicit different ways of keeping in touch in the last few hundred years. Then ask students to focus on pictures a–c and answer the questions. They can use their *Mini-dictionary* to look up unknown words or ask you.

> **ANSWERS**
> a   500 years ago; 5 months
> b   150 years ago; 2 weeks
> c   1969; 1.3 seconds

2 **a** Students put the items in order and compare with a partner.
b They read the text to check. Words to check or look up in their *Mini-dictionary*: *deliver, by hand, demonstrate, keyboard, enormous*.

> **ANSWERS**
> 1 pen and paper   2 the postage stamp
> 3 the typewriter   4 the telephone
> 5 the fax machine   6 e-mail   7 text messages

3 Students in pairs ask and answer the questions. They can do this orally or write down their answers. Circulate and help as needed.

> **ANSWERS**
> a   by hand
> b   one penny
> c   several times a day
> d   in the same way as in 1871; all the letters in the word 'typewriter' are on the top line.
> e   Around 1876
> f   because they were very heavy: around 13.5 kilos
> g   in 1992
> h   thirty-six billion

4 Do the first example with the students and ask them to continue individually.

> **ANSWERS**
> a the first stamp   b the telephone   c a fax machine
> d walkie-talkies

5 Students, in small groups, discuss the questions. Encourage them to speak freely. Circulate and collect examples of good language use and errors for feedback later.

ADDITIONAL PRACTICE

Workbook: Vocabulary booster: the post, page 87

Vocabulary (PAGE 122)

Ways of communicating

See *Teacher's tips: working with lexical phrases* on pages 9–10 of the *Teachers' Book*.

1 Focus students on the pictures or put these on an overhead transparency. Ask them the names of the items.

> **ANSWERS**
> a   a pen and paper
> b   a mobile
> c   a computer
> d   a fax/answering machine
> e   a letter/card in its envelope
> f   a digital camera

Ask *What can you do on a computer?* to elicit ideas. Ask them to match the phrases in the box with the photos. Circulate and help as needed. Early finishers can compare their answers with a partner.

> **POSSIBLE ANSWERS**
> a   **a pen and paper:** write a note; leave a message; check your messages
> b   **a mobile:** take/send a photo; make a phone call; send/get a text message; check your messages; call someone, etc.
> c   **a computer:** send a photo; write a letter; send/receive an e-mail; go on the Internet; check your messages
> d   **a fax/answering machine:** send a photo; make a phone call; leave a message; check your messages; call someone
> e   **a letter/card and envelope:** post a letter/card; send a card
> f   **a digital camera:** take/send a photo

2 Do the first example with the whole class. Then students, in pairs, write their answers. Circulate and help as needed.

> **POSSIBLE ANSWERS**
> a   send an e-mail; send a text message; make a phone call; call them
> b   send an e-mail; write a letter; send a card
> c   go on the Internet
> d   leave a message
> e   wrote a letter; sent a card
> f   send a card; send a text message; send an e-mail
> g   send an e-mail; send a (post)card; send a text message; call them
> h   write a note; leave a message
> i   send a card; write a letter; send an e-mail; send a text message
> j   make a phone call; send an e-mail; go on the Internet; call someone; send a text message

ADDITIONAL PRACTICE

Workbook: Ways of communicating, page 82; Improve your writing: writing a note, page 87.

Language focus 1 (PAGE 123)

Present perfect

1 [T14.1] Play the first extract and ask students: *What is he talking about: text messaging, writing letters, phone calls...?* (answer: *the Internet*). Then focus students on the list of questions and allow them time to read them. Then they listen and write the letter next to the question. Pause the recording after each extract, if needed. At this stage do not focus on the use of the Present perfect.

ANSWERS
a 3   b 6   c 8   d 5   e 7

2 [T14.2] Play the recording and students listen and complete the gaps. This time they listen in more detail and also focus on the Present perfect. Students can compare answers in pairs.

ANSWERS
a about thirty hours   b any TV   c three computers
d any letters   e five books

Grammar

1 Write on the board:

I _____ about ten e-mails so far today (send)

I _____ three computers in my life (own)

I _____ any letters this week (not write)

and elicit ideas from the students. Complete the sentences, tell them this is the Present perfect, and highlight:

- that the action or state is in the past but connected to the present
- that the time period in each case is not finished: draw a diagram and discuss how these three periods are unfinished. Note: This use of the Present perfect shows that the period of time is not finished and not the activity/action/state.
- that we do not know exactly, or it is not important when these things happened.

2 Use the second example to elicit how we form the Present perfect. Highlight:

- the use of *have/has*
- regular past participles
- irregular past participles

3 Focus students on the table or write it on the board. Students complete the gaps.

ANSWERS
+ 've/'s   – hasn't   ? Have, Has

Refer students to *Language summary A* on page 158.

PRACTICE

1 a Ask individuals some of the questions and demonstrate that they should write full answers to each. Circulate and help as needed.

b Students, in small groups, compare their sentences. Circulate and check their use of the Present perfect.

2 Demonstrate how to find the past participle from the *Mini-dictionary*. Either focus students on the list of verbs or dictate them and students look up the past participles. Circulate and help as needed.

ANSWERS
a lost   b forgotten   c phoned   d paid   e checked
f left   g received   h used   i bought   j taken
k kept   l had

3 Do the first example with the whole class. Elicit answers and introduce *I've never _____ and I've _____lots of___*. Get students to write true sentences about themselves. Words to check: *emergency services*, *buy online*, *a virus* /vaɪrəs/.

4 Elicit and drill the questions and short answers, and then ask students to work with a partner and ask and answer the questions. Demonstrate with the whole class and encourage people to add further information rather than just answering *yes* or *no*.

Pronunciation

See *Teacher's tips: helping students with pronunciation* on pages 7–8.

1 [T14.3] Play the recording and students write down the eight sentences. They check their answers on page 174.

2 Students listen again and underline the stressed words.

ANSWERS
1 I've <u>lost</u> my <u>mobile</u>.
2 He's <u>forgotten</u> to <u>post</u> this <u>letter</u>.
3 She's <u>phoned</u> <u>three</u> times to<u>day</u>.
4 We've <u>sent</u> her a <u>card</u>.
5 Have you <u>sent</u> that e-mail?
6 Has she <u>written</u> to you?
7 I <u>haven't</u> <u>spoken</u> to her this <u>week</u>.
8 He <u>hasn't</u> <u>called</u> to<u>day</u>.

3 Students listen and repeat, focusing on the stressed words. This helps them with the short (contracted) forms.

ADDITIONAL PRACTICE

RB **Resource bank:** Learner training worksheet D: Irregular verbs, page 162; 14A *The Travellers' Club* page 163

Workbook: Irregular past participles, page 82; Present perfect, page 83; Positive and negative, page 83; Questions and short answers, page 84; Pronunciation, page 84; Regular past participles, page 85

Language focus 2 (PAGE 124)

Time phrases with the Present perfect and Past simple

1 Ask students: *Who do you send the most e-mails to?* and *What kind of messages do you often send?* Students discuss in pairs. Then they read the two e-mails and answer the questions.

ANSWERS
E-mail to Mike: brother and sister; Katie is asking Mike to go round and check that their mother is okay because she has been ill.
E-mail to Grace: two friends; Rosie is asking Grace to come out for a meal because Rosie has just passed her driving test.

2 Ask students to underline the Past simple and Present perfect verbs in the e-mails in two different ways. Demonstrate with the first two examples from the e-mail to Mike. Students check their answers in pairs. Circulate and help as needed.

Grammar

1 Past simple

a Write the three examples on the board and in each case ask students *When...? e.g. When did I try to call you?* to focus students on the time expressions.

b Focus them on the use of the Past simple with *When* questions.

Use diagrams to highlight this use:

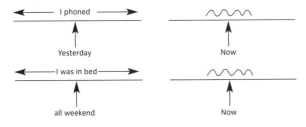

Highlight:
- that we use the Past simple when we know exactly when an action happened
- that the action is finished
- that it can be a short action *(phoned)* or a longer one *(was in bed/lived)*
- examples of past time phrases with the Past simple: *last night, yesterday afternoon, last month, in September, in 2004, all weekend*, etc.

2 Present perfect

a Ask students to write the question from these prompts: *you / speak / to Mum this week?*

Use a diagram to represent this:

Highlight:
- that we don't know exactly when in this week
- that this week is not finished
- some other examples of phrases: *this month, this year, today, so far this week, in my life, ever* and *never* (= in your life up to now)

b Point out other phrases we use with the Present perfect: *just, recently* and *ever/never*.

Refer students to *Language summary B* on page 159.

PRACTICE

1 Students choose the correct tense in the e-mails. Do the first two examples with them and then they work in pairs. Check: *pick up*. Circulate and help as needed, referring them back to the *Grammar* box as necessary. In the feedback check the time phrases which helped the students to decide on the correct answer.

ANSWERS
a we've just arrived b finally landed c stayed
d caught e has just picked us up f really enjoyed
g were fantastic h was great i has started
j has gone

2 **a** Do the first example with the students. Check by asking: *are we asking about an exact time? Are we asking about your life up to now?* Students continue individually and then compare in pairs. Circulate and help as needed.

ANSWERS
1 Have you passed your driving test? When did you pass?
2 Have you taken any exams recently? When did you take them?
3 Have you eaten in a restaurant this week? When and where did you go?
4 Have you been ill at all this year? When were you ill?
5 Have you ever been in hospital?
6 Have you ever been/gone on a long flight? When and where did you go?
7 Have you been/gone to stay with friends recently? Who did you visit?
8 Has anyone you know started a new job recently? When did they start?

Language note:

You could give a mini-lesson on the two past participles for *go*: *gone* and *been*. See Remember! section in *Language summary B* on page 159. In example 6 above both are possible.

b Students ask and answer the questions in pairs. Check the short answers: *Yes, I have* and *No, I haven't* before they start. Circulate and check that students use the correct tense. Collect examples of good language and errors for feedback later.

ADDITIONAL PRACTICE

RB Resource bank: 14B *Life boxes*, page 164

Workbook: Time words with the Present perfect, page 85; Word order, page 85; Time words with the Present perfect and Past simple, page 86

Real life (PAGE 125)

Telephoning

1 **a** Ask students *Have you ever made a phone call in English? Who to? Did you find it easy or difficult? Why?* Then focus students on the picture of Jane and ask them to read her notes. *Who is she going to call and why?* and check the answers.

b [cassette] [T14.4] Play conversation 1 and ask students to write 1 in the correct place on her list. Play the remainder of the recording and students put the numbers on the list.

> **ANSWERS**
> 2   1   4   3

c Students in pairs write the answers. Circulate to see if you need to play the recording again.

> **ANSWERS**
> 1 She didn't speak to Paul. She'll call again this afternoon.
> 2 She spoke to Julia at Thompson travel. There was a problem.
> 3 She didn't speak to Tania. She left a message.
> 4 She didn't speak to her Dad. He's going to call her back.

2 Play the conversations again and students complete the gaps. They compare their answers in pairs.

> **ANSWERS**
> a can I speak to   b he's not here   c he'll be back
> d this is; I'm calling about
> e I'm not here at the moment   f leave a message
> g can you call me   h it's me; Dad there
> i ask him to call me

Pronunciation

See *Teacher's tips: helping students with pronunciation* on pages 7–8.

1 [cassette] [T14.5] Play the first example. Highlight the polite intonation by repeating the question in a very flat tone, to sound less polite. Simply ask students to copy the questions. Or you use arrows to show the movement of the voice. Encourage students to start quite high and move their voice after the main stressed syllable:

Hello, can I speak to Paul please?

Is that Julia?   Can you call me back?

Is Dad there?   Can you ask him to call me?

2 [cassette] [14.6] Play the recording and students listen and repeat.

---

3 Students, in pairs or individually, complete the conversations. Circulate and help as needed.

> **POSSIBLE ANSWERS**
> a
> 1 Can I speak to Joe, please?
> 2 Can you ask him to phone me?
> 3 (give your phone number)
> 4 Thank you. Bye.
>
> b Hello, Sergio, this is....... Can you phone me back? It's about ... My number is..../
> Hello, Sergio, this is ...... I'm just ringing to .....

4 Students now practise both calls. Circulate and help with the pronunciation as needed.

ADDITIONAL PRACTICE

[RB] **Resource bank:** 14C *On the phone*, page 165
Workbook: Real life: Telephoning, page 86

Task: Analyse a questionnaire (PAGE 126)

Preparation: reading

Ask students to read the questionnaire and complete the answers. Encourage them to use their *Mini-dictionary* or ask you for unknown words. Check the meaning of: *to keep in touch with, essential, the main way, to chat, to spend hours chatting, a chat room, prefer, features (of a mobile), to pay attention*. Circulate and help as needed.

Task: speaking

1 Get a student to ask you Question 1. Explain why you feel the way you do. Then ask the students Question 2 and encourage them to expand on their answer. Then reply, using one of the phrases in *Useful language* box a. Drill the four phrases. Then students, in pairs, ask and answer the questions. Encourage students to explain their answers and respond naturally.

2 Ask a pair of students what was the same (introduce *similarities*) and what was different (introduce *differences*) in their answers. Point out that you want the most important points only. Focus students on *Useful language* b and check the use of the third person 's'. Students plan their summaries and write down ideas, Then they tell another student. Circulate and help as needed.

3 Students work in new groups but not with their original partner. They discuss each question and all summarise their own and their partners' answers. Weaker students read from their notes and stronger students try to remember the main points. Circulate and collect examples of good language and errors for feedback later.

4 Students work as a whole class or they remain in groups and discuss the question. This is an opportunity for freer practice so encourage students to express themselves without worrying too much about accuracy. If students have worked in small groups, end with a whole class feedback.

Study ... (PAGE 127)

Revising

1 This section focuses on revising what they have learnt during the course. Some students may already revise regularly whilst others never do anything or only revise before tests! Students work in pairs or small groups to discuss their choice of answer a or b in each case. Circulate, listening to their ideas.

2 Have a whole class discussion about their answers. Recommend the more systematic ideas (a,b,b). Tell them that research has shown that regular, small-scale revision is an effective way to help them remember. Elicit other ideas from the class or suggest some yourself.

Practise ... (PAGE 127)

Students can do this section independently to monitor their own learning. Or use it for further practice of the language covered in Module 14, or as a test. Make sure students do not look at the *Language summaries* until after they have finished all four exercises. Students can do this section for homework.

1—4 For each exercise, make sure students read the instructions carefully. Provide the answers either by checking as a whole class or by giving them a copy from the *Teacher's Book*.

1 Ways of communicating

> **ANSWERS**
> b leave a message
> c send a text message; make a phone call; call someone
> d check your messages
> e send her/him/them a card

2 Present perfect

> **ANSWERS**
> b 've never broken c 've missed d 've never stolen
> e 've gone / been f 've just had

3 Time phrases with the Present perfect and Past simple

> **ANSWERS**
> b PP c PS d PP e PS f PP

4 Telephone language

> **ANSWERS**
> a can I speak to b he's not here
> c ask him to call me
> d of course e call me back

Pronunciation spot

The sounds /æ/ and /ʌ/

a Show students the irregular verb list on page 149. They should complete the gaps.

> **ANSWERS**
> 2 sang sung 3 drank drunk 4 rang rung

b 📼 [T14.7] They listen to the recording or to you and check their answers. Model the difference between the two sounds and drill the students.

c 📼 [T14.8] Play the recording. Students listen and decide which sound they hear. They write the two sounds on two pieces of paper and hold up the one they hear or simply write down which sound in their notebook.

> **ANSWERS**
> 1 stamp   1
> 2 chat   1
> 3 month   2
> 4 worried   2
> 5 carry   1
> 6 camera   1
> 7 just   2
> 8 fantastic 1
> 9 love   2
> 10 study   2

Students can then listen again and repeat. Check their pronunciation of the two sounds.

Remember! (PAGE 127)

Ask students to tick all the items they understand and got correct. Encourage them to do extra study of areas that were weaker. Students then do the *Mini-check* on page 163 and tell you their scores.

> **ANSWERS**
> 1 Leila hasn't been to work this week because she's ill.
> 2 Have the others gone home? 3 I've broken my arm.
> 4 Anita has just called – can you call her back?
> 5 It hasn't rained this week. 6 went
> 7 haven't spoken 8 did you start 9 have never sent
> 10 was born 11 make 12 leave 13 take 14 post
> 15 send 16 Is Ed there? 17 Sorry, he's not here.
> 18 Is that Sonia? 19 Can I speak to Ahmed, please?
> 20 Can you ask him to call me, please?

module 15

Going places

Vocabulary (PAGE 128)

Things in a town

1 Ask students to tell their partner their favourite city, either in their own country or abroad, and why they like it. Then focus students on the vocabulary and ask them to find these things in the photos. They work in pairs and use their *Mini-dictionary* for unknown words or ask you. Circulate and identify any new words to check later.

ANSWERS

1	Venice	a canal, a square
2	Kyoto	a temple
3	Istanbul	a mosque, a river
4	Rio de Janeiro	a mountain, a statue, beautiful views
5	St Petersburg	a palace, a river

2 **a** [T15.2] Play the first extract and ask students to write the number 1 next to any of the vocabulary Fabrizio speaks about. Check the answers and then play the other extracts, pausing after each one for students to number the vocabulary. Students compare their answers in pairs. Circulate to see if you need to replay any parts of the recording.

ANSWERS

1 Venice: canals, a square, a cathedral, museums, palaces, bridges
2 Kyoto: traditional buildings, palaces, temples, gardens, modern buildings
3 Istanbul: hills, beautiful views, mosques, palaces, bridges, market, shopping centres, modern buildings
4 Rio de Janeiro: a beach, mountains, a statue, a sports stadium
5 St Petersburg: a palace, an art gallery, a river, churches and cathedrals

b Students, in small groups, discuss which cities they'd like to go to. Ask them to choose two out of the five and give their reasons.

Pronunciation

See *Teacher's tips: helping students with pronunciation* on pages 7–8.

[T15.2] Say *river* and ask students *How many syllables are there?* and *Where's the stress?* Put the table on the board and get students to copy it in their notebooks. Play the recording and students write the words in the correct column. Drill the vocabulary, paying attention to the stress.

ANSWERS

●•	•●	●••	•●•
mountain palace castle building market temple garden statue	canal	gallery stadium	cathedral museum

3 Students, in pairs, look at the postcards on page 145. Each student in turn takes a postcard and talks about it. (*There's a ...... It's got a ...... I can see some ....*) and their partner says which one it is.

Note to the teacher: The postcards show (clockwise from top left):

Sydney postcard: Sydney Harbour Bridge, Sydney Olympic Stadium, Sydney Opera House and Bondi Beach

Budapest postcard: a castle in the central park near Hero Square, Elizabeth Bridge over the River Danube, Vaci Utca – a famous shopping street

Barcelona postcard: Plaça Real, Gaudí House, a section of the Ramblas, a park

London postcard: Tower Bridge, Nelson's Column in Trafalgar Square, the Serpentine Gallery in Hyde Park

4 Students describe their town/city or a town/city they like very much to a partner. Circulate and help as needed.

ADDITIONAL PRACTICE

Workbook: Town facilities page 88; Listen and read: unusual places to visit, page 91

Listening (PAGE 129)

A tour of Edinburgh

1 Ask students as a whole class: *Where's Scotland? What do you know about it? What's the capital city?* Then ask students in pairs: *What do you know about Edinburgh?* Students look at the photos to get ideas.

Note to the teacher: Edinburgh /edɪnbʌrə/ is the capital of Scotland and is in the south-east of the country. It is built on a volcanic rock and has a castle and some interesting architecture. It is a university city and a tourist centre, famous for its castle, museum, whiskey, bagpipes, kilts, shops and pubs. In the summer, the Edinburgh Festival is an internationally famous festival of theatre and music.

2 [T15.3] Set the context of two tourists in Edinburgh, Rosa and Marcus. They are on a bus tour in the city. Play the recording so that students can match the pictures to the extracts. They work individually and then check with a partner.

ANSWERS

1 e 2 c 3 b 4 a 5 d

3 Allow students time to read the sentences and check any unknown vocabulary in their *Mini-dictionary*. Play the recording for students to complete the information. This practises their ability to extract specific information from a listening. They can hear certain sections more than once and you could pause the recording after each extract. They check their answers in pairs.

> **ANSWERS**
> a 900 b 1.6 kilometres c 500 d 1572
> e four thousand f nine o'clock g 1567

4 Students here practise making questions. Students work in pairs. Half the pairs write questions for a–d and half write questions for e–f above. Then students work with a new partner from the other half of the class and ask their questions. Students could close their books and try to remember the answers. Circulate and help as needed.

POSSIBLE QUESTIONS

How old is St Margaret's Chapel?
How long is the Royal Mile?
How old is John Knox's house?
When did John Knox die?
How many paintings are there in the Scottish National Gallery?
When does the Gallery open?
When did Mary Queen of Scots live in Holyrood?

5 Students, in small groups, discuss the questions. This is freer speaking practice so focus on communication rather than accuracy.

Language focus 1 (PAGE 130)

Prepositions of movement

1 Introduce *depressed* and ask students: *What do you usually do when you're depressed?* Then focus students on the first picture of Richard, establish he's very depressed and elicit ideas why. Then students, individually, look at the pictures and complete the gaps. They check their answers in pairs.

2 [T15.4] Play the recording for students to check their answers.

> **ANSWERS**
> b building c road d park e bridge f river
> g statue h steps i taxi j airport

Grammar

Allow students time to look at the prepositions and diagrams in the *Grammar* box. Then students close their books. Draw the diagrams on the board and elicit the correct prepositions.

Highlight:
• the use of *through / out of* also for looking *through/out of* a window
• the pronunciation of *through*
• the idea that *from/to* refer to points and *out of / into* usually refer to three dimensional objects. This explains why you walk *out of* an airport or station (seen as a building) but *from* Miami Airport seen as a point.

PRACTICE

Pronunciation

[T15.4] Play the recording again. Students listen to each phrase and repeat it, paying attention to the stress. Drill as necessary.

1 Students close their books and, in pairs, try and remember Richard's walk. Circulate and help as needed.

2 Students, in pairs, discuss the prepositions that can be used with the nouns. Check *under*. Have a whole class feedback.

> **POSSIBLE ANSWERS**
> **a bridge:** over, under, across, past, to, from
> **a field:** across, past, to, from
> **a square:** across, past, to, from
> **a shopping centre:** into, out of, through, past, to, from
> **the platform at a station:** along, to, from
> **a road:** along, across, up, down, past, to, from
> **a hill:** up, down, past, to, from
> **a river:** along, across, over, into, out of, up, down, to, from

3 a Focus students on the picture and tell them it is in Switzerland. Students, in pairs, identify the things in the box. They can use their *Mini-dictionary* to check unknown words. Drill the pronunciation as needed.

> **ANSWERS**
> All the items are in the picture.

b Do the first two examples with the students, then they continue individually and check their answers in pairs. Check the meaning of the *(Oberalp) Pass*.

> **ANSWERS**
> 1 out of 2 from 3 to 4 through 5 through
> 6 over 7 down 8 over 9 out of 10 past
> 11 into 12 up

4 a Students, in pairs, describe the journey covering the text. Their partner reads the text and corrects/prompts them. Circulate and help as needed.
b Students discuss the question.

ADDITIONAL PRACTICE

RB Resource bank: 15A *Prepositions pelmanism*, page 166
Workbook: Prepositions of movement, page 89

Language focus 2 (PAGE 132)

have to, don't have to, can and *can't*

1 Focus students on the signs and get them to match the signs with the places. They can use their *Mini-dictionary* for unknown words.

ANSWERS
a in the street   b in the street   c in the street
d in a hospital, in a museum
e at an airport, in a hospital, in a museum
f in a hospital, in a museum   g in a park
h at an airport   i in a museum
j at an airport, in a museum   k at an airport
l at an airport, in a hospital, in a museum
m in a park

2 Write these sentences on the board or use an overhead transparency and ask students to match them to the pictures. They should be able to do this without knowing *have to* and *don't have to*.

ANSWERS
a, c, b

Grammar

Write these explanations on the board or use an overhead transparency. Check students understand *necessary*, and then ask them to match the meanings with the verbs. They compare their ideas in pairs.

ANSWERS
1 *have to*   2 *don't have to*   3 *can*   4 *can't*

Highlight:
- the meaning of the four modal verbs by using the classroom situation: *You don't have to wear a uniform / bring a monolingual dictionary* etc., and by asking questions: *Is it necessary to bring a monolingual dictionary?* (No). *If you want to bring one, can you?* (Yes).
- the *he/she/it* form: *has to*
- the opposite of *have to* (necessary) is *can't* (not okay)

    Refer students to *Language summaries B and C on page 159.*

PRACTICE

1 **a/b** Students match the signs to the sentences then they complete the gaps. They work individually and then compare with a partner.

ANSWERS
1f can't   2g can't   3e can't
4i have to, don't have to   5l can't   6j can, can't
7k have to   8d can't   9m have to   10h can

2 **a** Ask students to write at least two sentences about each situation. Circulate and help as needed.

b Students compare their answers in pairs. Circulate and help as needed.

POSSIBLE ANSWERS
Note: Allow different answers as rules vary from country to country.

school
- You have to wear a uniform
- You have to obey instructions
- You can have short hair
- You don't have to earn your living
- You have to study
- You have to take exams
- You can't smoke
- You have to work hard

prison
- You have to wear a uniform
- You have to obey instructions
- You can't go out in the evening
- You can have short hair
- You don't have to earn your living
- You can study but you don't have to
- You can watch TV
- You can take exams
- You can smoke
- You have to get up early

the army
- You have to wear a uniform
- You have to do a lot of exercise
- You have to obey instructions
- You can't go out in the evening usually
- You have to have short hair
- You have to earn your living
- You can study
- You can watch TV
- You don't have to take exams
- You can't smoke
- You have to work hard
- You have to get up early

Pronunciation

1 🔊 [T15.5] Play the recording and students write down the sentences. Focus them on the pronunciation of *have to*. This is best done by concentrating on the stressed words and working backwards: *a uniform > wear a uniform > have to wear a uniform > you have to wear a uniform.*

ANSWERS
a You have to wear a uniform.
b You don't have to take exams.
c You don't have to study
d You have to get up early.
e You have to do a lot of exercise.
f You have to have short hair.
g You have to obey instructions
h You don't have to earn your living.

2 Play each sentence again for the students to listen and repeat.

ADDITIONAL PRACTICE

RB **Resource bank:** 15B *Springfield Hotel*, page 167

Workbook: *have to, don't have to*, page 89; Questions and short answers, page 90; *have to, don't have to, can, can't*, page 90

Real life (PAGE 133)

Following directions

1 Ask students the questions or put them in pairs to ask and answer and then have a whole class feedback.

2 Elicit these phrases by drawing a quick basic sketch of the local area and playing the part of a stranger. Model and drill the sentences as needed and write them on the board, paying attention to the prepositions and use of articles.

3 **a** [T15.6] Focus students on the four maps. Do the first example with the whole class, asking them the name of the place and where it is. They mark this with a cross. Play the remainder of the recording whilst students mark the destinations and names on the maps. They check in pairs. Check: *cashpoint*

b [15.7] Play the sentences for students to complete. They check their answers in pairs. Circulate to see if you need to replay any sentences. In the feedback, drill the phrases as needed.

> **ANSWERS**
> 1 near here   2 on the right   3 where's the nearest
> 4 near here; straight on; on the left; about 200
> 5 is this the way   6 the first street on the left
> 7 go straight on; a hundred metres
> 8 second street; the right.

4 Refer the students to the tapescript on page 175 and get students to read the conversations. Circulate and check their pronunciation and accuracy.

5 Demonstrate with an example and then students roleplay the situation in pairs. Circulate and collect examples of good language use and errors for feedback later.

ADDITIONAL PRACTICE

RB **Resource bank:** 15C *It's the first on the left*, page 168

Workbook: Real life: Following directions, page 92

Task: Plan a website about your town (PAGE 134)

Preparation: vocabulary and reading

1 Tell students you want to visit a particular city for a weekend and want ideas where to visit. Ask them *Where can I find information?* Elicit ideas from students and then ask them what they usually do.

2 Focus students on the vocabulary in the box; in pairs they check they understand the adjectives and use their *Mini-dictionary* or ask you about any unknown ones. Circulate and check the meanings of any new words. Refer them to 'website' on pages 134 and 135 and ask them to complete the gaps with suitable words. They work individually and then compare their answers.

> **POSSIBLE ANSWERS**
> b   traditional/interesting/attractive
> c   comfortable/friendly/traditional/modern/attractive/ lively/peaceful / value for money
> d   traditional/delicious / excellent food friendly /excellent service
> e   traditional/interesting/modern/fashionable/excellent
> f   friendly/traditional/interesting/attractive/lively
> g   difficult/asy
> h   friendly/lively / fashionable club / friendly/lively / fun atmosphere
> i   fun / value for money
> j   traditional/attractive/peaceful

> **Language note:**
> There are many possible answers but those above are the most likely collocations with each item. In example f, if students say *very excellent* you will need to explain we can't use *very* with a word that already means *very (good)*. You cannot use *very* with *delicious, value for money* or *fun*.

Task: speaking

1 **a** Explain the task and get students to think of one or two places they could choose.

b Students work in pairs, on the same town, or they choose to work individually if they have selected a town unknown to other people. Refer students to the different sections and get them to write down places to include under each section. Circulate and help as needed, especially with vocabulary and phrases.

2 Students refer to the website to help them describe the different places. They write these ideas down either in note form or fully. Circulate and help as needed.

3 Reorganise students so that they are working with a new partner. They choose one of the two options for speaking practice. Focus students on the relevant section of the *Useful language* box. Put the phrases on an overhead transparency, drill each one and then cover it and students try to remember it.
Circulate and collect examples of good language and errors for feedback later.

> **Follow up: writing**
> Choose the most relevant option for your class.
>
> **Option 1:** if you do this in class, circulate and check students' work as they write. Students can exchange their introductions with another student and comment on whether they'd like to visit the place. Alternatively, do this activity for homework.
>
> **Option 2:** introduce this the day before and ask students to bring in pictures of the town they will be talking about, possibly from the Internet. If they will be writing about the town where they are studying, you can bring in some pictures from a tourist brochure or a website. Students work in small groups to make the posters and then exhibit them around the classroom. Circulate and help as needed.

ADDITIONAL PRACTICE

Workbook: Vocabulary: Adjectives to describe towns, page 93;
Improve your writing: A postcard, page 94

Consolidation, Modules 11–15 (PAGES 136–137)

A Verb practice

You could introduce this with a picture of the Simpson family or
by playing an extract from a Simpsons cartoon and eliciting
what students already know about them.

> **ANSWERS**
> 2 watch   3 was born   4 was   5 started   6 invented
> 7 gave   8 has got   9 were   10 paid   11 made
> 12 have made   13 became   14 have appeared

B Articles

Check students know the basic story of Robin Hood. You could
bring in a picture to elicit information.

> **ANSWERS**
> 2 –   3 the   4 a   5 the   6 a   7 a   8 –   9 a
> 10 the   11 the   12 the   13 –   14 the   15 a
> 16 the   17 the   18 the

C Writing and speaking

1 Students can start by trying to write the dialogues from
memory and then refer back to the relevant pages to
improve what they have written. Circulate and check for accuracy.

2 Ask students to read the dialogues aloud and mark the
main stresses. They should also try to sound polite where
necessary. Circulate and help as needed.

3 Students act out their conversations and the rest of the
class say what the situation is. If your class is very large,
choose one pair for each situation.

D Listening: Song: *Trains and Boats and Planes*

1 Students check the words and predict the story of the
song. They can work in pairs and then have a whole class
feedback.

2 [C1] Play the song up to the end of the first red line
and then ask students *Is it the same?* Students should
circle the word that is different but at this stage should not try
to correct it.

3 Students listen again and write in the correct words.

> **ANSWERS**
> | a journey | a trip | Carried | took |
> |---|---|---|---|
> | are | were | ring | star |
> | carried | took you away | country | world |
> | come back | return | wait | 'm waiting |
> | wait | 'm waiting | watch | see |
> | land | sea | here | home |

4 Students decide, in pairs, which is the correct story.

> **ANSWER**
> b

5 Students discuss the questions together.

E Vocabulary: Word groups

Students work individually to find the words.

> **ANSWERS**
> **animals:** kangaroo, elephant
> **weather:** foggy, windy, snowing
> **school subjects:** engineering, maths, languages
> **ways of communicating:** letter, e-mail, phone
> **things in a town:** art gallery, sports stadium

Resource bank
Index of activities

Activity	Language point	When to use	Time (minutes)
1A Nice to meet you	Names and countries; *to be*	after *Language focus 1*, *Practice*, exercise 3, page 9 or after *Vocabulary*, *Nationalities*, *Pronunciation*, page 10	15–25
1B The English class	Personal information; third person of *to be*	after *Language focus 4*, *Grammar*, section on Questions with *be*, page 12	15–30
1C Short answer snap	Short answers with *to be*	after *Language focus 4*, *Practice*, exercise 2, page 13	15–20
2A What's this?	*This, that, these, those*	after *Vocabulary Pronunciation*, page 19	15–25
2B Who's got a Ferrari?	*Have got*	after *Language focus 2*, *Practice*, exercise 2, page 20	20–30
2C The family	Family vocabulary; possessive adjectives and *'s*	after *Language focus 3*, *Practice*, exercise 4, page 22	20–35
3A Pick four cards	Present simple questions with *you*	after *Language focus 1*, *Practice*, exercise 2, page 27	15–25
3B Pronoun stars	Subject and object pronouns	after *Language focus 2*, *Practice*, exercise 3, page 29	15–25
3C Time pelmanism	Ways of telling the time	after *Real life*, *Pronunciation*, page 30	15–25
4A Things you love and hate	Present simple; *like + -ing*	after *Language focus 1*, *Practice*, exercise 3, page 35	15–30
4B Three people I know	Present simple *yes / no* questions *he* and *she*	after *Language focus 2*, *Practice*, exercise 4, page 37	20–30
4C Always, sometimes, never	Present simple; adverbs of frequency	after *Language focus 3*, *Practice*, exercise 2, page 38	15–25
4D Verb dominoes	Verbs and nouns that go together	after *Language focus 3*, *Practice*, exercise 2, page 38	15–25
5A The perfect holiday	*Can* and *can't* for possibility	after *Language focus 1*, *Practice*, exercise 3, page 45	25–40
5B Transport crossword	Vocabulary related to transport	after *Real life*, page 49 i.e. at the end of the whole module as a general revision	20–30
Learner-training worksheet A	Using the *Mini-dictionary*	any time after the end of Module 5	15–30
6A Food battleships	*There is / there are*; food vocabulary; *some* and *any*	after *Language focus 2*, *Practice*, exercise 3, page 55	20–30
6B The recipe game	*Some* and *any*; food vocabulary	after *Language focus 2*, *Practice*, exercise 3, page 55	25–35
6C Sports stars	*How much* and *How many* with the Present simple	after *Language focus 3*, *Practice*, page 56	25–35
7A The history quiz	Past simple and past time phrases	after *Real Life*, exercise 3, page 65	15–25
7B Past tense bingo	Irregular past tenses	at the end of *Unit 7*, page 67	20–40
8A Looking back	Past simple *yes/no* questions	after *Language focus 2*, *Practice*, exercise 1, page 73	10–20

Activity	Language point	When to use	Time (minutes)
8B John Wayne	Past simple and question words	after *Language focus 2, Practice*, exercise 4, page 73	25–35
8C Safe at last!	Past simple	after *Language focus 2, Practice*, exercise 4, page 73	30–45
9A New Year's Eve	Comparative adjectives	after *Language focus 1, Practice*, exercise 2, page 79	20–30
9B A superlative survey	Superlative adjective	after *Language focus 2, Practice*, exercise 2, page 80	15–25
9C Shopping crossword	Vocabulary related to shopping	at the end of *Module 9*, page 85	20–30
Learner-training worksheet B	Present continuous: spelling the *-ing* form	after the *Grammar box* in Module 10, page 86	15–25
10A What's Sam doing?	Present continuous	after *Language focus 1, Practice*, exercise 3, page 87	20–30
10B A letter home	Present simple and continuous (question forms)	after *Language focus 2, Practice*, exercise 3, page 90	25–40
10C Identity parades	Vocabulary for describing people and clothes	after *Vocabulary*: describing people, *Practice*, exercise 4, page 90	25–40
11A Can you or can't you?	*Can* and *can't* for ability	after *Language focus 1, Practice*, exercise 2, page 97	15–25
11B The dinner party	Question words and tenses	after *Language focus 2, Practice*, exercise 2, page 99	25–40
11C The numbers game	Different ways of saying numbers	after *Real life*, exercise 3, page 99	15–30
Learner-training worksheet C	Recording new vocabulary	any time after the end of Module 11	20–30
12A Future walkabout	Future intentions: *going to, would like to* and *want to*	after *Language focus 1, Practice*, exercise 4, page 105	15–25
12B Collocation snap	Verb/noun collocations	after *Language focus 1, Practice*, exercise 4, page 105	15–25
12C The school party	Suggestions and offers	after *Language focus 2, Practice*, exercise 3, page 107	25–35
13A Education crossword	Vocabulary related to education	after *Vocabulary and speaking*, exercise 3, page 113	20–30
13B Looking into the future	Modal verbs for possibility: *might, will*	after *Language focus 2, Practice*, exercise 2, page 114	20–35
Learner-training worksheet D	Irregular verbs	after Module 14, *Language focus 1, Grammar* or *Practice 1*, page 123	15–30
14A The Travellers' Club	Present perfect questions with *ever*	after *Language focus 1, Practice*, exercise 4, page 123	20–30
14B Life boxes	Present perfect and Past simple	after *Language focus 2, Practice*, exercise 2, page 125	20–30
14C On the phone	Language for telephoning	after *Real life*, exercise 4, page 125	25–35
15A Preposition pelmanism	Prepositions of movement	after *Language focus 1, Practice*, exercise 4, page 131	15–25
15B Springfield Hotel	*have to, don't have to, can, can't*	after *Language focus 2, Practice*, exercise 2, page 133	25–35
15C It's the first on the left	Language for giving directions	after *Real life, Practice*, exercise 5, page 133	20–35
15D Revision board game	All the language in the Students' Book	after *Module 15*, page 135	25–45

Test one (modules 1–5) pages 172–174   **Test two** (modules 6–10) pages 175–177   **Test three** (modules 11–15) pages 178–180

Instructions for activities pages 101–113   **Resource bank key** pages 181–184

Instructions

1A Nice to meet you

You will need: One role card per student.

- If you do this activity after Practice exercise 2 on page 9, pre-teach the following countries: *France, Australia, Japan, Turkey, Korea.* If you do it after Vocabulary on page 10, pre-teach the following nationalities: *Mexican, Argentinian, Egyptian.*
- Give one role card to each student and deal with any pronunciation problems individual students may have. If you have more than sixteen students, distribute duplicate role cards or make your own.
- Students move around the room and ask each other questions to find out their classmates' new names and countries. If it is not possible for your class to move around the room, they should talk to as many people as possible sitting near them. **Students must try to remember the answers, but they are not allowed to write anything down.**
- Encourage students to include *Nice to meet you. / You too.* and *How are you? / I'm fine, thanks.* in their conversations, and to introduce students to each other using *This is ..., He's/She's from ...* wherever possible.
- Students work in pairs and ask each other the names/nationalities of the other people in the class using *What's his/her name?* and *Where's he/she from?* If necessary, students can make notes of their answers at this stage.
- Students check their answers with another.

You can also use the same cards to practise nationality adjectives. Follow the same procedure but in feedback stage encourage students to use nationalities: *She's Korean.*

The following names are male: *Diego, Wang Yong, Ahmed, Toshi, Peter, Ali, Ross, Jeff.* The others are female.

1B The English class

You will need: one copy of Worksheet A *and one copy of* Worksheet B *per pair of students*

- Students work in pairs. Give a copy of *Worksheet A* to Student A and a copy of *Worksheet B* to Student B. **Students are not allowed to look at each other's worksheets.**
- Students take it in turns to ask their partner questions about the people in the picture in order to complete the information boxes on their worksheets. For example, for the box about Frank, Student A needs to ask *How old is Frank?* and *What's his job?*, while Student B needs to ask *Where's Frank from?* and *Is he married?* If the box relates to two people, students should ask questions with *they* where appropriate.
- Students continue asking questions until both students have all the information. If a pair of students finishes early, they can check their answers by reading out the information on their worksheet to each other.

1C Short answer snap

You will need: one set of Question cards *and one set of* Answer cards *for each pair of students*

- Students work in pairs. Give a set of *Question cards* to Student A and a set of *Answer cards* to Student B. Tell students to shuffle the cards and put them face down in a pile in front of them. Students will also need a pen and paper to keep score.
- Both students turn over a card from their pile at the same time and place them down next to each other. If the answer matches the question, the first student to say *Snap!* gets a point. Students then pick up **their own cards only,** shuffle their pack, and play again. Students do **not** pick up their partner's cards.
- If the answer doesn't match the question, the students continue turning over cards from their piles until someone says *Snap!*
- If a student says *Snap!* when the answer **doesn't** match the question, his/her partner gets a point and the students continue with the activity. If there is disagreement about whether the cards match, the teacher adjudicates. The first student to get 10 points is the winner.
- It would be advisable to demonstrate this activity with the whole class before allowing the students to work in pairs.

2A What's this?

You will need: one copy of Worksheet A *and one copy of* Worksheet B *per pair of students*

- Check students know: *a computer*
- Divide the class into pairs. Give each pair a copy of *Worksheet A* and allow students two minutes to memorise where everything is in the picture. Students are not allowed to write anything down. Alternatively, show an overhead transparency of *Worksheet A.*
- Take away all the copies of *Worksheet A* and distribute a copy of *Worksheet B* to each pair. Tell the students they are sitting in the chair in the picture. Students take it in turns to point at the outline of a missing item and ask: *What's this/that?* or *What are these/those?* The other student responds by saying: *It's a ... (computer)* or *They're ... (pencils).* Encourage students to use *this/these* for items in the foreground of the picture on the desk and *that/those* for items in the background.
- If students are having difficulty remembering what all the items are, redistribute or reshow *Worksheet A* and allow the students to look at it for fifteen seconds.
- Students continue until they can both name all the items in the picture.

2B Who's got a Ferrari?

You will need: one worksheet per student; one role card per student

- Pre-teach the following items of vocabulary: *a Ferrari*; *a sportsman/sportswoman*; *a taxi driver*; *an elephant*; *famous*; *a swimming pool*; *a Stradivarius violin* (the most famous and expensive make of violin ever).
- Give each student a role card in random order, and allow them time to read the information on the card. **They are not allowed to look at one another's cards.** (If you have more than ten students, the cards can be duplicated without affecting the outcome of the activity.)
- Revise the following 'getting to know you' language from Module 1 of the Students' Book if necessary: *Hello, what's your name? My name's ... / Nice to meet you. You too. / Where are you from? I'm from ... / Are you married? No I'm single. What's your job? / I'm a ....*
- Give each student a copy of the worksheet. Tell the class that the line at the beginning of each sentence corresponds to a person's name.
- Students move around the room and have short conversations with one another in order to find out who has the items listed on the worksheet. Encourage students to introduce themselves and use 'getting to know you' questions to start the conversation, rather than just the questions required to complete the worksheet. When students find someone who has got a particular item, they write his/her name in the appropriate place on the worksheet. It is a good idea to do an example with them on the board first, encouraging them to guess what the person has got from other information they find out. This will make the activity more realistic.
- Finally, students check their answers in pairs or with the whole class.

2C The family

You will need: One copy of the family tree per student; one copy of Worksheet A *or* Worksheet B *per student*

- Give each student a copy of the family tree and check carefully, using the board, that they know how a family tree works and understand how the people are related.
- Divide the class into two groups, A and B. Give a copy of *Worksheet A* to all the students in group A and give a copy of *Worksheet B* to all the students in group B.
- Put students in pairs with someone who has the same worksheet. Students look at the information and write the names of the family in the correct place on their family trees (see **Key**). When they have finished, allow students to check their answers with another pair that has the same worksheet.
- Rearrange the class so that one student who has *Worksheet A* is working with a student who has *Worksheet B*. If you have extra students, have some groups of three.
- Students ask each other questions with *Who is ...?* in order to complete the family tree. For example: *Who is*

Molly's sister? Who is Tom's grandfather? Who is Mark and Laura's son?, etc. **Students are not allowed to look at each other's family trees.** When they have a new name, they should write it under the pictures in the space provided.
- Students should check each new name by referring to other people on the family tree. For example: *Have Jack and Emma got three children? Mark's got two sisters, Molly and Liz. Is that right?* etc.
- Check the answers with the whole group, either by using an overhead transparency or drawing the family tree on the board.
- As a follow-up activity, students can work in pairs and take it in turns to make up sentences about the family. The other student has to decide if the sentence is true or false.

3A Pick four cards

You will need: One set of cut-up cards per pair of students

- Before the class, cut up the cards and put them in a big envelope.
- Pre-teach the following items of vocabulary: *a town; fruit juice; food; business; languages.*
- Students take four cards from the bag. They must fill in the space in the speech bubble using one of the options provided, or their own ideas. Students may swap any cards they have duplicates of, or ones that they can't answer. Set a time limit of three or four minutes, and remove any blank cards in the envelope.
- Students put all their completed cards back in the envelope. Mix up the cards, then allow each student to take four completed cards from the envelope. Students should swap any cards they filled in themselves.
- Students move around the room and try to find the people who wrote the cards they are holding. In order to do this they must ask questions beginning with *Do you ...?* based on the sentence in the speech bubble.
- If Student A finds someone who says yes to his/her question, he/she shows Student B the card and asks: *Is this your card?* If it **is** Student B's card, Student A writes his/her name on it. If it **isn't** Student B's card, Student A must continue looking for the person who wrote the card.
- The activity continues until all the students have found the people who wrote the cards they are holding.

3B Pronoun stars

You will need: one set of Sentence cards *and two sets of* Pronoun cards *for each group of three students.*

- Pre-teach *star, Happy Birthday, stay* and check students know to use object pronouns after prepositions as well as in object position.
- Students work in groups of three. Give Student A a set of *Sentence cards*, face down in a pile. Give Students B and C a **complete set** of *Pronoun cards* **each**, and tell them to spread them out in front of them, face up. Shuffle the

cards beforehand. If you have extra students, have some groups of four, and give the extra student another set of *Pronoun cards*.

- Student A turns over the first *Sentence card* and reads **the sentence(s) in the speech bubbles only** out loud. Instead of using a pronoun, he/she should say *star* in the appropriate place.
- Students B and C must find the correct *Pronoun card* from their set as quickly as possible and give it to Student A, saying the pronoun at the same time. Student A should check the card against the answer on his/her *Sentence card*. The student who finds the correct card first takes both cards as a 'trick'. The student with the most tricks at the end is the winner.
- It is advisable to demonstrate this activity to the whole class before getting students to work in their groups.
- Students can repeat the activity with a different student turning over the *Sentence cards*.

3C Time pelmanism

You will need: one set of cards per pair of students

- Students work in pairs (or in groups of three). Give each pair/group a set of cards (shuffled) and tell them to spread them out in front of them **face down** without looking at them first.
- The students take it in turns to turn over any two cards. If a student finds two cards that match, he/she keeps the cards as a 'trick' and has another turn. If the cards do not match, he/she must put them back **in exactly the same place**.
- The activity continues until all cards are matched up. The student with the most tricks is the winner.
- At the end of the activity students can play again, or test each other on the times using the clock cards.

4A Things you love and hate

You will need: one copy of the worksheet per student

- Before distributing the worksheets, pre-teach the following vocabulary: *to wash up*; *to buy*; *ice cream*.
- Students mingle and ask questions beginning with *Do you like ...?* for each of the activities or items on the worksheet. They must find one student who likes/loves the item or activity, and one student who doesn't like / hates it.
- When they find someone, they write his/her name in the correct space on the worksheet. Students should try and collect as many different names as possible.
- Encourage students to use the following short answers during this stage of the activity: *Yes, I do. / Yes, I love it. / No, I don't. / No, I hate it. / It's okay*. If necessary, write them on the board before they begin.
- Students continue asking questions until they have filled in as many spaces as possible. Alternatively, set a time limit of ten minutes.
- Students work in pairs and tell each other what they have found out about the other people in the class. For

example: *Erika loves classical music, but she doesn't like watching football*. Finally, each student tells the whole group some things he/she has found out about his/her classmates.

4B Three people I know

You will need: one copy of the worksheet per student

- Give a copy of the worksheet to each student. Tell them to write the names of three people they know in the top line of the table in Question 1. Students should write names of friends and family, not acquaintances, classmates or famous people. Students should **not** write anything else in the table at this stage.
- Students write five things about each person they have named **in the boxes at the bottom of the page**. Students should write short answers (such as *France, swimming, a doctor* or *going to the cinema*) not whole sentences. They must also write the answers **in random order**.
- Students work in pairs and **swap worksheets** with their partners. They must ask yes/no questions about the people named, based on the information in the boxes at the bottom of their partner's worksheet. (Students are not allowed to ask questions with *What, Where*, etc.) For example, if Student A has written the names *Pedro, Susannah* and *Michel* in the table, and the word *Paris* appears in one of the boxes, Student B could ask: *Does Pedro come from Paris?*
- If the answer is *yes*, then Student B writes *Paris* in the table under Pedro's name. If the answer is *no*, then Student B must continue asking questions until he/she has found out which person *Paris* relates to, and in what way.
- Encourage students to use the correct short answers (*Yes, he/she does. No, he/she doesn't*.) when responding to their partner's questions.
- Students take turns asking yes/no questions until they have both completed the grid with five pieces of information about each person.
- At the end of the activity students can find a new partner and tell each other about the people on the worksheet. Alternatively, students can write a paragraph about each person on the worksheet, based on the information in the table.
- **Note:** It is useful to demonstrate this activity to the whole class before they begin, either by drawing the worksheet on the board or using an overhead transparency.

4C Always, sometimes, never

You will need: one copy of Worksheet A *or* Worksheet B *per student*

- Pre-teach the following items of vocabulary: *to go to sleep*; *to wake up*; *to go to the gym*; *the news*.
- Divide the class into pairs. If possible, pair students with someone they don't usually work with or don't know very well.

- Give one student in each pair a copy of *Worksheet A* and the other student a copy of *Worksheet B*. Each student should write their partner's name in the space at the top of the worksheet. **Students are not allowed to look at their partner's worksheets.**

- Students work individually and choose the word or phrase in italics that they think is true for their partner. Students are not allowed to ask their partners any questions at this stage of the activity.

- Students then take it in turns to tell their partner what they have written, beginning with *I think ... .* For example, Student A might say: *I think you sometimes listen to classical music. Is this true?*. Student B tells Student A if this statement is true or not. If the statement is not true, Student B should explain why. For example: *No, it's not true. I never listen to classical music. I hate it!*

- For each statement students get right they put a tick in the second column on the worksheet, and for each one they get wrong they put a cross. The student who gets the most statements correct is the winner.

- As a follow-up activity, students can find a new partner and tell each other what they found out about their original partners. For example: *Pablo usually watches TV in the evening, and he always goes to sleep after midnight.*

4D Verb dominoes

You will need: one set of dominoes per pair of students

- Students work in pairs. Give one set of dominoes to each pair, and ask them to share them out equally.

- One student places a domino in front of them, and the other student has to make a complete sentence by placing one of his/her dominoes at either end of the first domino. Students then take it in turns to put down their dominoes at either end of the domino chain, paying particular attention to the words in **bold**.

- If a student thinks his/her partner's sentence is not grammatically correct or doesn't make sense, he/she can challenge the other student. If the students cannot agree, the teacher adjudicates. If the sentence is incorrect, the student must take back the domino and miss a turn.

- If a student cannot make a sentence, the turn passes to his/her partner.

- The game continues until one student has used all his/her dominoes, or until neither student can make a correct sentence. The student who finishes first, or has the fewest dominoes remaining, is the winner.

- Students who finish early can test each other on the collocations in bold. One student says the noun, and his/her partner must say which verb is used with it.

5A The perfect holiday

You will need: one set of four worksheets for each group of four students

- Pre-teach the following items of vocabulary: *a swimming pool; a club; to hire a car/bicycle; a museum; on the coast; a jacuzzi.*

- Tell the class that they are going on a two-week holiday to Helena Island, and must decide which of four hotels to stay in. All the hotels cost the same!

- Divide the class into four groups and give copies of *Worksheet A* to all the students in the first group, copies of *Worksheet B* to all the students in the second group, etc. Allow students time to read the information and ask any questions.

- Students work together in pairs or groups with students who have the **same** worksheet, and decide what you can (and can't) do on holiday in the hotel **and** in the city/town/village nearby. Students should use *You can ...* and *You can't ...* during their discussion.

- For example, students with *Worksheet A* might say: *At the Ayala Hotel you can go swimming, and you can eat Italian food. In Helena City you can go to the cinema or you can visit a museum.* Students can make notes at this stage, but they do not need to write down all the sentences.

- Rearrange the class into groups of four, one student from each of the previous groups. If you have extra students make some groups of five. Students take it in turns to tell the group what you can and can't do in the hotel, and the place nearby. The whole group must then decide which hotel they are going to stay in. At this stage encourage students to discuss the advantages and disadvantages of each hotel, again using *You can ...* and *You can't ... .*

- Each group tells the whole class which hotel they have chosen, giving reasons for their decision.

5B Transport crossword

You will need: a copy of Crossword A *and* Crossword B *per pair of students*

- Divide the class into two groups, A and B. Give a copy of Crossword A to all students in group A, and a copy of Crossword B to all students in group B. Check that students understand how to refer to words in a crossword, e.g. *3 across* and *7 down*.

- Students work together in their separate groups to check they know all the meanings of the words on their worksheet. All the vocabulary is taken from Module 5 of the *Students' Book*. Students can refer to the *Mini-dictionary* if necessary.

- Put students into pairs, so that one student with Crossword A and one student with Crossword B are working together. **They are not allowed to look at each other's crosswords.**

- Students take it in turns to give clues (either verbal or visual) for the words that appear on their half of the crossword. The other student must guess the words and write them on his/her own crossword. They should tell their partner if the answer is one or two words, but they are not allowed to give letters as clues.

- The activity continues until both students have a completed version of the crossword.

Learner-training worksheet A

Using the *Mini-dictionary*

You will need: *one copy of the worksheet per student*

This worksheet gives students an overview of the type of information contained in the *Mini-dictionary* now they have begun to use it in the Modules and in the Study sections (*see Making the most of the* Mini-dictionary *on page 10 for more details*).

1 Students do part a) on their own, then discuss part b) in pairs. The aim is to show students that they don't always have to understand the definition to grasp the meaning – sometimes the example can be more useful.

2 Students work individually before checking the answers with the whole class.

3 Check students understand how the parts of speech are marked in the *Mini-dictionary* before they do the exercise on their own or in pairs. Check the answers with the whole class (see **Key**).

4 Check that students know where the pronunciation table is in their *Mini-dictionary*. You can go through the sounds with them. Many of the consonants are very easy to read, so you could concentrate on a few of the more difficult symbols. Students work in pairs before checking their pronunciation with the teacher.

6A Food battleships

You will need: *one copy of the **whole** worksheet per student*

- Distribute copies of the worksheet to each student. Allow students time to check they know the English words for all the food and drink items on the worksheet (all the words are taken from Module 6 of the *Students' Book*).
- Use the pictures to teach the following vocabulary items: *a fridge, a freezer, a cooker, a cupboard.*
- Divide the class into pairs and assign picture A to one student and picture B to his/her partner. If you have an odd number of students, allow two students to work together on one of the pictures.
- **Students work alone** and write the words for each of their eight items on their picture. They must write the words in the boxes provided, but they can put the items anywhere they like. **Students are not allowed to look at each other's pictures.**
- Students work in pairs. They take it in turns to ask their partner yes/no questions to find out where the items are hidden. Each student must begin each question with: *Is there a ...? / Is there any ...? / Are there any ...?* For example, Student A might ask: *Is there any cheese in the fridge?* or *Are there any sausages on the table?*. Encourage students to answer the questions with *Yes, there is / Yes, there are.* and *No, there isn't. / No, there aren't.* where appropriate.
- When a student guesses correctly, he/she writes the item in the correct place on his/her copy of the worksheet. The first student to find all his/her partner's items is the winner.

- At the end of the activity students can check their answers by telling each other what is in their partner's kitchen, using *There's a ... / There's some ... / There are some ...* where appropriate.

6B The recipe game

You will need: *one* Food card *and one matching* Recipe card *per student*

- Pre-teach the following items of vocabulary: *recipe; onion; green pepper; mushroom; carrot; rice; beans; potato; flour; strawberry; lemon; pineapple; ice cream.* Make sure students know which of these food words are countable and uncountable.
- Give each student a Food card and explain that these are the items each student has in his/her kitchen. Allow them time to check they know all the words on their card before continuing. (You will need a minimum of six students for this activity.) If you have more than six students you can use multiple copies of the cards without affecting the outcome of the activity.
- Give each student a Recipe card. **The letter on each student's Recipe card must be the same as the letter on their Food card** (i.e. a student with Food card A should also be given Recipe card A, etc.).
- Tell the class they are planning to make the food shown on their Recipe card. In order to do this, they must get the ingredients from the other students.
- Students move around the room and ask each other if they have got the food items they need, using *Have you got a/any ...?* and *I've got a/some ...* in their conversations. Encourage students to try and swap items, rather than merely giving them away.
- When a student hands over an item of food, he/she must cross the item off their Food card. **Each item on the Food card can only be given away once.** When students receive a food item, they must cross it off their Recipe card.
- Students are only allowed to obtain **one item at a time from each student**. Once they have obtained an item, they must move to talk to another student. If necessary, they can return to students they have already talked to later in the activity.
- The first student to find all the food they need for their recipe is the winner.
- Finally, students can work in pairs and tell their partners what they have and haven't got.

6C Sports stars

You will need: *one copy of* Worksheet A *or* Worksheet B *per student*

- Pre-teach the following items of vocabulary: *a medal; the marathon; a weightlifter; a tennis court; a bank; to train (for a sport).*
- Divide the class into two groups, A and B. Give a copy of *Worksheet A* to all the students in group A and a copy of *Worksheet B* to all the students in group B. Allow

students time to read their worksheets and ask any questions.

- Students work in pairs or groups with people who have the **same** worksheet, and write down the questions they will need to ask in order to complete the spaces on the worksheet. **Each question must begin with either *How much* or *How many*.** For example, students with *Worksheet A* should write: *How many Olympic gold medals has Sergei got?* for the first gap, while students with *Worksheet B* should write: *How many hours does he train every day?*
- Rearrange the class so that each student with *Worksheet A* is sitting next to a student with *Worksheet B*. **Students are not allowed to look at each other's worksheets.** They take it in turns to ask their partner the questions they have prepared, then write the answers on their worksheets.
- Finally, students check the answers with the whole class.

7A The history quiz

You will need: one copy of the worksheet per student

- Check/pre-teach the following items of vocabulary: **a car crash**; **a cartoon**; **a hit record**; **a journey**.
- Divide the class into teams of three or four, and give a copy of the worksheet to each student. Each team must decide on one correct answer for each question. Set a time limit of ten minutes.
- Check the answers with the whole class (see **Key**), and give one point for each correct answer. The team with the most points are the winners.

7B Past tense bingo

You will need: at least one Bingo card per student

- Give one Bingo card to each student, and allow them a few moments to check the past tenses on their cards.
- Sit or stand in front of the class with a copy of the Master bingo card. Call out the infinitives on the card in any order, and cross them off the card at the same time.
- If a student has the past tense of the infinitive on his/her card, he/she should put a line through it. For example, if the teacher calls out *buy*, all the students with *bought* on their Bingo Cards should cross it out.
- The first student who crosses out all the past tenses on his/her card is the winner. The card can be checked against the Master Bingo Card if necessary.
- To repeat the activity, distribute new cards to the students and play again.

8A Looking back

You will need: one copy of the worksheet per student

- Pre-teach the following items of vocabulary: *primary school; to give presents*.
- Give a copy of the worksheet to each student and check they understand the instructions. Make sure they write their answers in **random order**, and encourage them to

answer as many questions as possible. They should write single words, names or short phrases, not complete sentences.

- Put the students into pairs and tell them to swap worksheets with their partner. Students take it in turns to ask yes/no questions beginning with *Did you ...?* to find out why their partner has written the words in the bubbles at the bottom of the worksheet. For example, if Student A has written *Pedro*, Student B can ask: *Did you go on holiday with Pedro last month? / Did you talk to him on the phone last week?* etc. Students can refer back to the prompts if necessary.
- Encourage students to ask follow-up questions for each point if possible. For example, for 'a place in your country you went to last year', students could ask: *Did you enjoy it? What did you do there? Where did you stay?* etc.
- At the end of the activity, students report back to the class on the most interesting things they found out about their partner.

8B John Wayne

You will need: one copy of Worksheet A *or* Worksheet B *per student*

- Ask the class what they know about John Wayne and write their ideas on the board. Pre-teach the following items of vocabulary: *ugly; a film studio; a western; to appear in a film; a director; a role in a film; a success*.
- Divide the class into two groups, A and B. Give a copy of *Worksheet A* to each student in group A and a copy of *Worksheet B* to each student in group B. Allow students time to read their worksheets and ask any questions about the vocabulary.
- Students work in pairs or groups with people who have **the same worksheet** and write down the questions (in the Past simple) they will need to ask in order to complete their version of the text. For example, students with *Worksheet A* should write *When was John Wayne / he born?* and *Where did his family move to when he was a child?* for questions a and b.
- Rearrange the class so that each student with *Worksheet A* is working with a student with *Worksheet B*. **Students are not allowed to look at each other's worksheets.** Students take it in turns to ask the questions they have prepared. They should write the answers in the spaces on their worksheet.
- When they have finished they can look at each other's worksheets and check their answers.
- As a follow-up activity, students can see how much their partner remembers.

8C Safe at last!

You will need: one copy of the newspaper article per student; one set of role cards per pair of students

- Pre-teach the following items of vocabulary: *to sail; a sailor; an island; sand; to rescue somebody; a pilot; to interview somebody; a reporter*.

- Give each student a copy of the newspaper article to read, and check they have understood the main points.
- Divide the class into pairs. You need an **even number of pairs** for this activity. If there are extra students, have some groups of three. Give half the pairs/groups Reporters' role cards and the other half Sailor role cards.
- Students prepare questions and answers in their pairs, following the instructions on the card. Allow about ten or fifteen minutes for this and help students with vocabulary as necessary.
- Rearrange the class so that each pair of 'reporters' can interview a pair of 'sailors'. (With a strong class, reporters can interview sailors individually.) The reporters should make brief notes during the interview, in order to report back later.
- Reporters tell the whole class the most interesting things they have found out about their sailor.
- Finally, each reporter can work with one of the sailors they interviewed and write the newspaper article together.

9A New Year's Eve

You will need: one copy of each picture per student

- Pre-teach the following items of vocabulary: *a sofa; a plant; curtains; a moustache; a toy car; champagne.*
- Give each student a copy of picture A, and tell the class that this is a picture of the Jones family on New Year's Eve 2000. Set a time limit of three minutes, and tell the students that they must remember as much as possible about the picture.
- Collect in the copies of picture A and distribute copies of picture B. Check the class understand that picture B is the same family on New Year's Eve in the year 2005.
- Students work in pairs and write down as many differences as possible between picture B and picture A. There are 16 differences in total (see **Key**), not including the fact that all the people are older. Students must use comparative adjectives in their answers, for example: *In picture B Mr Jones is fatter.*
- If students are finding it hard to remember the differences, collect in picture B and redistribute picture A. Allow the class one minute to look at picture A again, then collect them back and redistribute picture B. Alternatively, you can allow students to see both pictures at the same time.
- The students who find all the differences first, or who find the most differences in a set time, are the winners.
- Students check their answers with another pair or with the whole class.

9B A superlative survey

You will need: one card per student

- Pre-teach the following items of vocabulary: *a relative; large; near.*
- Give one card to each student. If you have more than twelve students in the class, use duplicate cards.

Students must find out the answer to the question on the card by talking to all the other students in the class.

- Allow students time to write down either one or two questions with 'you' they will need to ask the other students. For example, a student with Card A will need to ask **two** questions: *Have you got any brothers and sisters?* and *How old are they?*, but a student with Card B will only need to ask one question: *What time did you go to bed last night?* Go round the class and check that all the students have appropriate questions before continuing.
- Students move around the room and ask the questions they have prepared. They must talk to every student in the class, and should make brief notes of the answers on the back of their cards or in a notebook.
- Students work out the answers to the questions on the cards and report back to the class. For example, a student with Card A might say: *Julia's got the oldest brother or sister. Her brother Antonio is 37.*

9C Shopping crossword

You will need: a copy of Crossword A and Crossword B per pair of students

- Divide the class into two groups, A and B. Give a copy of Crossword A to all students in group A, and a copy of Crossword B to all students in group B. Check that students understand how to refer to words in a crossword, e.g. *3 across* and *7 down*.
- Students work together in their separate groups to check they know all the meanings of the words on their worksheet. All the vocabulary is taken from Module 9 of the Students' Book. Students can refer to the *Mini-dictionary* if necessary.
- Put students into pairs, so that one student with Student A crossword and one student with Student B crossword are working together. **They are not allowed to look at each other's crosswords.**
- Students take it in turns to give clues for the words that appear on their half of the crossword. For example: *You can buy bread there. / You buy this in a pharmacy.* etc. The other student must guess the words and write them on his/her own crossword. Students should tell their partner if the answer is more than one word, but they are not allowed to give letters as clues.
- The activity continues until both students have a completed version of the crossword.

Learner-training worksheet B

Present continuous: spelling the *-ing* form

You will need: one copy of the worksheet per student

The aim of this activity is to encourage students to use the *Mini-dictionary* to find the spelling of the *-ing* form and also to learn the rules for spelling the *-ing* form.

1 Go through the dictionary entries with the whole class, and check that students understand how the *Mini-dictionary* shows the *-ing* form.

2   Students work individually before checking their answers with a partner and then with the whole class (see **Key**).

3   Focus students on the rules and elicit an example for rules b and c. Students then categorise the verbs in the box into three sets according to which rule they follow. Highlight the fact that verbs ending with -*y* are regular and simply take -*ing* (see **Key**).

4   Students work in pairs and use the rules to work out the -*ing* forms. They can then check their answers in the *Mini-dictionary*: Student A can check half and Student B the other half (see **Key**).

10A What's Sam doing?

You will need: one copy of the picture per student; one Activity card per student

- Pre-teach the following items of vocabulary: *to steal; a sandcastle; to play volleyball; to windsurf*.

- Give each student a copy of the picture and one of the Activity cards. **Students are not allowed to look at each other's pictures or cards.** Tell them to write the person's name in the correct box in the picture. They must also cross the person's name off the list next to the picture. If you have less than sixteen people in your class, give two cards to some of the students. If you have more than sixteen students, distribute duplicate cards.

- Students move around the room and ask questions to find out what all the people in the list are doing. For example: *What's Joe doing? He's selling ice cream. / I don't know.* When students find out what someone is doing, they write their names in the space on the picture and cross them off their list. Again, students are not allowed to look at each other's pictures.

- **The aim of the activity is to find out what Sam is doing.** (Sam is the girl eating an ice cream, and is the only one without a card.) In order to find this out students need to have written the other sixteen names on their picture, so Sam is the only one left.

- Students are only allowed to obtain **one** name at a time from each person they speak to. When they have written the name on their picture they must find a new partner. When a student discovers what Sam is doing, he/she sits down.

- Students work in pairs and check they have all the names in the correct places. The answers should be checked with the whole group.

- As a follow-up activity students can test each other. Student A turns over the picture and Student B asks him/her what the people are doing. Students can then swap over, so that Student B turns over the picture and Student A asks the questions.

10B A letter home

You will need: one copy of Letter A or Letter B per student

- Pre-teach the following items of vocabulary: *a square (in a town); to play cards; dangerous; to carry something; a box; souvenirs*.

- Divide the class into two groups, A and B. Give a copy of Letter A to all the students in group A, and a copy of Letter B to the all the students in group B. Allow students time to read their version of the letter and ask any questions.

- Students work in pairs or groups with people who have **the same worksheet** and write down the questions they need to ask to complete their version of the letter. The questions should be either in the Present simple or Present continuous. For example, students with Letter A should write: Where is she sitting (at the moment)? for number 1, and What time do (their) classes start? for number 5.

- Pair one student with Letter A with one student with Letter B. **Students are not allowed to look at each other's letters.** Students take it in turns to ask the questions they have prepared, and write the answers in the spaces on their worksheet.

- When they have finished they can look at their partner's letter and check their answers.

10C Identity parades

You will need: one copy of the worksheet per student

- Distribute copies of the worksheet to each student, and allow them a few moments to study the pictures.

- Put students into pairs. Students take it in turns to describe a person on the worksheet to their partner. They should describe the person's appearance and clothes **in as much detail as possible**, using the vocabulary on pages 81 and 84 of the Students' Book (and the word *T-shirt*). Students are not allowed to say the person's name, or where they are in the pictures. If necessary, demonstrate this beforehand by describing one of the people to the whole class and asking them to guess who it is.

- When Student A has finished his/her description, Student B must guess who his/her partner is describing. If Student B is unsure, he/she should ask questions about the person. For example: *Is he wearing a jacket? Has she got a ponytail?*

- Students take it in turns to describe a person until all the people have been discussed.

- For further practice, allow students a further two minutes to look at the pictures and tell them to remember as much detail about the people as possible.

- Student A turns over his/her worksheet, and Student B says the name of one of the people. Student A must try to describe that person in as much detail as possible. After describing four or five people, students swap over so that Student A is saying the names of people and Student B is describing them from memory.

- Finally, students can write descriptions of some of the people in class or for homework.

11A Can you or can't you?

You will need: one copy of Worksheet A *or* Worksheet B *per student*

- Pre-teach the following items of vocabulary: *to add*; *to multiply*; *chess*; *backgammon*; *to type*; *a keyboard*; *to ski*.
- Divide the class into pairs. If possible, put students with someone they don't usually work with or don't know very well.
- Give one student in each pair *Worksheet A* and the other student *Worksheet B*. Each student should write their partner's name in the space at the top of the worksheet. Students are not allowed to look at their partner's worksheets.
- Students work individually and try to guess if their partner can or can't do the activities listed on their worksheet. **Students are not allowed to ask their partners any questions at this stage of the activity.**
- Students then take it in turns to ask their partner if they can do the activities listed on their worksheet. For example, students with *Worksheet A* should ask: *Can you swim 100 metres? / Can you say all the months in English?*, etc.
- For each statement students have guessed right they put a tick in the second column on the worksheet, and for each one they get wrong they put a cross. Students should ask for proof that their partner can do these things if possible!
- The student in the pair who gets the most answers correct is the winner.
- As a follow-up activity students can work with a new partner and tell him/her about the person they have just been talking to. For example: *I talked to Yoko. She can swim a hundred metres, but she can't play a musical instrument.*

11B The dinner party

You will need: one copy of the worksheet per student; one role card per student

- Pre-teach the following items of vocabulary: *an inventor*; *to invent*; *a sailor*; *a diplomat*; *a marathon runner*; *a millionaire*; *a translator*; *a film director*; *to win the lottery*; *a painting*.
- Tell the class that they are all going to a dinner party, and give each student a copy of the worksheet. Also tell them that the gap at the beginning of each line corresponds to a person's name.
- Students work in pairs or small groups and write down the questions they will need to ask in order to complete the second gap for each person. Students must begin each question with one of the question words in the box above the picture. For example students should write: *What did you invent last month?* for number 1 on the worksheet. Note that all these questions should have 'you' as the subject. Check these questions with the whole group before continuing (see **Key**).

- Give each student a role card in random order and allow them time to read the information on the card. **They are not allowed to look at one another's cards.** (If you have more than ten students, the cards can be duplicated without affecting the outcome of the activity.)
- Students move around the room and have short conversations with each other. Encourage students to begin by introducing themselves and using 'getting to know you' questions (*Where are you from? What do you do?*, etc.), rather than just asking the questions required to complete the worksheet.
- When a student finds out who someone is, he/she writes the person's name in the first gap on the worksheet. Then he/she must ask the question he/she has prepared and write the answer in the second gap. The activity continues until the students have filled in all the gaps on their worksheet.
- Students check their answers in pairs or with the whole class.

11C The numbers game

You will need: one copy of both sets of cards per three students

- Before class cut out the two sets of cards, ensuring that you keep the cards for Game 1 and Game 2 **separate**.
- Divide the class into groups of three and distribute the cards for Game 1. Give the first student Card A, the second student Card B, and the third student Card C. If you have extra students, put two students together so that they are working with one card.
- Students must listen to the numbers their partners say and find them in the **HEAR** column on their card. They must then say the corresponding number in the **SAY** column for the other students to recognise. Tell students that there are some years (e.g. 1690) on the cards as well as numbers.
- The student with **START** on his/her card begins by saying the number indicated. The turn then passes from student to student until they reach the **FINISH** square. Students can tick off the numbers on their cards if they wish.
- If necessary, demonstrate the activity before students begin working in their groups.
- When the students have finished, distribute the cards for Game 2 and allow the groups to repeat the activity with the new cards. Alternatively, this second set of cards can be used for revision later in the course.

Learner-training worksheet C

(Recording new vocabulary)

You will need: one copy of the worksheet per student

Students at this level often record vocabulary in lists, with a translation in their own language. In the Study section of Module 11, they are encouraged to try new ways of organising their vocabulary. This worksheet aims to make students aware of other information they can include in their vocabulary books, such as parts of speech and word stress.

1 Go through the extracts with the students and identify how grammar is shown in the *Mini-dictionary.*

2 Students do the exercise individually before checking the answers in pairs or with the whole group (see **Key**).

3 Students do the exercise in pairs or small groups. Check the answers with the whole group. List B contains the following extra information: part of speech (including putting *to* in front of a verb and *a/an* in front of a countable noun); common word combinations and examples; regular/irregular verbs; countable/uncountable nouns; opposites; word stress.

4 Students do the exercise in pairs or small groups. Encourage them to use the *Mini-dictionary* to find more information. Check the answers with the whole class (see **Key**).

5 Students work on their own before comparing their ideas in groups. Alternatively, this exercise can be set for homework.

12A Future walkabout

You will need: one copy of the worksheet per student

- Distribute one copy of the worksheet to each student. Tell the class that they must find one student who is going (to)/would like to/wants to do each activity on the worksheet.

- Check that the students can make the correct questions with 'you' as the subject for each sentence. For example: *Are you going away for the weekend? Do you want to stay in this evening and watch TV?*, etc. With a weak class, tell them to write down the questions before continuing.

- Students move around the room asking each other questions based on the prompts. When they get a positive answer, they write the student's name in the second column on the worksheet. Students should then ask at least one follow-up question. For example: *Where are you going? / Who are you going with?*, etc. for prompt number 1.

- When they have written someone's name down and asked a follow-up question, they should move on and talk to another student. Students should collect as many different names as possible on their worksheet.

- Students work in pairs or small groups and tell each other what they have found out about their classmates. Finally, students can share.

12B Collocation snap

You will need: one set of Snap! cards per pair of students

- Check/Pre-teach the following collocations: *to have a meal; to watch the news / a video; to stay at home; to do an exam / an exercise / some studying.* All the other collocations in the activity are taken from Module 12 in the Students' Book (pages 98–100).

- Write the following verbs on the board: *GO TO; DO; WATCH; STAY; HAVE; GO.*

- Students work in pairs. Give one set of *Snap!* cards to each pair. Tell them to share the cards out equally and

put the cards face down in a pile in front of them. (If you have a group of three, two students should work together and take turns in playing the game with the third student.)

- Students turn over a card from the top of their pile at the same time and place them down in front of them. If a student thinks both words or expressions on the cards collocate with one of the verbs on the board, he/she says *Snap!*. The student must then say which verb goes with the two words or expressions. For example, if the two cards say SHOPPING and ON HOLIDAY, then a student can say Snap because they both collocate with the verb GO. (Note that *A PARTY* can collocate with both *HAVE* and *GO TO.*)

- If the student is correct, he/she picks up all the cards in front of them and puts them at the bottom of his/her pile. If both students say *Snap!*, then the student who says it first takes the cards.

- If the student is not correct, his/her partner picks up all the cards instead. If the students cannot agree, the teacher adjudicates (see **Key**).

- If neither student says *Snap!*, then they both continue turning over cards until there is a match. If students use all their cards and there is still no match, they collect up their own cards, shuffle them and play again.

- The student who collects all the cards first is the winner.

- It is advisable to demonstrate this activity with the whole class before allowing the students to work in pairs.

12C The school party

You will need: one copy of the worksheet per student

- Pre-teach the following items of vocabulary: to organise a party; to invite people to a party; entertainment; a DJ (disc jockey); balloons; to put up decorations.

- Distribute copies of the worksheet and put students into pairs. (You need **an even number of groups** for this activity, so include some groups of three if necessary.)

- Students work in pairs and do **Part A** of the worksheet. Encourage students to use the language for making suggestions from page 101 of the Students' Book (*Let's ... / Shall we ...? / We could ...*), and write these expressions and suitable responses on the board if necessary.

- Put two pairs together so that students are now working in groups of four. Students do **Part B** on the worksheet, using ideas and suggestions from both pairs. Students should write the details of their party, and which student is going to organise each part, in the boxes provided.

- Encourage students to use the language for making suggestions (see above), and also the language for making offers from page 101 of the Students' Book (*Shall I ...? / I'll ...*) in their discussions. Again, write these expressions and suitable responses on the board if necessary.

- Rearrange the class so that each student is sitting next to another student from a different group. Students work with their new partner and tell each other about the party they have planned, using *going to / want to / would like to* where appropriate.

- Finally, each group can tell the whole class about the parties they have planned, and the class can decide which party they think would be the best.

13A Education crossword

You will need: a copy of Crossword A *and* Crossword B *per pair of students*

- Divide the class into two groups, A and B. Give a copy of Crossword A to all the students in group A, and a copy of Crossword B to all the students in group B. Check that students understand how to refer to words in a crossword. For example: *3 across* and *7 down*.
- Students work together in their separate groups to check they know all the meanings of the words on their worksheet. All the vocabulary is taken from Module 15 of the Students' Book. Students can refer to the *Mini-dictionary* if necessary.
- Put students into pairs, so that one student with Student A crossword and one student with Student B crossword are working together. **They are not allowed to look at each other's crosswords.**
- Students take it in turns to give clues for the words that appear on their half of the crossword. For example: *It's a subject you do at school, about things that happened in the past. If you study a lot, you will ____ your exam.* etc. The other student must guess the words and write them in his/her own crossword. Students can tell their partner if the answer is more than one word, but they are not allowed to give letters as clues.
- The activity continues until both students have a completed version of the crossword.

13B Looking into the future

You will need: one worksheet per student

- Pre-teach the following items of vocabulary: *pollution; to be extinct; petrol; videophone.* Distribute a copy of the worksheet to each student. Check students understand that all the sentences relate to the year 2100. Students work individually, and choose a word or expression from the box of each gap.
- Put students into groups of three or four. Students tell each other what they have written for each point, giving reasons for their answers. Students should discuss any differences of opinion they have and come to a consensus for each point. When they have reached agreement each student should write *Yes* or *No* in the second column on the worksheet, depending on whether the group agrees with their original opinion or not.
- Each group shares their ideas with the whole class, giving reasons for their answers.

Learner-training worksheet D

(Irregular verbs)

You will need: one worksheet per student

The aim of this worksheet is to encourage students to look up and learn past tenses and past participles of irregular verbs, and to raise their awareness of common sound patterns.

1 Check that students know how to find the past tense and past participles of irregular verbs in the *Mini-dictionary*.

2 Students do the exercise individually before checking the answers with the whole class.

3 Students work individually and complete the table. They can refer to the **Irregular verb table** on page 149 of the Students' Book during the activity (note that not all of these verbs are in the *Mini-dictionary*). The first student to complete the table correctly is the winner. Check the pronunciation of the verbs with the whole class.

4 Check the students know how to pronounce the irregular verbs in the boxes. Draw students' attention to the phonemic symbols in the first row of the table, which represent the **vowel** sounds in each verb.

5 Students work in pairs or small groups. Note that in Groups B and C the infinitive can have any vowel sound. Check the answers with the whole class (see **Key**). Practise saying the verbs in each group with the whole class. Finally, students can work in pairs and test each other on irregular verbs from the worksheet.

14A The Travellers' Club

Present perfect questions and short answers.

You will need: one role card per student

- Pre-teach the following items of vocabulary: *to climb a mountain; a whale; a temple; a sunrise.* Also check that students know the past participles of the following irregular verbs: *swim; drink; ride; sleep; work; drive,* and that they can pronounce all the place names that appear on the role cards.
- Tell the students they are all members of The Travellers' Club, which is for people who have travelled all over the world. They are going to a meeting at the club, where they will meet lots of other travellers.
- Give each student a role card and allow them time to check the information. (Role cards 1 to 8 are needed to for all students to complete the activity; Role cards 9 to 12 are optional. If you have more than 12 students, use duplicate role cards.)
- Students move around the room and start conversations with each other. **The aim of the activity is for each student to find at least one person who has done each of the things on his/her own role card.** In order to do this, they must ask questions with *Have you ever ...?* based on the points on the cards.
- When they find someone who has done the same thing as them, they should write his/her name on their role card. Encourage students to ask suitable follow-up questions where appropriate.

- The activity continues until all the students have found at least one person for each of the activities on their role card.
- Finally, students discuss their answers in small groups or with the whole class.

14B Life boxes

You will need: one worksheet per student

Give each student a copy of the worksheet. Students work individually and write their answers in the boxes. Make sure they write their answers in **random order**, and encourage them to write nine answers if possible. They should write single words or short phrases, not complete sentences, and can write film titles and names of countries in their own language if necessary.

- Students work in pairs and swap worksheets with their partner. Students take it in turns and ask questions to find out why their partner has written the words in the boxes. For example: *Why have you written 'Madrid' here? / Who's Petra?* etc. The other student must reply using the Present perfect tense. For example: *I've been to Madrid twice, and I liked it a lot. I've seen it five times!* etc.
- Students must ask at least one natural follow-up question on each topic (e.g. *When was that? Why did you buy it? Why?*). You may need to elicit some ideas for this before students start.
- At the end of the activity, students report back to the class on the most interesting things they found out about their partner.

14C On the phone

You will need: one set of role cards per pair of students

- Pre-teach the following items of vocabulary: *to collect something*; *to repair something*.
- Put students into pairs. Give one student in each pair a set of Student A role cards and the other student a set of Student B role cards. Each set of cards should be placed face down in a pile **in order**, with role card 1 on the top and role card 4 at the bottom.
- Students turn over the top card of their pile (role cards 1A and 1B). Allow students time to read the information on the card before doing roleplay 1. Encourage students to use the language for telephoning on page 125 of the Students' Book where appropriate.
- When students have finished the roleplay 1, they turn over the second cards in their piles and do roleplay 2. Students continue until they have done all four roleplays.
- Finally, Student A and Student B can swap their sets of cards and repeat the activity.

15A Preposition pelmanism

You will need: one set of cards per pair of students

- Put students into pairs. Give each pair a set of cards and tell them to spread them out in front of them **face down**, with the bigger cards on one side and the smaller cards on the other. Shuffle the cards before the class. (All the prepositions of movement and vocabulary items are taken from the Students' Book pages 130–131.)
- Students take it in turns to turn over one big card and one small card. If the preposition is the correct one to fill the gap in the sentence, the student keeps the cards as a 'trick' and has another turn. If the cards do not match, the student must put them back **in exactly the same place**. If the students cannot agree on the correct answers, the teacher adjudicates.
- The activity continues until all the cards are matched up. The student with the most tricks is the winner.
- If one group finishes early, they can test each other by holding up the picture cards and asking their partner for the correct sentence.

15B Springfield Hotel

You will need: one worksheet per student

- Pre-teach the following items of vocabulary: *a guest*; *staff (plural noun)*; *reception*; *to check out*; *to be ill*.
- Distribute one worksheet to each student. Allow them to read the advertisement at the top of the worksheet and check they have understood the main points.
- Tell the class that they have bought the Springfield Hotel, and are going to decide what rules to have in the hotel, both for guests and for staff.
- Put the students into pairs (or groups of three) and tell them to work out the rules using the prompts provided. Students should write the rules in the second column of the worksheet, using the expressions in bold in the Useful language box where appropriate.
- If necessary, do one or two examples with the whole class beforehand. For example: *Guests have to check out before 12 o'clock. Guests can pay by cash or credit card.*
- Students who finish early can think of some more rules and put them in the Other rules box at the bottom of the worksheet.
- Put two pairs/groups together and tell them to compare rules. Students should make a note of which rules are the same and which are different. If one pair/group doesn't agree with a rule, they can try to persuade the other pair/group to change it!
- Finally, students compare their rules with the whole class and discuss any different or unusual rules they have discovered.

15C It's the first on the left

You will need: one Worksheet A *and one* Worksheet B *per pair of students*

- Check that your students know how to ask for directions. For example: *Excuse me, where's the (nearest) bookshop? How do I get to the art gallery?*
- Put students into pairs. Give a copy of *Worksheet A* to one student, and a copy of *Worksheet B* to the other. **Students are not allowed to look at each other's worksheets.**
- Check that students know where they are on the map (at the railway station). Tell the class that the places that are shaded (the bus station, the shops, the bank, the coffee shop, the Sun Restaurant and the cinema) are on *both* maps, so they may refer to them when giving directions. For example: *Go past the bus station and turn left. When you come to the Sun Restaurant, turn right*.
- Students take it in turns to ask each other for directions to the places listed on the worksheet. Encourage students giving directions to use expressions from the *Useful language* box where possible.
- When a student has found the place he/she wants to go to, he/she writes the name of the place on his/her copy of the map. Students are not allowed to look at each other's worksheets until they have both found all five places listed.
- Finally, students compare their maps and see if they have marked the places correctly.

15D Revision board game

You will need: one copy of the board and one set of Question cards *per group of three students; dice and counters*

- Put students into groups of three. Give each group a copy of the board, a set of *Question cards* (shuffled), dice and counters. Tell students to put the *Question cards* face down in a pile on the appropriate space on the board, and their counters on the *Start* square.
- Students take it in turns to throw a number. If Student A lands on a square with a question mark on it, he/she must pick up a *Question card*. He/She should place the card down so that all the students can read it, then attempt to answer the question.
- If the other students think that the answer is correct, Student A stays on the square. If the answer is not correct, or Student A cannot answer the question, he/she should move back to his/her original square. If the students cannot agree, the teacher adjudicates (see **Key**).
- If a student lands on a square with a speech bubble on it, he/she must talk about that topic for fifteen seconds without stopping. (If one of the students in each group has a watch with a second hand, make him/her the timekeeper.) If he/she cannot think of anything to say, or stops talking before the fifteen seconds are up, he/she must return to his/her original square.
- The first student to reach the *Finish* square is the winner. Groups who finish first can go through the Question cards and check their answers.

1A Nice to meet you

Names and countries; *to be*

Name: Ana

Country: Mexico

Name: Diego

Country: Argentina

Name: Olga

Country: Russia

Name: Stefan

Country: Germany

Name: Marie-Claire

Country: France

Name: Wang Yong

Country: China

Name: Jeff

Country: Australia

Name: Ahmed

Country: Egypt

Name: Victoria

Country: Italy

Name: Toshi

Country: Japan

Name: Magda

Country: Poland

Name: Peter

Country: Britain

Name: Elena

Country: Spain

Name: Ali

Country: Turkey

Name: Ross

Country: the USA

Name: Sun

Country: South Korea

1B The English class

Personal information; third person of *to be*

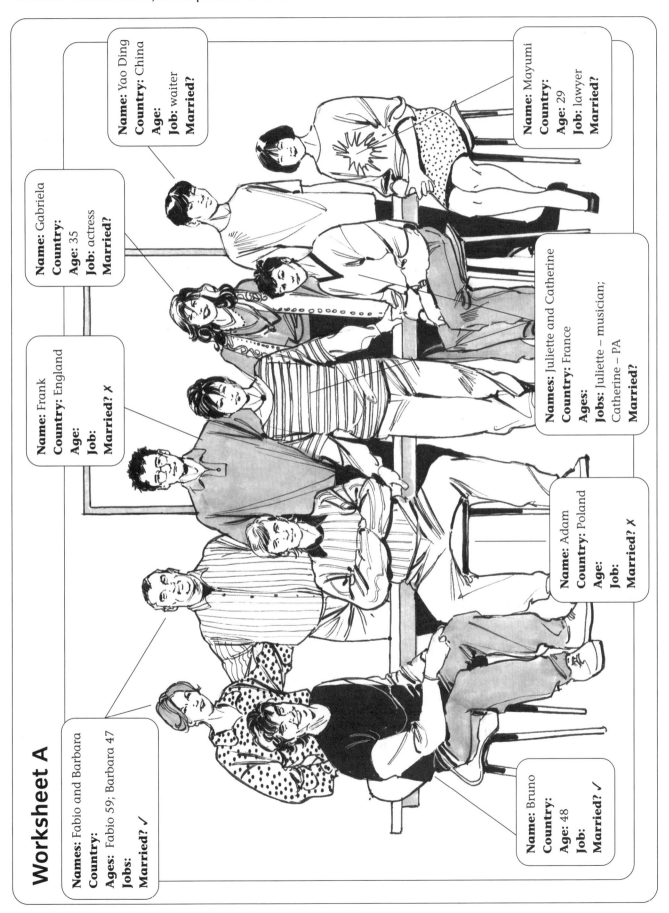

Worksheet A

Names: Fabio and Barbara
Country:
Ages: Fabio 59; Barbara 47
Jobs:
Married? ✓

Name: Frank
Country: England
Age:
Job:
Married? ✗

Name: Gabriela
Country:
Age: 35
Job: actress
Married?

Name: Yao Ding
Country: China
Age:
Job: waiter
Married?

Name: Mayumi
Country:
Age: 29
Job: lawyer
Married?

Names: Juliette and Catherine
Country: France
Ages:
Jobs: Juliette – musician;
Catherine – PA
Married?

Name: Adam
Country: Poland
Age:
Job:
Married? ✗

Name: Bruno
Country:
Age: 48
Job:
Married? ✓

Worksheet B

Names: Fabio and Barbara
Country: Italy
Ages:
Jobs: Fabio – police officer; Barbara – nurse
Married?

Name: Frank
Country:
Age: 30
Job: doctor
Married?

Name: Gabriela
Country: Spain
Age:
Job:
Married? ✓

Name: Yao Ding
Country:
Age: 19
Job:
Married? ✗

Name: Mayumi
Country: Japan
Age:
Job:
Married? ✓

Names: Juliette and Catherine
Country:
Ages: both 21
Jobs:
Married? ✗

Name: Adam
Country:
Age: 27
Job: engineer
Married?

Name: Bruno
Country: Brazil
Age:
Job: electrician
Married?

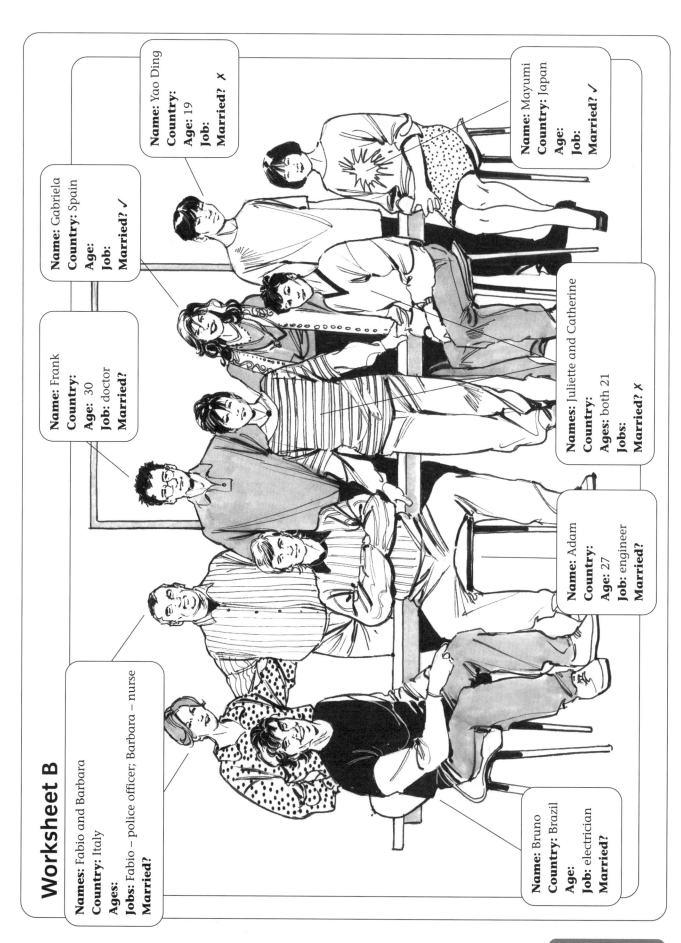

1C Short answer snap

Short answers with *to be*

Question cards

Are you from Argentina?	Is Manuel Spanish?	Are you police officers?
Are you an actor?	Is Rachel married?	Are you and your friend on holiday?
Are you a shop assistant?	Is your mother a businesswoman?	Are Sue and Tim at university?
Is Tom at university?	Is she Japanese?	Are his friends from the USA?
Is your father an engineer?	Are you from Italy?	Are they tourists?

Answer cards

Yes, I am.	No, he isn't.	No, we aren't.
No, I'm not.	Yes, she is.	Yes, we are.
Yes, I am.	No, she isn't.	No, they aren't.
Yes, he is.	Yes, she is.	Yes, they are.
No, he isn't.	Yes, we are.	No, they aren't.

2A   What's this?

This, that, these, those

Worksheet A

Worksheet B

PHOTOCOPIABLE

2B Who's got a Ferrari?

Have got

WHO'S GOT WHAT?

1 .... has got a Ferrari.

2 .... has got twenty cats.

3 .... has got ten children.

4 .... has got an elephant.

5 .... has got a famous girlfriend/boyfriend.

6 .... has got a big swimming pool.

7 .... has got a restaurant.

8 .... has got a Stradivarius violin.

9 .... has got a famous father.

10 ....has got ten thousand books.

Role card 1

Your name is Tom/Sally and you live in London, England. You're a musician, you're married and you've got a Stradivarius violin!

Role card 2

Your name is Tom/Sally, you live in Liverpool, England and you're single. You're a teacher and you've got twenty cats!

Role card 3

Your name is Franco/Francesca and you live in Rome, Italy. You're married, you're a police officer and you've got ten children!

Role card 4

Your name is Ali/Gita and you live in Calcutta, India and you're married. You're a taxi driver and you've got an elephant!

Role card 5

Your name is Nick/Nicola and you live in Hollywood, in the USA. You're an actor/ actress and you've got a famous girlfriend/boyfriend.

Role card 6

Your name is Martin/Suzannah. You're married and you live in São Paulo, Brazil. You're an engineer and you've got a big swimming pool.

Role card 7

Your name is Nikam/Niki and you live in Chang Mai, Thailand. You're married. You're a businessman/businesswoman and you've got a restaurant.

Role card 8

Your name is Toshi/Yumi and you live in Tokyo, Japan. You're single and you're a sportsman/sportswoman. You've got a Ferrari!

Role card 9

Your name is Junior/Rosa and you live in Madrid in Spain. You're single, you're a singer and you've got a famous father.

Role card 10

Your name is Hans/Rita and you live in Berlin, Germany. You're a doctor and you've got ten thousand books!

2C The family

Family vocabulary; possessive adjectives and 's

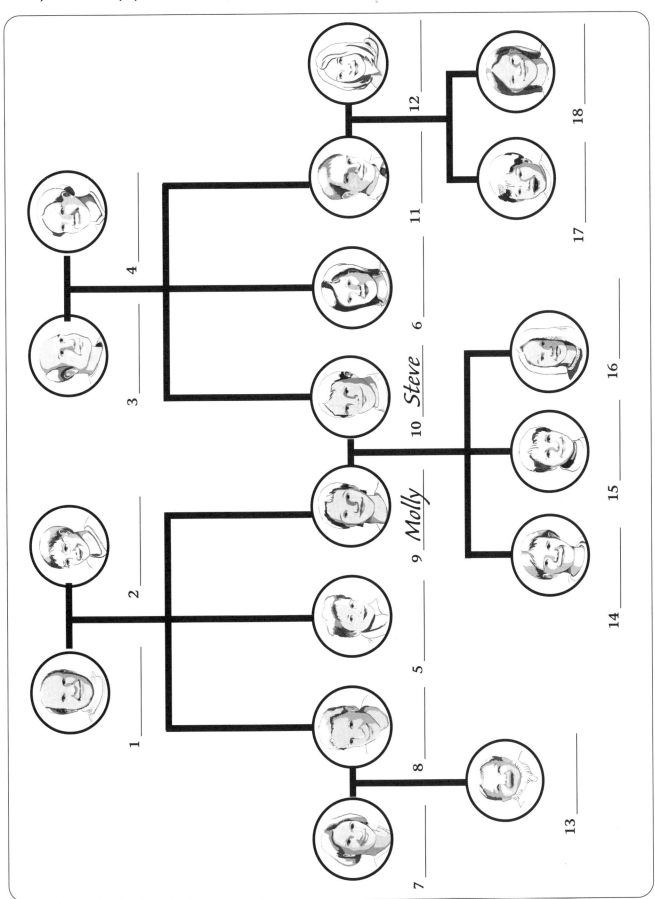

Worksheet A

1   Bob is Steve's brother.

2   Bob is married. His wife's name is Sally.

3   Molly and Steve have got one daughter. Her name's Sue.

4   Molly's got one sister. Her name's Liz.

5   Sally and Bob have got one son. His name's Tom.

6   Tom's got a sister. Her name's Maria.

7   Mike is Liz's father.

8   Jack is Tom's grandfather.

9   Tom is Steve's nephew.

10 Jack's got two granddaughters, Maria and Sue.

11 Sue and Maria are cousins.

12 Mike's got two daughters, Molly and Liz.

Worksheet B

1   Steve's got one sister. Her name's Pam.

2   Steve and Molly are Peter's parents.

3   Billy is Peter's brother.

4   Molly's got a brother. His name's Mark.

5   Mark is married. His wife's name is Laura.

6   Emma is Pam and Steve's mother.

7   Laura and Mark have got one son. His name's Frank.

8   Victoria is Frank's grandmother.

9   Molly is Frank's aunt.

10 Frank and Billy are cousins.

11 Peter and Billy are Emma's grandchildren.

12 Molly is Victoria's daughter.

3A Pick four cards

Present simple questions with *you*

I live in _____ .

a big house	a small house
a big flat	a small flat
a big city	a small town

(or the name of your town/city)

I go _____ .

out a lot	to English classes
to the cinema a lot	on holiday a lot
swimming a lot	to restaurants a lot

(or your own answers)

I drink a lot of _____ .

milk	tea
coffee	water
fruit juice	coke

(or your own answer)

I speak _____
a little / very well.

French	Spanish
Italian	Russian
Chinese	German
another language	

(*Don't* write your first language!)

I work _____ .

for a small company	for a big company
in an office	long hours
at home	

(or your own answer)

I eat a lot of _____ .

apples	chocolate
sweets	hamburgers
pizzas	Indian food

(or your own answer but *don't* write the food from your country)

I study _____ .

at university	at school
economics	languages
business	law

(or your own answer)

I live with my _____
(and my _____ *).*

parents	brother(s)
sister(s)	children
son	daughter

(or your own answer)

© Pearson Education Limited 2005

3B Pronoun stars

Subject and object pronouns

My name is Joe, and ☆ am from Scotland.

Answer: **I**

A: Do you live here?
B: No, ☆ are on holiday.

Answer: **we**

Peter's our teacher, and we like ☆ very much.

Answer: **him**

A: Do ☆ live in a big city?
B: No, we don't.

Answer: **you**

A: John and I are at university.
B: What do ☆ study?

Answer: **you**

Look, that's Madonna! Go and speak to ☆.

Answer: **her**

This is my son. ☆ is a teacher.

Answer: **He**

My parents are Brazilian, but ☆ live in Italy.

Answer: **they**

I like coffee, and I drink ☆ every morning.

Answer: **it**

My sister's 28 years old and ☆ is married.

Answer: **she**

I've got a big house, and my parents live with ☆.

Answer: **me**

Sue and I live in Monaco. Come and stay with ☆!

Answer: **us**

A: What's this?
B: ☆ is a mobile phone.

Answer: **It**

Happy Birthday, Jane! This is for ☆.

Answer: **you**

My children like cats, but I don't like ☆.

Answer: **them**

Pronoun cards

I	**WE**	**HIM**
YOU	**YOU**	**HER**
HE	**THEY**	**IT**
SHE	**ME**	**US**
IT	**YOU**	**THEM**

© Pearson Education Limited 2005

3C Time pelmanism

Ways of telling the time

four o'clock		half past five	
five past nine		twenty-five to one	
ten past twelve		twenty to eight	
a quarter past two		a quarter to ten	
twenty past six		ten to three	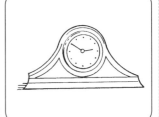
twenty-five past eleven		five to seven	

© Pearson Education Limited 2005

4A Things you love and hate

Present simple; *like* + *-ing*

	Someone who likes/loves this	Someone who doesn't like / hates this
1 doing homework		
2 classical music		
3 washing up		
4 Chinese food		
5 getting up early		
6 watching football on TV		
7 doing housework		
8 buying new shoes		
9 chocolate ice cream		
10 living in this town/city		

© Pearson Education Limited 2005   **PHOTOCOPIABLE**

4B   Three people I know

Present simple *yes*/*no* questions; *he* and *she*

1 Write the names of **three** people you know (either friends or people in your family) in the boxes below. Do **not** write anything else in the table.

Name:	Name:	Name:

2 Write **five** things about each person **in the boxes below**. Write short answers, not whole sentences. Write your answers in any box you want, but not in the same order as the questions. Choose from the following:

- the country (or city) he/she comes from
- something he/she likes doing
- where he/she works or studies
- a sport he/she likes watching
- the town or city he/she lives in now
- some food or drink he/she likes
- a foreign language he/she speaks
- something he/she hates

4C Always, sometimes, never

Present simple; adverbs of frequency

Worksheet A

Underline the answer in *italics* that you think is correct for your partner. You can only choose **one** answer for each sentence. You cannot ask him/her any questions.

Partner's name	Right or wrong?
1 He/She *often listens / sometimes listens / doesn't often listen / never listens* to classical music.	
2 He/She *often goes / sometimes goes / doesn't often go / never goes* to the gym.	
3 He/She *always/often/sometimes/never* goes to the cinema at the weekend.	
4 He/She *always drinks / usually drinks / doesn't often drink / never drinks* coffee in the morning.	
5 He/She *always/usually/sometimes/never* goes to sleep before ten o'clock.	
6 He/She *often plays / sometimes plays / doesn't often play / never plays* tennis at the weekend.	
7 He/She *always/usually/sometimes/never* wakes up before seven o'clock.	
8 He/She *always does / usually does / doesn't often do / never does* his/her English homework!	

Worksheet B

Underline the answer in *italics* that you think is correct for your partner. You can only choose **one** answer for each sentence. You cannot ask him/her any questions.

Partner's name..	Right or wrong?
1 He/She *always/usually/sometimes/never* wakes up after nine o'clock at the weekend.	
2 He/She *often goes / sometimes goes / doesn't often go / never goes* to expensive restaurants.	
3 He/She *always/usually/sometimes/never* watches the news on TV in the evening.	
4 He/She *often goes / sometimes goes / doesn't often go / never goes* dancing at the weekend.	
5 He/She *often/sometimes/never* writes e-mails or letters in English.	
6 He/She *always/usually/sometimes/never* goes to sleep after midnight.	
7 He/She *always has / sometimes has / doesn't usually have / never has* toast for breakfast.	
8 He/She *always/usually/sometimes/never* studies English at the weekend!	

© Pearson Education Limited 2005

4D Verb dominoes

Verbs and nouns that go together

... **her homework** for about two hours.	I often **read** ...
... **a magazine** when they travel by train.	Sally always **plays** ...
... **the guitar** in her friend's rock band.	Many Japanese men like **playing** ...
... **the radio** when he drives to work.	My daughter **listens to** ...
... **videos** at her boyfriend's house.	Do you usually **watch** ...
... **shopping** with her friends on Saturdays.	My grandfather **goes** ...
... **home.** They don't like this place at all!	Most people **have** ...
... **a shower,** at 6 a.m. He gets up very early.	My friend Laura **writes** ...
... **letters** to all her grandchildren every month.	Jimmy hates **going to** ...
... **the cinema** with my girlfriend.	My husband and I **visit** ...
... **his grandparents** in the summer holidays.	My mother never **drinks** ...
... **tea** in the afternoon. They love it!	At the weekend I often **do** ...

... **a newspaper** when I have my breakfast.	Many people **read** ...
... **tennis** on Tuesday evenings with her friends.	Alice's sister **plays** ...
... **golf** in their free time.	Richard usually **listens to** ...
... **CDs** on her **personal stereo.**	Katy often **watches** ...
... **television** at the weekend?	His sister sometimes **goes** ...
... **swimming** in the sea every day, and he's 78!	All the children want **to go** ...
... their evening **meal** at 8 o'clock.	My husband **has** ...
... **about 100 e-mails** a day!	Nick's grandmother **writes** ...
... **school.** He wants to stay at home and watch TV!	On Wednesday evening I usually **go to** ...
... **our friends** in Australia every Christmas.	Neil's son usually **visits** ...
... **coffee.** She hates it!	Old people often **drink** ...
... **nothing,** just relax!	In the evenings Julia usually **does** ...

© Pearson Education Limited 2005   **129**

5A The perfect holiday

Can and *can't* for possibility

Worksheet A

Read the information below and decide what you can (and can't) do if you stay at this hotel.

Helena Island – Ayala Hotel

Going on holiday? Then come to the beautiful *Ayala Hotel* on Helena Island.

* swim in three swimming pools
* eat in two restaurants
  (we have the best Italian food on the island)
* go to the *Club Ayala* every evening
* hire cars and bicycles
* walk to three quiet beaches
  (only five minutes from the hotel)
* go by bus to the beautiful Helga mountains

The Ayala Hotel is only twenty minutes from **Helena City**, where there are cinemas, museums, clubs and lots of interesting shops.

For the perfect holiday, come to The Ayala Hotel!

Worksheet B

Read the information below and decide what you can (and can't) do if you stay at this hotel.

Helena Island – Bella Hotel

The Bella Hotel on Helena Island – for the holiday of your dreams.

* eat in four excellent restaurants
  (including French and Chinese)
* visit the beautiful beach next to the hotel
* swim in two big swimming pools
* play tennis or golf
* hire cars and motorbikes
* go by boat to Bird Island – the most
  beautiful place in the world!

The Bella Hotel is only half an hour from **Perilla**, an old town on the coast. In Perilla there are interesting old buildings, restaurants, cafés, a cinema and lots of shops.

The Bella Hotel – where the beautiful people go!

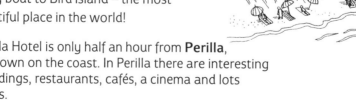

PHOTOCOPIABLE

Worksheet C

Read the information below and decide what you can (and can't) do if you stay at this hotel.

Helena Island – Romina Hotel

Come on holiday to **The Romina Hotel** – the best place to stay on Helena Island!

* walk to four different beaches
  (only 5 or 10 minutes from the hotel)
* relax in our swimming pool and jacuzzi
* eat in three wonderful restaurants
  (one is open 24 hours a day!)
* hire boats, cars and bicycles
* watch free films every night
* go by bus to the beautiful Helga mountains

The Romina Hotel is ten minutes' walk from **Selia**, a small fishing village. In Selia there are some restaurants, two excellent clubs and lots of cafés on the beach.

For the holiday of a lifetime, come to The Romina Hotel!

Worksheet D

Read the information below and decide what you can (and can't) do if you stay at this hotel.

Helena Island – Stella Hotel

Come to the wonderful **Stella Hotel** on Helena Island!

* a beautiful long beach next to the hotel
* eat in four restaurants
  (including Japanese and Italian)
* hire cars and scooters
* dance all night at *Club Stella*
* swim in three swimming pools
  (one is open 24 hours a day!)
* go by boat to Bird Island – the most beautiful place in the world

The Stella Hotel is 25 minutes from **Vandana**, an old town on the coast. In Vandana there are very good restaurants and shops, an art gallery and lots of places to walk.

Come and stay in The Stella Hotel – and enjoy life!

5B Transport crossword

Vocabulary related to transport

Crossword A

Crossword B

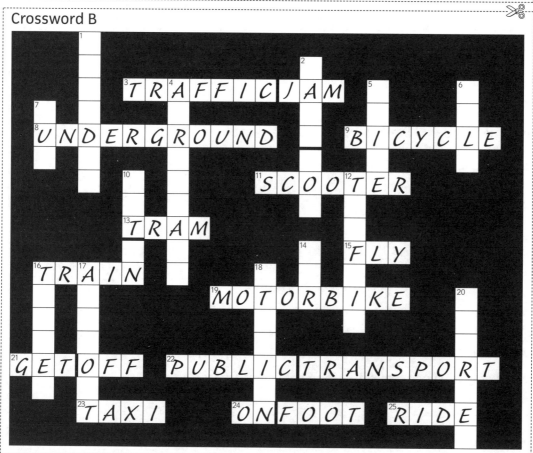

 PHOTOCOPIABLE

Learner-training worksheet A

Using the *Mini-dictionary*

MEANING

1 **a)** Find these words in your *Mini-dictionary* and read the definitions and examples.

- thirsty
- packet
- shave

b) Do you understand the words? If you do, is this because of the definition, the example, or both?

GRAMMAR

2 Look at the words in Exercise 1 again.

Which word is: a a noun? ....

b a verb? ....

c an adjective? ....

3 See how the *Mini-dictionary* shows you that a word is a noun, verb or adjective.

meal /miː/ *noun* [C] past tense **meals** food that you eat at a particular time: *We usually have a big meal in the evening.* | *Cara is going to cook her boyfriend a meal.*

favourite /ˈfeɪvərət/ *adjective* your favourite thing or person is the one that you like most: *We chose Jose's favourite music for the party.* | *She's my favourite teacher.*

walk /wɔːk/ *verb* third person singular **walks,** present participle **walking,** past tense **walked,** past participle **have walked** to move forwards by putting one foot in front of the other: *I usually **walk to** college.*

Look at these words from Modules 1 and 5 of the *Students' Book* and write **noun, verb** or **adjective** next to the word. Use your *Mini-dictionary* to check your answers.

a home ....   c great ....   e married ....

b live ....   d carry ....   f life ....

PRONUNCIATION

4 Pronunciation is shown like this in the *Mini-dictionary*.

cousin /ˈkʌzən/ *noun* [C] plural **cousins** the son or daughter of your AUNT or UNCLE: *When I was little my cousin used to come over to my house.*

Use the pronunciation table on the inside of the front cover of the *Mini-dictionary* to help you pronounce words correctly. Find these words in the *Mini-dictionary* and say them to your partner.

- fantastic
- married
- relatives
- crowded
- excellent
- arrive
- professional

6A Food battleships

There is / there are; food vocabulary; *some* and *any*

Picture A

Picture B

© Pearson Education Limited 2005

6B The recipe game

Some and *any*; food vocabulary

Food card A

You've got …

Food card B

You've got …

Food card C

You've got …

Food card D

You've got …

Food card E

You've got …

Food card F

You've got …

Recipe card A

Lasagne

You need:

- pasta
- an onion
- a green pepper
- tomatoes
- meat
- flour
- milk
- butter
- cheese

Recipe card B

Curry with Rice

You need:

- rice
- tomatoes
- an onion
- carrots
- beans
- mushrooms
- meat
- a green pepper
- a lemon

Recipe card C

Hawaiian Pizza

You need:

- flour
- ham
- sausages
- tomatoes
- cheese
- a green pepper
- mushrooms
- meat
- a pineapple

Recipe card D

Fish and Potato Pie

You need:

- fish
- potatoes
- milk
- eggs
- an onion
- carrots
- cheese
- butter
- flour

Recipe card E

Fruit Surprise

You need:

- apples
- bananas
- grapes
- strawberries
- eggs
- sugar
- a lemon
- cream
- ice cream

Recipe card F

Mixed Fruit Pie

You need:

- sugar
- flour
- eggs
- apples
- strawberries
- bananas
- grapes
- cream
- ice cream

PHOTOCOPIABLE

6C Sports stars

How much and *How many* with the Present simple

Worksheet A

Sergei Bugalov

Sergei is a weightlifter, and he lives in Bulgaria. He's got .... Olympic gold medals, and trains for six hours every day. He usually eats .... eggs and ten kilos of meat a week. He also drinks .... milk a day! He lives in a big flat in Sofia with his wife and nine children.

Christina Jones

Christina is from the USA, and is a marathon runner. She runs two hundred kilometres every week, and has got .... World Championship medals. She usually eats one kilo of fish and drinks .... water a day. Every year she goes to twenty different countries. She hasn't got a car, but she's got .... Harley Davidson motorbikes!

Silvia Martínez

Silvia is a tennis player from Spain. She lives near Madrid, and there are .... swimming pools and six tennis courts in her garden. She trains for .... hours every day. She drinks three litres of fruit juice a day, and eats .... bananas a week. She's very rich, and has got $10 million in the bank!

Antonio Crespo

Antonio is a footballer, and he lives in Italy. He plays about fifty matches every year and visits .... different countries. He usually eats five kilos of pasta a week, and drinks .... wine on Sunday night. He's very rich, and has got three houses and .... Ferraris!

Worksheet B

Sergei Bugalov

Sergei is a weightlifter, and he lives in Bulgaria. He's got three Olympic gold medals, and trains for .... hours every day. He usually eats forty eggs and .... meat a week. He also drinks twelve litres of milk a day! He lives in a big flat in Sofia with his wife and .... children.

Christina Jones

Christina is from the USA, and is a marathon runner. She runs .... kilometres every week, and has got two World Championship medals. She usually eats .... fish and drinks eight litres of water a day. Every year she goes to .... different countries. She hasn't got a car, but she's got three Harley Davidson motorbikes!

Silvia Martínez

Silvia is a tennis player from Spain. She lives near Madrid, and there are two swimming pools and .... tennis courts in her garden. She trains for four hours every day. She drinks .... fruit juice a day, and eats fifty or sixty bananas a week. She's very rich, and has got $.............. in the bank!

Antonio Crespo

Antonio is a footballer, and he lives in Italy. He plays about .... matches every year, and visits about ten different countries. He usually eats .... pasta a week, and drinks one or two bottles of wine on Sunday night. He's very rich, and has got .... houses and seventeen Ferraris!

7A The history quiz

Past simple and past time phrases

THE HISTORY QUIZ

Choose the correct answer to the questions below.

1   George Lucas made the first *Star Wars* film in:
    a) the sixties   b) the seventies   c) the eighties

2   Leonardo da Vinci was born in:
    a) the eleventh century   b) the thirteenth century   c) the fifteenth century

3   Princess Diana died in a car crash in:
    a) 1994   b) 1997   c) 1999

4   Bruce Lee made his first film when he was:
    a) six   b) seventeen   c) thirty-one

5   The First World War was from:
    a) 1910 to 1916   b) 1914 to 1918   c) 1916 to 1920

6   Walt Disney made the first Mickey Mouse cartoon about:
    a) 100 years ago   b) 75 years ago   c) 50 years ago

7   Margaret Thatcher was Prime Minister of the United Kingdom from:
    a) 1971 to 1983   b) 1979 to 1990   c) 1985 to 1997

8   The nuclear accident at Chernobyl happened in:
    a) the sixties   b) the seventies   c) the eighties

9   Elizabeth the First became Queen of England in:
    a) the sixteenth century   b) the eighteenth century   c) the twentieth century

10 The Berlin Wall came down in:
    a) 1984   b) 1989   c) 1995

11 Madonna had her first hit record with *Holiday* when she was:
    a) fifteen   b) nineteen   c) twenty-five

12 The first journey by train was about:
    a) 200 years ago   b) 300 years ago   c) 400 years ago

PHOTOCOPIABLE

7B Past tense bingo

Irregular past tenses

BINGO CARD A

HAD	SAID	SPOKE
WENT	COULD	WAS/WERE
BECAME	STOLE	DID
GOT	MET	DRANK

BINGO CARD B

BOUGHT	BEGAN	FOUND
LEFT	TOOK	READ
MADE	WON	SAW
WROTE	CAME	ATE

BINGO CARD C

DRANK	MET	GOT
SAW	WON	MADE
WAS/WERE	COULD	WENT
FOUND	BEGAN	BOUGHT

BINGO CARD D

ATE	CAME	WROTE
DID	STOLE	BECAME
READ	TOOK	LEFT
SPOKE	SAID	HAD

BINGO CARD E

BOUGHT	WON	HAD
BECAME	SPOKE	LEFT
WROTE	READ	GOT
COULD	DRANK	BEGAN

BINGO CARD F

WENT	MET	STOLE
MADE	FOUND	CAME
SAID	DID	WAS/WERE
TOOK	ATE	SAW

BINGO CARD G

WON	HAD	BOUGHT
MET	STOLE	WENT
READ	GOT	WROTE
DID	WAS/WERE	SAID

BINGO CARD H

SPOKE	LEFT	BECAME
FOUND	CAME	MADE
DRANK	GOT	COULD
ATE	SAW	TOOK

MASTER BINGO CARD

DID	DRANK	CAME	BEGAN	MADE	GOT
SAID	LEFT	TOOK	COULD	ATE	WENT
HAD	READ	WON	MET	WROTE	SPOKE
BOUGHT	SAW	BECAME	STOLE	WAS/WERE	FOUND

© Pearson Education Limited 2005

8A Looking back

Past simple *yes/no* questions

Write **short answers** to the following points in the bubbles below. You can write your answers in any bubble you want, but **not** in the same order as the questions.

- a place in your country you went to last year
- someone you talked to on the phone last week
- something you liked (or hated) doing when you were a child
- something you bought last month
- the town or city you lived in ten years ago
- a place you went on holiday to when you were a child
- someone you were friends with at primary school
- a present you gave to someone in your family last year
- something you did last month that you enjoyed
- someone you went on holiday with last year (or the year before)

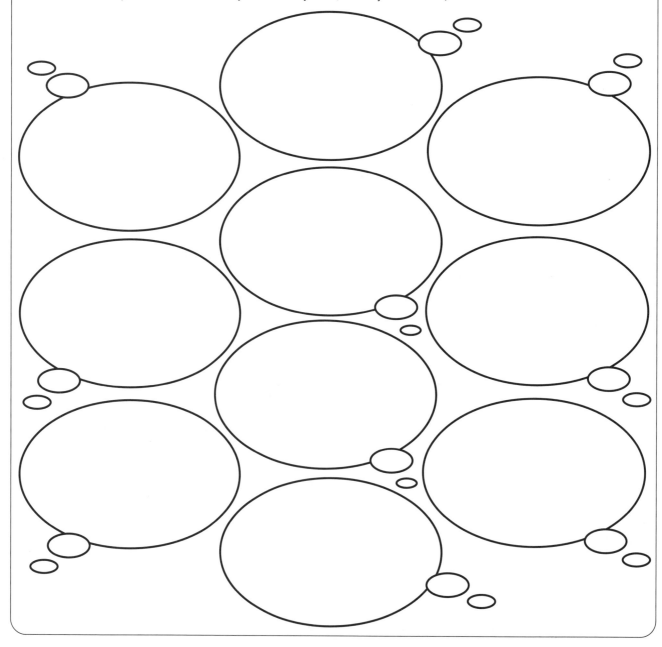

PHOTOCOPIABLE

8B John Wayne

Past simple and question words

Worksheet A

John Wayne – An All-American Hero

John Wayne was born on (a) .... in Iowa, USA, but his real name was Marion Robert Morrison. When he was a child his family moved to (b) .... because his father was ill, and at that time Marion usually (c) .... to school. He went to the University of Southern California, and in the summer he worked (d) .... Here Marion met John Ford, a famous film director, and they became good friends. In 1930 the director offered Marion a role in his new movie *The Big Trail* because (e) .... Marion decided to change his name to John Wayne when he made *The Big Trail*, and over the next eight years he appeared in (f) .... films.

Then in 1939 he made *Stagecoach*, which became an instant success. *Stagecoach* won (g) .... Oscars, and suddenly John Wayne was a star. In his career he appeared in nearly two hundred films, and he won (h) .... in 1970 for his role in the classic western *True Grit*. He made his last film in (i) 19......, and died of cancer in 1979. He was married three times and had (j) .... children.

Write questions for each of the gaps in the text above.

a When was ....?

b Where did his family .... when he was ....?

c How .... usually go ....?

d Where ....?

e Why ....?

f ....?

g ....?

h ....?

i ....?

j ....?

© Pearson Education Limited 2005 **141**

Worksheet B

John Wayne – An All-American Hero

John Wayne was born on May 26th 1907 in (1) ...., but his real name was Marion Robert Morrison. When he was a child his family moved to California because (2) ...., and at that time Marion usually rode a horse to school. He went to the University of (3) ...., and in the summer he worked at the Fox Film Studios. Here Marion met (4) ...., a famous film director, and they became good friends. In (5) 19...... the director offered Marion a role in his new movie *The Big Trail* because he was 'tall, strong and ugly'. Marion decided to (6) .... before he made *The Big Trail*, and over the next eight years he appeared in fifty-six films.

Then in (7) 19...... he made *Stagecoach*, which became an instant success. *Stagecoach* won two Oscars, and suddenly John Wayne was a star. In his career he appeared in (8) .... films, and he won the Oscar for best actor in 1970 for his role in the classic western *True Grit*. He made his last film in 1976, and died of cancer in (9) 19...... . He was married (10) .... times and had seven children.

Write questions for each of the gaps in the text above.

1 Where was...?

2 Why did his family...?

3 Which university did...?

4 Which famous ....?

5 When ....?

6 ....?

7 ....?

8 ....?

9 ....?

10 ....?

PHOTOCOPIABLE

8C Safe at last!

Past simple

Safe at last!

Three years ago two friends, Alex Brown and P.J. Kelly, decided to sail to Australia in a boat they made themselves. Three weeks later, they disappeared in the middle of the Indian Ocean. Boats and planes spent three weeks looking for them, but nobody could find Alex and P.J.

Then last week the pilot of an Indian Army plane saw the word HELP! written in the sand on a small island. A rescue boat went to the island – and found Alex and P.J. alive and well!

We sent our reporters to talk to the two sailors, and you can read their exclusive interview in next week's *Daily Planet!*

The island where Alex and P.J. lived for three years.

Reporter role card

You are going to interview Alex or P.J. With your partner(s), write down the questions you are going to ask. Write at least **ten** questions.

Make sure you include questions to find out the following information.

- why they were on the island
- what they ate and drank
- where they lived and slept
- what they did every day
- the problems they had on the island
- any people (or animals) they saw
- what they liked and didn't like about living on the island
- how they tried to get off the island
- if they want to go sailing again!

Now add three more questions of your own.

Sailor role card

You are P.J. or Alex. Some reporters from the *Daily Planet* are going to interview you. With your partner, make notes to help you in your interview.

Here are some things the reporter will ask you about.

- what happened to the boat
- what you ate and drank
- where you lived and slept
- what you did every day
- the problems you had on the island
- any people (or animals) you saw
- what you liked and didn't like about living on the island
- how you tried to get off the island
- if you want to go sailing again!

Now think of three more things to tell the reporters.

9A New Year's Eve

Comparative adjectives

Picture A

Picture B

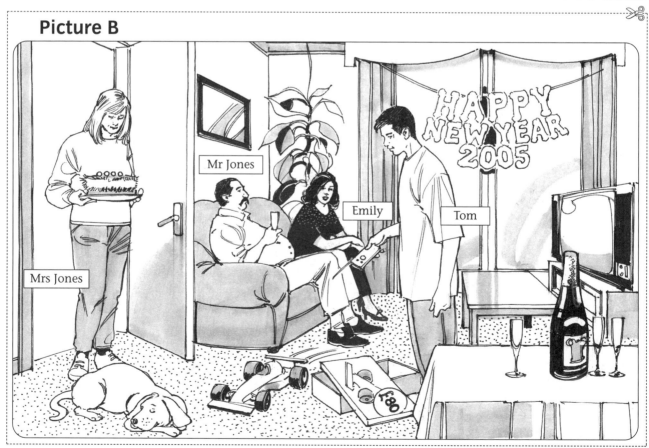

 PHOTOCOPIABLE

9B A superlative survey

Superlative adjectives

Card A

Which student has got the oldest brother or sister?

Card B

Which student went to bed the latest last night?

Card C

Which student has got the oldest car, motorbike, scooter or bicycle?

Card D

Which student takes the longest to come to school?

Card E

Which student lives in the largest house or flat?

Card F

Which student had the biggest breakfast this morning?

Card G

Which student usually wakes up the earliest?

Card H

Which student has got the youngest parent?

Card I

Which student has got the newest pair of shoes?

Card J

Which student went to the most beautiful place on holiday last year?

Card K

Which student has got the oldest relative?

Card L

Which student lives nearest to the school?

9C Shopping crossword

Vocabulary related to shopping

Crossword A

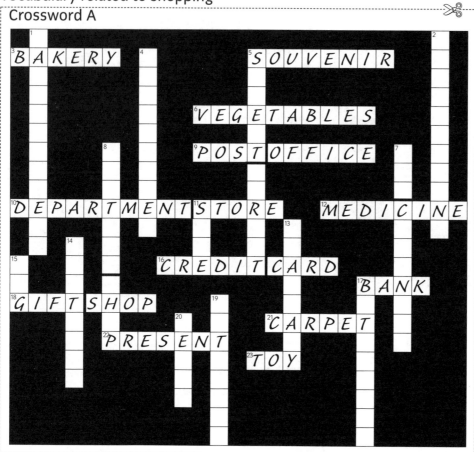

Crossword B

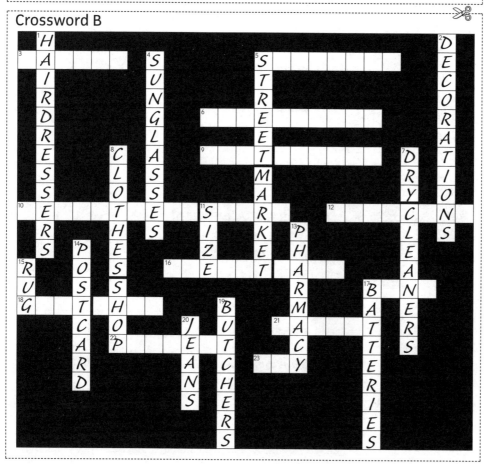

 PHOTOCOPIABLE

Learner-training worksheet B

Present continuous: spelling the *-ing* form

1 You can find the *-ing* form of verbs in your *Mini-dictionary*.

> **read** /riːd/ *verb* third person singular **reads**, present participle (reading) past tense **read**, /red/ past participle **have read** /red/ to look at something that is written down and understand what it means: *Dad sat in his chair, reading the paper.* | *My little brother is learning to read.* | *I like reading*

> **live** /lɪv/ *verb* third person singular **lives**, present participle (living) past tense **lived**, past participle **have lived**
> **1** if you live in a place, that place is your home: *Where do you live?* | I live in New York.
> **2** to be alive: *How long can you live without water?* | *My grandfather lived until he was ninety.*

2 Find the *-ing* form of these verbs in your *Mini-dictionary*.

walk	make	finish	travel	meet
leave	win	try	drive	play

3 Read the rules of how to spell the *-ing* form. Match the verbs in the box with the rules.

a   Most verbs add *-ing*: walking,
b   Verbs ending with *e*, lose the *e* and add *-ing*:
c   Verbs ending consonant + vowel + consonant, double the final consonant and add *-ing*:

4 Work with a partner and use the rules to write the *-ing* form of these verbs. Check your answers in your *Mini-dictionary*.

a   start _____
b   take _____
c   work _____
d   get _____

e   stay _____
f   stop _____
g   meet _____
h   watch _____

i   write _____
j   wait _____
k   buy _____
l   begin _____

 © **Pearson Education Limited** 2005

10A What's Sam doing?

Present continuous

Wendy John Philip Tania Peter Joe Vanessa Martin Mark Karen Claire Fred Vicky Susan Tim Jenny Sam

© Pearson Education Limited 2005

PHOTOCOPIABLE

Activity cards

✂

Card A Vicky is making a sandcastle.	**Card B** Peter is coming out of the sea.	**Card C** Wendy is playing football with her brother.	**Card D** Karen is talking on her mobile phone.
Card E Joe is selling ice cream.	**Card F** Claire is playing volleyball with her boyfriend.	**Card G** Vanessa is sleeping on the beach.	**Card H** Fred is running along the beach.
Card I Martin is stealing someone's bag.	**Card J** Tania is listening to music on her personal stereo.	**Card K** Mark is swimming in the sea.	**Card L** Philip is writing a postcard to a friend.
Card M Tim is playing football with his sister.	**Card N** Jenny is windsurfing.	**Card O** Susan is reading a book.	**Card P** John is playing volleyball with his girlfriend.

10B A letter home

Present simple and continuous (question forms)

Letter A

C/Juan Canalejo 3° A
28017 Madrid
24th June

Dear Jennifer

Greetings from sunny Madrid! At the moment I'm sitting (1) ...., drinking coffee and eating (2) .... I sit in the same café every afternoon and watch the people – it's really interesting. Two old men are (3) ...., and a young girl is playing the guitar. Oh, I love it here...

But this isn't a holiday! Peter and I are studying (4) .... for a month at the university. We're really enjoying it, but it's very hard work. We study for four hours every morning, and classes start at (5) .... We normally get up at six o'clock! Peter and I go to the university by (6) ...., which is quite dangerous. The traffic is crazy here! We're staying with Franco (a friend from school), who lives (7) ....

Peter is enjoying it here too, and at the moment he's looking for souvenirs in the street markets. We usually (8) .... in the evening and eat meat or fish – food is very cheap here. We want to .... next year.

Well, I can see Peter walking across the square, and he's carrying a very big box! I'll say goodbye now. See you next month!

Lots of love

Penny

Letter B

C/Juan Canalejo 3° A
28017 Madrid
24th June

Dear Jennifer

Greetings from sunny Madrid! At the moment I'm sitting in a beautiful square, drinking (a) .... and eating chocolate cake! I sit (b) .... every afternoon and watch the people – it's really interesting. Two old men are playing cards, and a young girl is (c) .... Oh, I love it here...

But this isn't a holiday! Peter and I are studying Spanish for a month at the university. We're really enjoying it, but it's very hard work. We study for (d) .... hours every morning, and classes start at seven thirty. We normally get up at (e) .... o'clock! We go to the university by scooter, which is quite dangerous. The traffic is crazy here! We're staying with (f) ...., who lives in the centre of Madrid.

Peter is enjoying it here too, and at the moment he's looking for (g) .... in the street markets. We usually go to a restaurant in the evening and eat (h) .... – food is very cheap here. We want to come back again next year.

Well, I can see Peter walking across the square, and he's carrying a .... (i) .... I'll say goodbye now. See you next month!

Lots of love

Penny

10C Identity parades

Vocabulary for describing people and clothes

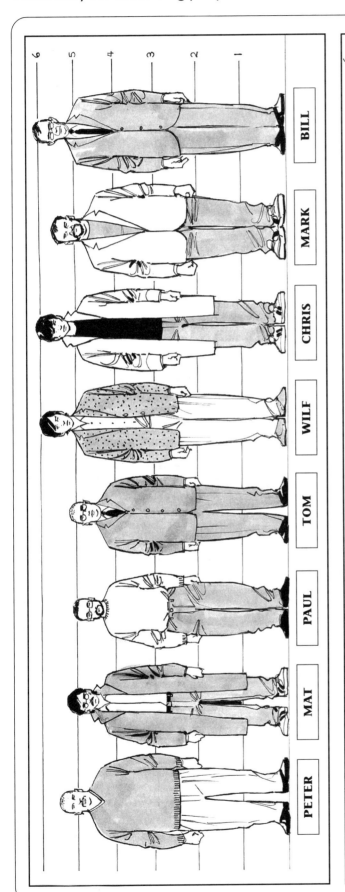

11A Can you or can't you?

Can and *can't* for ability

Worksheet A

Partner's name	Right or wrong?
1 My partner *can/can't* swim a hundred metres.	
2 My partner *can/can't* say all the months in English.	
3 My partner *can/can't* play a musical instrument.	
4 My partner *can/can't* cook well.	
5 My partner *can/can't* add 134 and 87 without writing anything. (the answer is 221)	
6 My partner *can/can't* name three English football teams.	
7 My partner *can/can't* play chess.	
8 My partner *can/can't* drive a car.	
9 My partner *can/can't* ride a horse.	
10 My partner *can/can't* remember where the Olympics were in 1996. (the answer is Atlanta, USA)	

Worksheet B

Partner's name	Right or wrong?
1 My partner *can/can't* run a kilometre without stopping.	
2 My partner *can/can't* say 'Hello' in five languages.	
3 My partner *can/can't* play tennis well.	
4 My partner *can/can't* type without looking at the keyboard.	
5 My partner *can/can't* multiply 9 by 12 without writing anything. (the answer is 108)	
6 My partner *can/can't* name five states in the USA (in English, of course!).	
7 My partner *can/can't* play backgammon.	
8 My partner *can/can't* ride a motorbike or scooter.	
9 My partner *can/can't* ski.	
10 My partner *can/can't* remember who was President of the United States in 1991. (the answer is George Bush)	

11B The dinner party

Question words and tenses

DINNER PARTY GUESTS

1 .... is an inventor. He/She invented a _____ last week.

2 .... is a millionaire. He/She won £ _____ on the lottery three months ago.

3 .... is a politician. He/She became president of his/her country in 19____.

4 .... is a sailor. He/She lived on his/her boat for _____ years.

5 .... is a diplomat. He/She visited _____ countries last year.

6 .... is a marathon runner. He/She runs _____ kilometres every day.

7 .... is an artist. He/She sells one of his/her paintings every _____.

8 .... is an Olympic swimmer. He/She can swim 100 metres in _____ seconds.

9 .... is a translator. He/She can speak _____ , _____ and _____.

10 .... is a film director. He/She makes _____ films.

| What ...? | When ...? | What kind of ...? | Which ...? | How long ...? |
| How often ...? | How much ...? | How many ...? | How far ...? | How fast ...? |

Role card A

You are an inventor, and you live in Germany. Last week you invented a machine that does English homework! You think this machine will make you rich!

Role card B

You're from London, and three months ago you lived in a very small flat and worked in a bank. Then you won £4,000,000 on the lottery! Now you live in a big house in Hawaii.

Role card C

You are a famous politician from Argentina, and you became president of your country in 1999. Everybody thinks you're a wonderful president (well, that's what they tell you!).

Role card D

You are a famous sailor from Holland. You sailed around the world in the 1970s. After that you lived on your boat for 27 years! Now you live in Amsterdam.

Role card E

You are a diplomat for your country. You spend a lot of time travelling around the world visiting important people. Last year you visited 74 countries!

Role card F

You are a marathon runner from South Africa. You won the New York Marathon in 1998. You run 30 km every day, including Sundays. You're very tired!

Role card G

You are an artist, and you live in Russia. You are very poor, because you only sell one painting every year. Maybe someone at the party wants to buy your paintings?

Role card H

You are from Australia, and you're a swimmer. You won two gold medals in the Sydney Olympics. You are the fastest swimmer in the world, and you can swim 100 metres in 54 seconds.

Role card I

You are a translator for the United Nations, and you live in the centre of New York. You can speak three languages – French, Russian and English (of course!).

Role card J

You are a famous film director from Hollywood. You only make one kind of film – action films. You are good friends with Bruce Willis and Arnold Schwarzenegger.

PHOTOCOPIABLE

11C The numbers game

Different ways of saying numbers

GAME 1 CARD A	
HEAR	**SAY**
14	1960
17,000	400
3,000,000,000	13,000
4,000,000	40
403	40,000
700,000	5.9
1749	90
START ➡	70,000
70	1.4
900,000	1690

GAME 1 CARD B	
HEAR	**SAY**
13,000	1947
40	9,000
1690	3,000,000
19	4,000,000,000
70,000	9.5
400	900,000
30,000	70
304	14
1.4	90,000
14,000	403

GAME 1 CARD C	
HEAR	**SAY**
5.9	17,000
90	3,000,000,000
1960	4,000,000
90,000	**FINISH!**
9,000	700,000
4,000,000,000	1749
3,000,000	14,000
9.5	304
1947	30,000
40,000	19

GAME 2 CARD A	
HEAR	**SAY**
808	62
5.8	1,500
START ➡	80,000
8.5	16
260	500,000
88,000	660
6,000,000,000	6.2
220	60,000
1680	600
18	200,000

GAME 2 CARD B	
HEAR	**SAY**
2,000,000,000	80
6.2	1860
600	1.8
12	6,000,000,000
1,500	22
16	88,000
2,000	18
60,000	**FINISH!**
5,000,000	1680
620	666

GAME 2 CARD C	
HEAR	**SAY**
200,000	620
62	5,000,000
660	5.8
80,000	12
80	2,000
1.8	260
666	8.5
1860	808
500,000	2,000,000,000
22	220

Learner-training worksheet C

Recording new vocabulary

1 Look how the *Mini-dictionary* shows the grammar of words.

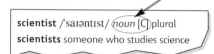

scientist /ˈsaɪəntɪst/ *noun* [C] plural
scientists someone who studies science

lively /ˈlaɪvli/ *adjective* comparative **livelier**,
superlative **liveliest** interesting and exciting:
The student bar has a really lively atmosphere.

2 Match these words with the correct part of speech. Check your answers in the *Mini-dictionary*.

a funny
b sell
c girlfriend
d juice
e between
f enjoy

1 a countable noun
2 a preposition
3 an irregular verb
4 a regular verb
5 an uncountable noun
6 an adjective

3 When you write new vocabulary in your notebooks, it is useful to include extra information about the words. Look at these two lists of words and decide what **extra** information is included in List B.

List A

ride = andar
ugly = feo
moustache = bigote
wait = esperar
toothpaste = pasta de dientes
uniform = uniforme

List B

to ride (irreg) (past: rode)   = andar
(e.g. to ride a bicycle / scooter)

ugly (adj)   = feo
(opposite of 'beautiful')

a moustache (noun C)   = bigote

to wait (reg)   = esperar
(e.g. to wait <u>for</u> a bus)

toothpaste (noun U)   = pasta de dientes

a uniform (noun C)   = uniforme
(e.g. to wear a uniform)

4 Look at these words from Module 10 and 11 of the Students' Book. Write them in your notebook and include more information about each word. Use your *Mini-dictionary* to help you, and write the translations in your own language.

aftershave   noisy   prefer   pet   keep   lazy

12A Future walkabout

Future intentions: *going to, would like to* and *want to*

Find someone who ...	Name(s)
1 ... is going away for the weekend.	
2 ... wants to stay at home this evening and watch TV.	
3 ... is going to have a big party for his/her next birthday.	
4 ... would like to become a language teacher.	
5 ... is going to a concert or a club in the next two weeks	
6 ... wants to go shopping this weekend.	
7 ... is going out with some friends on Saturday night.	
8 ... would like to live in an English-speaking country.	
9 .... is going to visit friends or relatives.	
10 ... would like to marry a famous film star.	
11 ... is going to fly somewhere in the next three months.	
12 ... wants to study English at this school next year.	

12B Collocation snap

Verb/noun collocations

Snap cards

A MUSEUM	**THE GYM**	**THE CINEMA**	**A CLUB**
AN EXERCISE	**SOME STUDYING**	**THE HOUSEWORK**	**HOMEWORK**
SPORT ON TV	**A VIDEO**	**THE NEWS**	**TELEVISION**
WITH FRIENDS	**AT A HOTEL**	**AT HOME**	**IN BED**
A MEAL	**A PARTY**	**A CIGARETTE**	**A BUSY WEEKEND**
SHOPPING	**DANCING**	**ON HOLIDAY**	**AWAY FOR THE WEEKEND**

PHOTOCOPIABLE

12C The school party

Suggestions and offers

Part A

You are going to organise a party for the whole school. Don't worry about money – the school is going to pay for everything! With your partner, decide the following things:

when to have the party	
where to have the party	
what kind of **food** you want	
what kind of **drinks** you want	
entertainment (eg a band, a DJ, games)	
things to **buy/get/make** (e.g. balloons, glasses, food)	
things to **do** before the party (e.g. put up decorations, invite people)	
any other ideas for the party	

Part B

Discuss your ideas with another pair/group, and plan your party together. Make notes about the party in the boxes below, and decide who is going to organise each part.

Where	Food	Entertainment	Things to do
When	**Drink**	**Things to buy/ get/make**	**Other ideas**

© **Pearson Education Limited 2005**

13A Education crossword

Vocabulary related to education

Crossword A

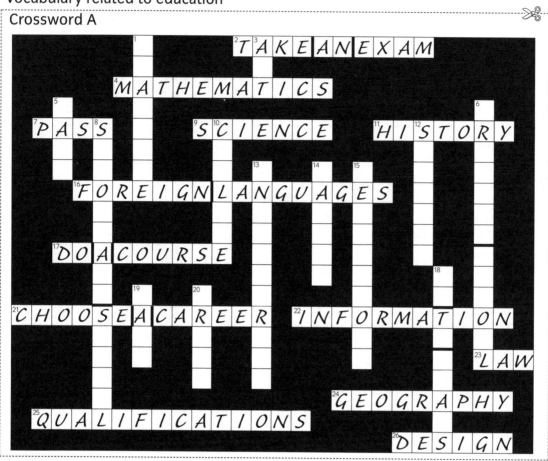

Crossword B

 PHOTOCOPIABLE

13B Looking into the future

Modal verbs for possibility: *might, will*

LIFE IN THE YEAR 2050

Look at the sentences below and put one of the following expressions in the gaps.

| will | will probably | might | might not | probably won't | won't |

In the year 2050 ...	Does the group agree?
1 ... every family in your country .... have a videophone in their homes.	
2 ... people .... live on the moon or other planets.	
3 ... there .... be big changes in the weather in your country.	
4 ... people .... be healthier.	
5 ... lions and elephants .... be extinct.	
6 ... there .... be more pollution than now.	
7 ... cars .... use petrol.	
8 ... children .... do all their school lessons on the Internet.	
9 ... most people .... work from home.	
10 ... life .... be more enjoyable than now.	

 © Pearson Education Limited 2005

Learner-training worksheet D

Irregular verbs

1 Notice how the past tenses and past participles of irregular verbs are shown in the *Mini-dictionary*.

> **fall** /fɔːl/ *verb* third person singular **falls**, present participle **falling**, past tense **fell**/fel/ past participle **have fallen**/ˈfɔːlən/ **fall in love** to start to love someone in a romantic way: *They were falling in love.* | *She fell in love with her friend's boyfriend.*

2 Find the past tenses and past participles of these verbs in your *Mini-dictionary* and write them in the spaces provided.

a lose _____ _____   c choose _____ _____
b sleep _____ _____   d catch _____ _____

3 Irregular verb race! Complete the table as quickly as you can. You can use the **Irregular verb table** on page 150 of the Students' Book to help you. (NOTE: You must spell all the words correctly to win.)

INFINITIVE	PAST TENSE	PAST PARTICIPLE
speak		
give		
steal		
come		
read		
think		
win		
hear		
bring		

4 Some irregular verbs have similar sound patterns. Look at the verbs in the boxes below and check you can pronounce them.

Group A /iː/ /e/ /e/	Group B any /ɔː/ /ɔː/	Group C any /əʊ/ /əʊ/
meet met met	buy bought bought	break broke broken

5 Put these verbs in the correct boxes above and write the past tenses and past participles. There are four verbs for each box. Use the **Irregular verb table** in the Students' Book to help you if necessary.

catch	read	bring	steal	speak	leave
choose	feel	think	wake up	fight	sleep

© Pearson Education Limited 2005 PHOTOCOPIABLE

14A The Travellers' Club

Present perfect questions with *ever*

Role card 1

You've climbed Mount Everest.
You've been to the North Pole.
You've lived in the Amazon jungle.
You've met the President of Peru.

Role card 2

You've climbed Mount Everest.
You've swum in the Nile.
You've sailed across the Atlantic Ocean.
You've drunk water from the River Ganges.

Role card 3

You've lived in the Amazon jungle.
You've seen a whale.
You've eaten sheep's eyes.
You've travelled from Beijing to Moscow by train.

Role card 4

You've seen a whale.
You've sailed across the Atlantic Ocean.
You've worked in a coffee shop in Amsterdam.
You've watched the sunrise from the top of Mount Fuji.

Role card 5

You've been to the North Pole.
You've ridden an elephant.
You've walked across South America.
You've watched the sunrise from the top of Mount Fuji.

Role card 6

You've ridden an elephant.
You've swum in the Nile.
You've eaten sheep's eyes.
You've driven across the Sahara Desert.

Role card 7

You've drunk water from the River Ganges.
You've slept in an Indian temple.
You've travelled from Beijing to Moscow by train.
You've walked across South America.

Role card 8

You've met the President of Peru.
You've slept in an Indian temple.
You've driven across the Sahara Desert.
You've worked in a coffee shop in Amsterdam.

Role card 9

You've climbed Mount Everest.
You've travelled from Beijing to Moscow by train.
You've driven across the Sahara Desert.
You've watched the sunrise from the top of Mount Fuji.

Role card 10

You've met the President of Peru.
You've seen a whale.
You've swum in the Nile.
You've walked across South America.

Role card 11

You've lived in the Amazon jungle.
You've drunk water from the River Ganges.
You've ridden an elephant.
You've worked in a coffee shop in Amsterdam.

Role card 12

You've been to the North Pole.
You've sailed across the Atlantic Ocean.
You've eaten sheep's eyes.
You've slept in an Indian temple.

14B Life boxes

Present perfect and Past simple

Write **short answers** to the following points in the boxes below. You can write your answers in any box you want, but **not** in the same order as the questions.

- a town or city you've been to that you liked a lot
- the most expensive thing you've bought this year
- a film you've seen more than once
- something you've eaten today
- the best birthday present you've received in your life
- an interesting television programme you've seen this week
- a place you haven't been to, but would like to visit
- the most exciting thing you've done in your life
- a café or restaurant you've been to this month

© Pearson Education Limited 2005   **PHOTOCOPIABLE**

14C On the phone

Language for telephoning

Student A – Role card 1

Your name is Sam Cook. You are going to call a travel agency called *Australia Travel*. You booked two plane tickets to Sydney three weeks ago, and want to know when they will be ready. The person you spoke to last time was Alex Marsh. You are leaving on Monday next week, so you want the tickets as soon as possible.

Student B – Role card 1

Your name is Alex Marsh, and you work for a travel agency called *Australia Travel*. Three weeks ago you sold two plane tickets to Sydney to a person called Sam Cook. The tickets will be ready on Friday of this week. Customers can collect tickets if they want to. Your address is 224, King Street.

Student A – Role card 2

Your name is Tom/Susan, and you are at home. You've got a sister called Vanessa, but she is out at the moment, and won't be back until 5 or 6 p.m. (it is now 3 p.m.). She has asked you to take any messages for her, including the person's phone number.

Student B – Role card 2

You are going to call your friend Vanessa. You are going to a concert tonight, and have an extra ticket. You want to ask Vanessa to come with you. The concert starts at 8 o'clock (it is now 3 p.m.). You are calling from your mobile phone, and the number is 01764 242197.

Student A – Role card 3

You are going to call a television repair company called *Fixit Limited*. Last week someone from this company came to your house and repaired your television, but now it doesn't work again. You are quite angry, and you want to speak to the manager, Mr Jones. Your phone number is 020 81695 4398.

Student B – Role card 3

You are the secretary of a television repair company called *Fixit Limited*. Your boss, Mr Jones, is out of the office all day, but will be back tomorrow. If any customers phone to speak to him, you must take a message and the customer's phone number.

Student A – Role card 4

You have got a new job as a waiter/waitress in a French restaurant. You work every evening except Tuesdays and Sundays – on these days you finish work at 6.30 p.m. There is a very good coffee shop next door to your restaurant where you often meet friends.

Student B – Role card 4

You are going to call a friend, who has just got a job as a waiter/waitress. You want to ask him/her to go to the cinema with you on Monday evening. (If you can, think of a film that you want to see.) When you speak to him/her, decide a time and a place to meet before the film.

15A Preposition pelmanism

Prepositions of movement

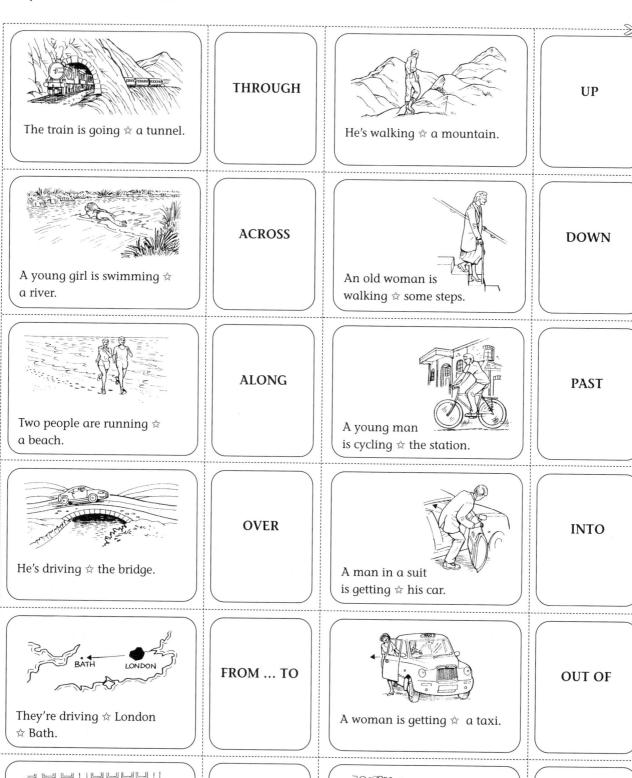

The train is going ☆ a tunnel.	THROUGH	He's walking ☆ a mountain.	UP
A young girl is swimming ☆ a river.	ACROSS	An old woman is walking ☆ some steps.	DOWN
Two people are running ☆ a beach.	ALONG	A young man is cycling ☆ the station.	PAST
He's driving ☆ the bridge.	OVER	A man in a suit is getting ☆ his car.	INTO
They're driving ☆ London ☆ Bath.	FROM ... TO	A woman is getting ☆ a taxi.	OUT OF
They're driving ☆ some shops.	PAST	Two people are walking ☆ the road.	ALONG

PHOTOCOPIABLE

15B Springfield Hotel

Have to, don't have to, can, can't

FOR SALE:

Springfield Hotel, close to town centre and railway station. 10 guest rooms (6 double and 4 single), excellent restaurant and beautiful garden. Call 04653 211762 for details.

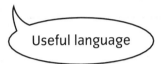

Useful language

'Guests **have to**... (check out before 12).'

'Staff **don't have to** ... (wear a uniform).'

'Guests **can** ... (smoke in their rooms).'

'Staff **can't** ... (smoke in the restaurant).'

You and some friends have bought the hotel! With your partner(s), look at the following information and decide what the rules are going to be in your hotel. Write your rules in the second column.

GUESTS	
Checking out • check out before 10/11/12 ...? • pay by cash / cheque / credit card ...? • if a guest checks out late? • if a guest wants the room for an extra day?	
Meals • book a table for lunch/dinner? • wear smart clothes for dinner? • smoke in the restaurant? • use mobile phones in the restaurant?	
In the rooms • have visitors (when)? • play music? • eat in the room? • leave keys when they go out? • smoke cigarettes in the room?	
STAFF	
Working hours • work weekends (how often?) • work evenings (how often?) • if they are ill?	
Clothes • wear a uniform? • wear a suit and tie (men)? • wear trousers/skirt (women)? • clothes for kitchen staff?	
Other rules?	

© Pearson Education Limited 2005

15C It's the first on the left

Language for giving directions

Worksheet A

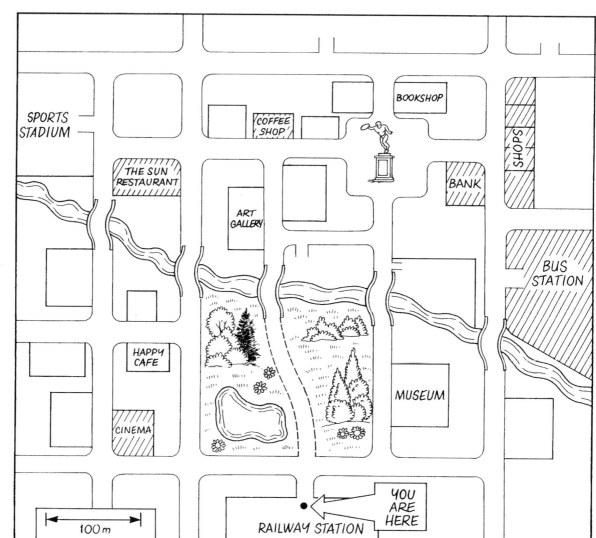

Ask your partner directions to:

1. the theatre
2. the Sunday market
3. the post office
4. the shopping centre
5. the city museum

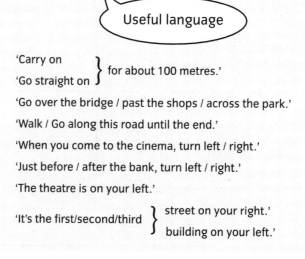

Useful language

'Carry on
'Go straight on } for about 100 metres.'

'Go over the bridge / past the shops / across the park.'

'Walk / Go along this road until the end.'

'When you come to the cinema, turn left / right.'

'Just before / after the bank, turn left / right.'

'The theatre is on your left.'

'It's the first/second/third } street on your right.'
building on your left.'

© Pearson Education Limited 2005

Worksheet B

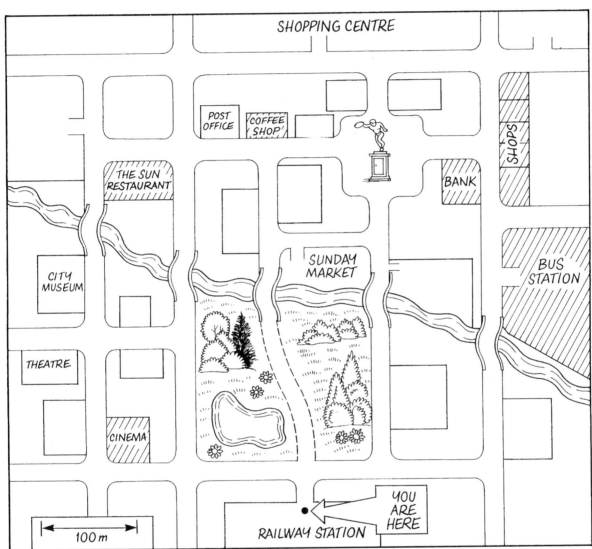

Ask your partner directions to:

a the museum
b the nearest bookshop
c the sports stadium
d the art gallery
e the Happy Cafe

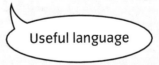
Useful language

'Carry on
'Go straight on } for about 100 metres.'

'Go over the bridge / past the shops / across the park.'

'Walk / Go along this road until the end.'

'When you come to the cinema, turn left / right.'

'Just before / after the bank, turn left / right.'

'The theatre is on your left.'

'It's the first/second/third } street on your right.'
                              } building on your left.'

15D Revision board game

All the language in the Students' Book

How much do you remember?

Start

GO FORWARD TWO SQUARES

your last holiday

MISS A TURN

what you've got in your bag or pockets

THROW AGAIN

what you usually do at the weekend

the most beautiful place you've visited

something you like doing

your family

GO BACK THREE SQUARES

your town or city

something interesting you did last week

MISS A TURN

describe someone you know well

GO FORWARD TWO SQUARES

QUESTION CARDS

what you'd like to do in the future

something you hate doing

what you did last weekend

what you do in your spare time

what you're going to do next weekend

THROW AGAIN

GO BACK THREE SQUARES

finish

Question cards

1

Which is correct?

Q: Do you *like/likes* playing
   tennis?
A: Yes, I *do/like*, but my brother
   don't/doesn't.

2

How much **or** *how many*?

a) _____ people are there in your
   class?
b) _____ money have you got?
c) _____ countries have you visited?

3

A, the **or** *Ø*?

My sister's ____ teacher, and she lives
in ____ Boston, in ____ United States.

4

How do you say these numbers?

23.8   15,000,000

706   1918 (year)

5

'My father's name is Jim, and he has
two brothers, Tim and Tom. Tim is
married to Mandy, and they have
two daughters, Mindy and Cindy. So
Mandy is my _____ and **Cindy** is
my _____.'

6

**What is the past tense of these
verbs?** (you must get at least **3**
correct!)

sleep   fall   leave   wear

7

**What are the past tenses and
past participles of these verbs?**
(you must get at least **3** correct!)

lose   break   write   meet

8

Choose the correct answer:

I *have to / don't have to* get up at 7.00
to go to school, but on Saturdays I
have to / can get up when I want.

9

**What are the comparatives and
superlatives of these adjectives?**

funny   boring   good
comfortable   small

10

Match the verb and the noun:

play   a film on TV
go   basketball
go to   swimming
watch   the gym

11

**Put the words in the correct
order to make a question.**

ago on where years you holiday
go three did ?

12

Put these in order:

sometimes   never
not ... often   always
usually   often

13

The **or** *Ø*?

I work in ___ city centre, and I go to
___ work by ___ train.

14

**Put these words in order to
make a sentence.**

will my pass teacher exam the
we probably thinks

15

Think of **seven** types of transport
(e.g. by car) in thirty seconds.

16

Which question word?

How ____ is it from Rome to Pisa?
How ____ can an elephant run?
How ____ do you play tennis?

17

Name **ten** animals in thirty seconds.

18

Which is correct?

My sister and her husband *live/lives*
in Poland. He *speak/speaks* Polish,
but she *doesn't/don't*.

19

**Present Simple or Present
Continuous?**
I (live) in London, but at the
moment I (stay) with a friend in
Holland. My friend (work) now and
he (like) his job very much.

20

Is **or** *has got*?

Janet ____ tall and thin, and she
_____ blue eyes. She ____ long hair
and she ____ in her thirties.

21

Countable or uncountable?

cheese   banana
cereal   roll
butter   jam
egg   sausage

© Pearson Education Limited 2005

Test one

TIME: 45 MINUTES

modules 1–5

A Plurals

Write the plural forms of the nouns.

For example:

computer *computers*

1 sweet ....
2 man ....
3 child ....
4 bottle ....
5 family ....
6 watch ....
7 sportswoman ....

| 7 |

B Questions

Look at the answers and write the questions.

For example:

A: *What's your first name?*

B: John.

1 A:...?
  B: MacDonald.
2 A: ....?
  B: I'm from Scotland.
3 A: ....?
  B: I'm an actor.
4 A: ....?
  B: No, I'm single.
5 A: ....?
  B: I live in London.
6 A: ....?
  B: 020 7854 6000

| 6 |

C Grammar and vocabulary

Circle the correct word in the following sentences.

For example:

Stefan *speak/speaks* two languages.

1 What are *they're/their* names?
2 He's *a/an* engineer.
3 Are *those/that* your keys?
4 I don't like *spiders/spider*.
5 Your cat likes *me/my*.
6 I go to *work/the work* at 8 o'clock every day.
7 My mother lives in Egypt. I speak to *she/her* every Sunday.
8 Do you travel *by/with* bus or train?

| 8 |

D Pronunciation

Where is the stress? Put the words in the correct column.

~~beautiful~~	~~teacher~~	tourist	married
manager	lesson	languages	excellent
business	holiday		

● ○	● ○ ○
teacher	*beautiful*

| 4 |

E Vocabulary

Write the opposite word.

For example:

married / *single*

1 start/.................
2 uncle/.................
3 husband/.................
4 love/.................
5 son/.................
6 depart/.................
7 parent/.................

| 7 |

172

F Prepositions

Write the correct preposition from the box in the following sentences.

about   on   in   at   on   ~~in~~   at

For example:

My school's ..*in*.. Rome.

1   Ross and I are students .... university.
2   It's 11 o'clock .... night here.
3   Maria's in Australia .... business.
4   My grandmother is .... 85.
5   The students are .... holiday this week.
6   My girlfriend phones me .... the evenings.

6

G Vocabulary and Present simple

Complete the gaps with a verb (for example: *listen, be, go*) in the Present simple.

On Saturday I (1) ..*listen*.. to the radio in the morning and then (2) .... shopping. We (3) .... lunch at 1 o'clock and then Peter (4) .... football on television in the afternoon and I usually (5) .... a book or a newspaper. In the evening we often (6) .... friends or we (7) .... to the cinema.

6

H Short answers

Write the short answers for the questions.
For example:

A: Is she a doctor?   B: Yes, ...*she is*.......

1   A: Are you Italian?   B: No, we ....
2   A: Have they got a car?   B: No, ...
3   A: Do you like classical music?   B: Yes, I ....
4   A: Does Anna study law?   B: Yes, ...
5   A: Can I take a bus?   B: Yes, ...

5

I Pronunciation

Look at the underlined sounds. Three sounds are the same and one sound is different. (Circle) the word with the different sound.

For example:

fr<u>ie</u>nd l<u>e</u>tter (j<u>ou</u>rney) cass<u>e</u>tte player

1   c<u>a</u>mera politici<u>a</u>n <u>a</u>ctor <u>a</u>rchitect
2   ph<u>o</u>to d<u>o</u>ctor c<u>o</u>mb ph<u>o</u>ne card
3   tr<u>a</u>ffic b<u>a</u>by w<u>ai</u>t f<u>a</u>vourite
4   lunch l<u>o</u>ve c<u>o</u>mfortable c<u>o</u>ffee
5   f<u>ou</u>r d<u>oo</u>r l<u>aw</u> kn<u>ow</u>

5

J Vocabulary

Write the missing letters in these means of transport.
For example:

c *a* r

1   m _ t _ _ b _ k _   4   b _ c _ c _ e
2   a _ r _ p _ _ n _   5   u _ d _ r _ r _ u _ d t r _ _ _
3   s c _ _ _ _ r

5

K Grammar

Correct the mistakes.
For example:

Do we can take a train?
Can we take a train .... ?

1   Do you like swim?
.... ?

2   She no got a dog.
....

3   Washington is in United States.
....

4   Mr Jenson no drink coffee.
....

5   What time close the bank?
.... ?

6   My brother's police officer.
....

7   Do you have got a brother?
.... ?

8   What means 'traffic jam'?
....

8

L Vocabulary

Match the verbs and the nouns.

1	live	a	open all night
2	study	b	public transport
3	start	c	in a flat
4	go	d	school at 9
5	stay	e	to the cinema
6	use	f	economics

1 ..c.   2 ...   3 ...   4 ...   5 ...   6 ...

[5]

M Real life

Underline the correct answer.

For example:

What's Mark's e-mail address?

a) Yes, he has.   b) No, he isn't.   c) I don't know.

1 A single to Cambridge, please.
    a) Single or return?   b) How much is it?
    c) That's £25 please.
2 How do you say this word?
    a) 'Musician.'   B) m,u,s,i,c,i,a,n
    c) It's a person who plays a musical instrument,
       for example, the guitar.
3 How can I get to the station?
    a) You can fly.   b) Go in a train.   c) You can walk.
4 Have you got the time?
    a) Yes it's 12 o'clock.   b) I'm sorry I'm not.
    c) Yes, I have.
5 What do you think of your English lessons?
    a) I don't think.   b) These are very good.
    c) They're okay.

[5]

N Numbers and times

Write the numbers and times in words.

For example:

62 ...*sixty-two*...   5.10 ..*five past ten*..

1	48	....
2	6.35	....
3	100	....
4	9.30	....
5	1.15	....
6	73	....

[6]

O Vocabulary

Circle the word that doesn't match the others.

For example:

red green big white

1	parent	friend	grandfather	mother
2	tourist	musician	actress	police officer
3	brilliant	excellent	perfect	crowded
4	platform	taxi	station	train
5	snack	meal	dinner	diary

[5]

P Questions

Complete the questions using *What, Who, How, How old,
How much, Where, What time.*

For example:

..*What's / What is*.. the name of your school?

1 A: .... are you? B: I'm fine thanks
2 A: .... is your father? B: He's 48.
3 A: .... is that man? B: Oh, that's my cousin.
4 A: .... do your parents live? B: In Sydney.
5 A: .... is the Moscow train? B: At 5.30, I think.
6 A: .... is this computer? B: $800.
7 A: .... do you like doing at the weekends?

[7]

Q Grammar

Put the word in brackets in the correct place.

For example:

We visit our grandmother. (*often*)
We often visit our grandmother.

1 My dog watches TV with me. (*always*)
    ....
2 Our teacher plays his guitar in class. (*sometimes*)
    ....
3 I write letters but I write a lot of e-mails. (*never*)
    ....
4 Do you play computer games? (*often*)
    ....
5 Parents don't read books to their children. (*often*)
    ....

[5]

TOTAL [100]

Test two

modules 6–10

A Countable and uncountable nouns

Circle the correct word.

For example:

I'd like *some*/*any* tea please

1   I'm sorry, Sir, but we haven't got *any/no* fish.
2   Natalya ate some *toasts/toast* but I didn't have any.
3   *There's/There are* some cheese on the table.
4   I didn't give Fiona *an/any* apple.
5   We had *some/any* hot chocolate last night before we went to bed.
6   They didn't see *some/any* bread in the market.
7   Oh dear – there's *no/any* milk.
8   I haven't got *some/any* money for new clothes.

	8

B Question words

Complete the sentences with a question word from the box.

Who	What	~~Where~~	How
How much	How many	How often	When

For example:

Where are you from?

1   .... children has Eleanor got?
2   A: .... was your holiday?   B: It was brilliant!
3   .... did you do last night?
4   A: .... coffee do you drink in one day?
5   .... did you and your husband first meet?
6   A: .... is in the film?   B: Harrison Ford, I think.

	6

C Numbers and dates

Write the numbers and dates in words.

For example:

56th *fifty-sixth*

1 42nd .... 2 1969 .... 3 3rd ....
4 21st .... 5 5th .... 6 2005 ....

	6

D Vocabulary

Write the missing letters.

For example:

The opposite of good is b _a_ _d_

1   Everybody knows Elvis Presley. He's really f _ _ _ _ _.
2   The opposite of *started* is f _ _ _ _ _ _ _.
3   You can buy meat at a b_ _ _ _ _ _'s
4   You can buy jeans in a c_ _ _ _ _ _   s _ _ _.
5   I fell asleep at 11 o'clock and w _ _ _   u _ next morning at 7.
6   The opposite of beautiful is u _ _ _.
7   My f _ _ _ _ _ _ _ colour is red.
8   Tim Berners Lee i _ _ _ _ _ _ _ the World Wide Web.

	8

E Past simple

Put the verbs in brackets into the Past simple.

William Shakespeare (1) ....*was*.... (*be*) born at Stratford-Upon-Avon in 1564 and (2) .... (*study*) at the town school. He married Anne Hathaway and they (3) .... (*have*) three children but he (4) .... (*not stay*) in Stratford. In 1587 he (5) .... (*decide*) to go to London and he (6) .... (*leave*) Anne and Stratford and (7) .... (*travel*) to the capital city. In London he (8) .... (*become*) an actor. Shakespeare (9) .... (*write*) many poems, and thirty-five plays. His plays (10) .... (*be*) very popular. He (11) .... (*die*) in 1616 back in Stratford.

	10

F Pronunciation

Put the words in the correct column.

~~hamburgers~~	popular	sausages	bananas
oranges	attractive	tomatoes	difficult
important	interesting	successful	

○ ● ○	● ○ ○
	hamburgers

	5

G Questions

Write the questions for each answer

For example:

A: What / last night?
What did you do last night?
....
B: I watched television and went to bed early.

1 A: You / nice weekend?
....
B: Yes, I went to Paris!

2 A: Oh! Who / go with?
....
B: With my brother, Jim.

3 A: Be / good?
....
B: Yes, it was fantastic!

4 A: What / do?
....
B: On Saturday we walked around the city centre
and we had a wonderful meal at a little restaurant.

Now complete the answers with the verb in the Past simple.

5 A: And what about Sunday?
B: We .... the Eiffel Tower and the Louvre. (see)

6 A: Did you buy anything in Paris?
B: I didn't, but Jim .... some wine and
cigarettes. (buy)

6

H Comparative adjectives

Write the comparative form of the adjective in brackets.

For example:

My brother's bedroom is ...*smaller*.... than mine. (*small*)

1 The new James Bond film is .... than the last
one. (*good*)

2 It's .... to eat fruit than to eat sweets.
(*healthy*)

3 Tokyo's .... than Sydney. (*big*)

4 My English is .... now than it was a year
ago! (*bad*)

5 I like these blue sunglasses, but they're ....
than the green ones. (*expensive*)

6 My name's Xiang Hu, but please call me John
because it's .... to pronounce. (*easy*)

6

I Pronunciation

Look at the underlined sounds. Three sounds are the same
and one sound is different. Circle the word with the
different sound.

For example:

fr<u>ie</u>nd   l<u>e</u>tter   (j<u>ou</u>rney)   cass<u>e</u>tte player

1 s<u>i</u>x   bisc<u>ui</u>ts   d<u>i</u>fficult   kn<u>i</u>fe
2 <u>a</u>pples   gr<u>a</u>pes   st<u>a</u>mps   p<u>a</u>sta
3 sh<u>ir</u>t   f<u>ir</u>st   l<u>ear</u>n   <u>ear</u>ring
4 y<u>o</u>ghurt   t<u>oo</u>thpaste s<u>ou</u>p   fr<u>ui</u>t
5 sm<u>a</u>ll   f<u>ou</u>r   s<u>au</u>ce   sl<u>ow</u>
6 b<u>ee</u>r   n<u>ear</u>   w<u>ear</u>   b<u>ear</u>d

6

J Real life

<u>Underline</u> the correct answer.

For example:

What's Mark's e-mail address?
a) Yes, he has.   b) No, he isn't.   c) <u>I don't know.</u>

1 Do you like coffee?
a) Yes, I'd like.   b) Yes, I love it.   c) No, thank you.

2 Would you like some orange juice?
a) Yes, I'd like.   b) Yes, I love it.   c) No, thank you.

3 Do you sell shampoo?
a) Yes, do you like some?   b) No, we aren't
c) I'm sorry, we don't

4 Have you got this T-shirt in blue?
a) Yes, we have got.   b) Yes, we do.
c) Let me look.

5 Can I have two of those cakes please?
a) These ones?   b) That one?   c) Yes, you have.

6 Is this seat free?
a) I'm sorry, it isn't.   b) Yes thank you.
c) Yes, please.

7 Is it OK to smoke here?
a) You can.   b) No, it's a no smoking area.
c) Would you like a cigarette?

7

K Superlative adjectives

Write the superlative form of the adjective in brackets.
For example:
What's the ...*fastest*.... car in the world? (*fast*)

1 Who's the .... teacher in the school? (*nice*)
2 Where's the .... post office? (*near*)
3 What's the .... way to get to the airport? (*good*)
4 How much is the .... ticket to Oslo? (*cheap*)
5 What's the .... word to spell in English ? (*difficult*)
6 Who's got the .... car? (*big*)

| | 6 |

L Vocabulary

Cross out the word which does **not** go with the word in the circle.
For example:

have
eat
~~do~~   (breakfast)

1 watch
   visit   (football)
   play

2 ride
   drive   (a car)
   use

3 go
   make   (abroad)
   live

4 watch
   sell   (a newspaper)
   read

5 win
   take   (money)
   do

| | 5 |

M Be or *have got* and vocabulary

Put *is / are / has got / have got* in the gaps.
For example:
My car ......*is*......... very comfortable.

1 Sandra .... tall and slim.
2 Paul's children .... black hair.
3 Mrs. Jackson .... 37.
4 Jordan .... green eyes.
5 Mark and Rita .... in their fifties.

| | 5 |

N Present simple and continuous

Underline the correct verb.
For example:
I don't like / *I'm not liking* fish.

1 Oh no! *It rains* / *It's raining*!
2 *Do you often wear* / *Are you often wearing* jeans to work?
3 My uncle *loves* / *is loving* black and white films.
4 I'm sorry, Tania can't come to the phone. *She has* / *She's having* a bath.
5 Look at that man! *He dances* / *He's dancing* in the street.
6 On Friday nights *we watch* / *we're watching* a video.
7 *I don't usually go* / *I'm not usually going* to school by train.
8 A: What *do you read* / *are you reading?*
    B: It's a letter from Sonia. Do you want to read it?

| | 8 |

O Spelling

Write the *-ing* form of these verbs.
For example:
eat *eating*

1 have ....   5 swim ....
2 wait ....   6 play ....
3 run ....   7 get ....
4 study ....   8 take ....

| | 8 |

TOTAL | | 100 |

Test three

TIME: 45 MINUTES

modules 11–15

Ⓐ Questions

Complete the questions below with the question words in the box.

How much	How fast	Which	How long
What kind of	What	How often	How many
~~How old~~	How far		

For example:

A: ...*How old*... is your cat?   B: She's three.

1 A: .... did you stay in Uruguay?   B: One week.
2 .... is Budapest from Vienna?
3 A: .... do the United States have a new President?
   B: Every four years.
4 .... TV did British people watch last year?
5 .... did you do last weekend?
6 A: .... is the Eurostar train between France
   and Britain?
   B: I'm not sure, about 100 km an hour?
7 .... do you like best, Thailand or Indonesia?
8 A: .... countries have you visited?
   B: Let me see … About twelve, I think.
9 A: .... food do they have in Poland?
   B: They eat a lot of meat.

| 9 |

Ⓑ Grammar

Three of the sentences below are correct. Tick (✓) the correct ones and correct the others.

For example:

Don can to swim. ✗ *Don can swim.*

1 Can you sing? No, I don't can.
2 What you are going to do after the lesson?
3 Sofie don't want to study tonight.
4 I'm studying Spanish for find a better job.
5 What do you like to do tomorrow?
6 I don't often go to concerts.
7 I might to see Vanessa next Friday.
8 Do you want watch TV tonight?
9 Where you go on holiday next year?
10 It won't rain tomorrow.

| 10 |

Ⓒ Numbers

Write the numbers in words.

For example:

80 km / hr   *eighty kilometres per hour*

1 101   ....
2 2,000   ....
3 30,000   ....
4 2.5   ....
5 4,000,000 ....
6 1966 (year) ....

| 6 |

Ⓓ Real life

Make full sentences in these dialogues.

Dialogue 1

A: I / hungry
I'm hungry.
....

B: Me too. Shall / order a pizza?
....

A: Good idea. Have / a menu?
....

B: Yes, we have. What kind / pizza / like?
....

A: Four seasons.
B: Okay, I / order it.
....

Dialogue 2

A: Hello / speak / Pete please.
....

B: Sorry / out.
....

A: Oh, can / leave / message?
....

B: Sure.
A: Can you ask him / phone / me?
....

B: Yes. What / number?
....

| 9 |

E Prepositions 1

Put a preposition from the box in the correct place in the sentences.

| at | to | on | ~~off~~ | in | for |

For example:

off
I got / the train at Munich.

1 Did you go the gym?
2 I'd like to watch the golf television.
3 I feel bad. I'm going to stay bed.
4 We had a party our mother's 50th birthday.
5 What did you do the weekend?

| | 5 |

F Articles

Complete the story with *a / an / the* or Ø (zero article).

This is (1) ....*a*......... true story about (2) .... young doctor who lived in (3) .... Chicago in (4) .... United States about a hundred years ago. (5) .... young man fell in love with (6) .... attractive young woman. (7) .... young woman's family were very rich and (8) .... doctor was poor, but they really loved each other. One Saturday he decided to speak to her father. Her family's house was in (9) .... city centre and he arrived at (10) .... 7 o'clock in (11) .... evening, but (12) .... family were having (13) .... dinner, so he went home.

On Sunday he came back but everyone was out, so he waited in (14) .... big room. It was very quiet in (15) .... room and he felt tired, so he sat down on (16) .... small chair by the window.

He was a big man and (17) .... chair broke! He felt very bad about this and he sat down on (18) .... different chair, a big, comfortable one. Unfortunately there was (19) .... cat on (20) .... chair. Very unfortunately, he was a really big man and (21) .... cat didn't live! (22) .... doctor decided to find another wife and he left immediately!

| | 11 |

G Vocabulary

Complete the gaps with the missing word.
For example:
He's a very f *a m o u s* actor; everyone knows him.

1 I had a r _ _ _ _ _ _ _ evening. I had a bath and read.
2 It's raining! My jacket is really w _ _.
3 You can see lots of paintings by artists in the Art G _ _ _ _ _ _.
4 I didn't like m _ _ _ _ _ _ _ _ _ at school. I can't count!
5 I have bought a lot of CDs o _ _ _ _ _. You order on the computer and it's much cheaper than in the shops.
6 I'm sorry, I can't see you tomorrow. I'm b _ _ _.
7 Janine f _ _ _ _ _ all her exams because she didn't do any work.
8 I'm doing a French c_ _ _ _ _ on Monday evenings.

| | 8 |

H Present perfect

Put the verbs into the corrrect form of the Present perfect in the following sentences.
For example:
Barcelona / ever / win / the competition?
Has Barcelona ever won the competition?

1 I don't think we / meet. I'm Harry.
....

2 Pat / never / see / a James Bond film.
....

3 Luke / do / a lot of jobs in his life.
....

4 He / be / a sportsman, an actor and a politician.
....

5 I / never / have / a dog before.
....

6 You / ever / broke / your arm?
....

| | 6 |

I Pronunciation

Match the words in the box with the correct stress pattern.

castle	typewriter	qualification	exhibition
interesting	museum	technology	

1 ○○○●○ ....
2 ●○ *castle* ....
3 ●○○ ....
4 ○○●○ ....
5 ○●○ ....
6 ●○○ ....
7 ○●○○ ....

☐ **6**

J Prepositions 2

Ⓒircle the correct preposition in the following sentences.
For example:
I walked *along* / *⟨down⟩* / *through* the steps.

1 The underground station? You go *out of* / *out* / *across* the front door and turn left.
2 The President flew *to* / *from* / *past* Cape Town to Johannesburg this morning.
3 Walk *past* / *across* / *along* Oxford Street for about ten minutes and you'll see Selfridges.
4 There are more than twenty bridges *through* / *over* / *up* the River Thames.

☐ **4**

K Have to / Can

Complete the gaps with the correct form of *have to* or *can*.
For example:
You ...*don't have to*.... pay now. You can pay tomorrow.

1 Is your computer broken? You .... use mine.
2 In this job we .... speak English because all the tourists are from Britain and Australia.
3 You .... wear a suit when you go to the cinema.
4 I'm sorry, but you .... speak to Mr Stevens now. He's out of the office.
5 Karen .... come to the party. She can stay at home if she wants.
6 We .... get Portuguese TV here! It's fantastic!

☐ **6**

L Verbs

Put the verbs in brackets into the correct tense. You can use the Present simple, the Present continuous, the Past simple or the Present perfect.

Rob: This (1) .....*is*..... (be) Rob Taylor and you (2) .... (*listen*) to *Music Radio Live*. The time is 8 o'clock here in Edinburgh and opposite me in the studio today is the singer Mel Yates! Our first question (3) .... (*be*) from Ana in Holland.
Anna: Yes, Mel. My question is : What (4) .... (*wear*) today?
Mel: (5) .... (*wear*) a long black dress and sunglasses.
Rob: And now a question from Paul in Belgium:
Paul: (6) .... (*have*) a boyfriend?
Mel: Yes, his name's Sam and we (7) .... (*meet*) a year ago.
Rob: Here's Sonja from Sweden:
Sonja: (8) .... (*play*) a musical instrument?
Mel: Yes, I (9) .... (*play*) the guitar, but not very well.
Rob: Now here are Jess and Vic from Ireland:
Jess: Hi, Mel. My question is: (10) .... (*ever / be*) in a film?
Mel: No, but I'd like to make a film one day.
Vic: (11) .... (*ever / had*) a bad concert?
Mel: Let me think. Oh yes. In Berlin in 1999. We (12) .... (*be*) in an outdoor stadium and it (13) .... (*rain*) all evening. After an hour people (14) .... (*start*) going home.
Rob: Thanks Mel. This is Rob Taylor and I (15) .... (*sit*) here with Mel Yates ...

☐ **14**

M Pronunciation

Look at the <u>underlined</u> sounds. Three sounds are the same and one sound is different. Ⓒircle the word with the different sound.
For example:
fri<u>e</u>nd l<u>e</u>tter ⟨j<u>ou</u>rney⟩ cass<u>e</u>tte player

1	stat<u>ue</u>	cl<u>ou</u>dy	sh<u>oe</u>s	thr<u>ough</u>
2	sn<u>ow</u>	w<u>o</u>n't	cl<u>o</u>thes	w<u>a</u>nt
3	l<u>i</u>brary	w<u>i</u>ndy	p<u>i</u>cture	b<u>ui</u>lding
4	r<u>ai</u>ning	st<u>a</u>dium	w<u>ar</u>m	str<u>aig</u>ht
5	c<u>i</u>ty	f<u>ee</u>d	rec<u>ei</u>ve	b<u>ea</u>ch
6	sc<u>ie</u>nce	mob<u>i</u>le	t<u>ie</u>	h<u>i</u>ll

☐ **6**

TOTAL ☐ **100**

Resource bank key

2C The family

1 Mike	6 Pam	11 Bob	16 Sue
2 Victoria	7 Laura	12 Sally	17 Tom
3 Jack	8 Mark	13 Frank	18 Maria
4 Emma	9 Molly	14 Billy/Peter	
5 Liz	10 Steve	15 Billy/Peter	

Learner-training worksheet A

2
a packet
b shave
c thirsty

3
a noun
b verb
c adjective
d verb
e adjective
f noun

7A The history quiz

1 b (*Star Wars* was made in 1977)
2 c (he was born in 1452)
3 b (she died on August 31st 1997)
4 a (he was a childhood movie star)
5 b
6 b (*Steamboat Willie* in 1928)
7 b
8 c (it happened on April 26, 1986)
9 a (she became Queen in 1558)
10 b (it came down in November 1989)
11 c (Madonna was born on August 16th 1958;
    Holiday was a hit in October 1983)
12 a (The first public railway in the world opened
    in England in 1823.)

9A New Year's Eve

In Picture B:
1 Mr Jones has got a longer moustache
2 Mr Jones is fatter
3 Mrs Jones has got longer hair
4 Mrs Jones is thinner
5 Emily is more beautiful
6 Emily has got shorter hair
7 Tom is taller
8 The toy car is bigger
9 The toy car is more expensive
10 The dog is fatter
11 The bottle of champagne is bigger
12 The cake is smaller
13 The sofa is more comfortable
14 The curtains are longer
15 The TV is bigger
16 The plant is taller

Learner-training worksheet B

2 walking
   making
   finishing
   travelling
   meeting
   leaving
   winning
   trying
   driving
   playing

3
a finishing meeting trying playing
b making, leaving, driving
c travelling, winning

4
a starting	d getting	g meeting	j waiting
b taking	e staying	h watching	k buying
c working	f stopping	i writing	l beginning

11B The dinner party

1 *What* did you invent last month?
2 *How much* (money) did you win on the lottery
   three months ago?
3 *When* did you become president of your country?
4 *How long / How many years* did you live on your
   boat (for)?
5 *How many countries* did you visit last year?
6 *How far / How many kilometres* do you run every
   day?
7 *How often* do you sell one of your paintings?
8 *How fast* can you swim 100 metres?
9 *Which / What* languages can you speak?
10 *What kind of* films do you make?

Learner-training worksheet C

2
a 6
b 3
c 1
d 5
e 2
f 4

4 suggested answers:

- aftershave (noun U) e.g. Do you use aftershave?

- noisy (adjective) noisier, the noisiest, e.g. The city's very noisy at night.

- prefer (verb regular) prefers, preferring, preferred, e.g. Which do you prefer – lemonade or Coke?

pet (noun C), e.g. Have you got any pets?

keep (verb irregular) keeps, keeping, kept, e.g. Where do you keep your milk?

- lazy (adjective) lazier, the laziest, e.g. My brother's really lazy.

12B Collocation snap

GO TO: a museum; the gym; a party; the cinema; a club
DO: an exercise; some studying; the housework; homework
WATCH: sport on TV, a video; the news; television
STAY: with friends; at a hotel; at home; in bed
HAVE: a meal; a party; a cigarette; a busy weekend
GO: shopping; dancing; on holiday'; away for the weekend

Learner-training worksheet D

Group A			Group B		
/iː/	/e/	/e/	any	/ɔː/	/ɔː/
meet	met	met	buy	bought	bought
read	read	read	catch	caught	caught
leave	left	left	bring	brought	brought
feel	felt	felt	think	thought	thought
sleep	slept	slept	fight	fought	fought

Group C		
any	/əʊ/	/əʊ/
break	broke	broken
steal	stole	stolen
speak	spoke	spoken
choose	chose	chosen
wake up	woke up	woken up

15D Revision board game

QUESTION CARDS
1 like; do; doesn't
2 a) How many b) How much c) How many
3 a; ∅; the
4 twenty-three point eight; fifteen million; seven hundred and six; nineteen eighteen
5 Mandy is my aunt and Cindy is my cousin.
6 slept; fell; left; wore

7 lost, lost; broke, broken; wrote, written; met, met
8 have to; can
9 funnier, the funniest; more boring, the most boring; better, the best; more comfortable, the most comfortable; smaller, the smallest
10 play basketball; go swimming; go to the gym; watch a film on TV
11 Where did you go on holiday three years ago?
12 always, usually, often, sometimes, not ... often, never
13 the; ∅; ∅
14 My teacher thinks we will probably pass the exam.
15 train; bus; taxi; tram; aeroplane/plane; motorbike; scooter; bicycle/bike; ferry; underground/subway (train); on foot
16 far; fast; often
17 various answers
18 live; speaks; doesn't
19 live; am staying; is working; likes
20 is; has got; has got; is
21 banana, roll, egg and sausage are countable; cheese, cereal, butter and jam are uncountable

Test one (modules 1–5)

A
1 sweets   2 men   3 children   4 bottles   5 families
6 watches   7 sportswomen

B
1 What's your surname?
2 Where are you from?
3 What's your job?
4 Are you married?
5 Where do you live?
6 What's your telephone number?

C
1 their   2 an   3 those   4 spiders   5 me   6 work
7 her   8 by

D

● ○	● ○ ○
tourist	manager
married	languages
lesson	excellent
business	holiday

E
1 finish   2 aunt   3 wife   4 hate   5 daughter
6 arrive   7 child

F
1 at   2 at   3 on   4 about   5 on   6 in

G

2 go   3 have   4 watches   5 read   6 visit   7 go

H

1 aren't.   2 they haven't.   3 I do.   4 she does.
5 Yes, you can.

I

1 politician   2 doctor   3 traffic   4 coffee   5 know

J

1 motorbike   2 aeroplane   3 scooter   4 bicycle
5 underground train

K

1   Do you like swimming?
2   She hasn't got a dog.
3   Washington is in the United States.
4   Mr Jenson doesn't drink coffee.
5   What time does the bank close?
6   My brother's a police officer.
7   Have you got a brother?
8   What does 'traffic jam' mean?

L

2 f   3 d   4 e   5 a   6 b

M

1 c   2 a   3 c   4 a   5 c

N

1 forty-eight   2 twenty-five to seven
3 one hundred / a hundred   4 half past nine
5 quarter past one   6 seventy-three

O

1 friend   2 tourist   3 crowded   4 taxi   5 diary

P

1 How   2 How old   3 Who   4 Where   5 What time
6 How much   7 What

Q

1   My dog always watches TV with me.
2   Our teacher sometimes plays his guitar in class.
3   I never write letters, but I write a lot of e-mails.
4   Do you often play computer games?
5   Parents don't often read books to their children.

Test two (modules 6–10)

A

1 any   2 toast   3 There's   4 an   5 some   6 any
7 no   8 any

B

1 How many   2 How   3 What   4 How much
5 When   6 Who

C

1 forty-second   2 nineteen sixty-nine   3 third
4 twenty-first   5 fifth   6 two thousand and five

D

1 famous   2 finished   3 butcher's   4 clothes shop
5 woke up   6 ugly   7 favourite   8 invented

E

2 studied   3 had   4 didn't stay   5 decided   6 left
7 travelled   8 became   9 wrote   10 were   11 died

F

○ ● ○   ● ○ ○
bananas   popular
attractive   sausages
tomatoes   oranges
important   difficult
successful   interesting

G

1   Did you have a nice weekend?
2   Oh? Who did you go with?
3   Was it good?
4   What did you do?
5   saw
6   bought

H

1 better   2 healthier   3 bigger   4 worse
5 more expensive   6 easier

I

1 knife   2 grapes   3 earring   4 yoghurt   5 slow
6 wear

J

1 b   2 c   3 c   4 c   5 a   6 a   7 b

K

1 nicest   2 nearest   3 best   4 cheapest
5 most difficult   6 biggest

L

1 visit   2 ride   3 make   4 watch   5 do

M

1 is   2 have got   3 is   4 has got   5 are

N

1 It's raining   2 Do you often wear   3 loves
4 She's having   5 He's dancing   6 we watch
7 I don't usually go   8 are you reading

O

1 having 2 waiting 3 running 4 studying
5 swimming 6 playing 7 getting 8 taking

Test three (modules 11–15)

A

1 How long 2 How far 3 How often 4 How much
5 What 6 How fast 7 Which 8 How many
9 What kind of

B

1 No, I can't
2 correct
3 Sofie doesn't want to study tonight.
4 I'm studying Spanish to find a better job.
5 What would you like to do tomorrow?
6 correct
7 I might see Vanessa next Friday.
8 Do you want to watch TV tonight?
9 Where are you going (to go) on holiday next year?
10 correct

C

1 a/one hundred and one 2 two thousand
3 thirty thousand 4 two point five 5 four million
6 nineteen sixty-six

D

Dialogue 1
B: Me too. Shall I/we order a pizza?
A: Good idea. Have we got a menu?
B: Yes, we have. What kind of pizza would you like?
A: Four seasons.
B: Okay, I'll order it.

Dialogue 2
A: Hello, can I speak to Pete please?
B: Sorry, he's out.
A: Oh, can I leave a message?
B: Sure.
A: Can you ask him to phone me?
B: Yes. What's your number?

E

1 Did you go to the gym?
2 I'd like to watch the golf on television.
3 I feel bad. I'm going to stay in bed.
4 We had a party for our mother's 50th birthday.
5 What did you do at the weekend?

F

2 a 3 Ø 4 the 5 The 6 an 7 The 8 the 9 the
10 Ø 11 the 12 the 13 Ø 14 a 15 the 16 a
17 the 18 a 19 a 20 the 21 the 22 The 23 the

G

1 relaxing 2 wet 3 Gallery 4 mathematics
5 online 6 busy 7 failed 8 course

H

1 I don't think we've (have) met. I'm (am) Harry
2 Pat's (has) never seen a James Bond film.
3 Luke's (has) done a lot of jobs in his life.
4 He's (has) been a sportsman, an actor and a
   politician.
5 I've (have) never had a dog before.
6 Have you ever broken your arm?

I

1 qualification 3 typewriter/interesting 4 exhibition
5 museum 6 typewriter/interesting 7 technology

J

1 out of 2 from 3 along 4 over

K

1 can 2 have to 3 don't have to 4 can't
5 doesn't have to 6 can

L

2 're / are listening 3 is 4 are you wearing
5 I'm / am wearing 6 Have you got / Do you have
7 met 8 Do you play 9 play 10 Have you ever been
11 Have you ever had 12 were 13 rained 14 started
15 'm / am sitting

M

1 cloudy 2 want 3 library 4 warm 5 city 6 hill